Politics and Foreign Direct Investment

The proliferation of foreign direct investment has raised questions about its impact on local economies and politics. Here, seven scholars bring together their wide-ranging expertise to investigate the factors that determine the attractiveness of a locale to investors and the extent of their political power. Multinational corporations prefer to invest where legal and political institutions support the rule of law, protections for property rights, and democratic processes. Corporate influence on local institutions depends, in turn, on the relative power of other players and the types of policies at issue.

Nathan M. Jensen, Associate Professor, Department of Political Science, Washington University in St. Louis

Glen Biglaiser, Associate Professor, Department of Political Science, University of North Texas

Quan Li, Professor, Department of Political Science, Texas A&M University

Edmund Malesky, Associate Professor, Department of Political Science, Duke University

Pablo M. Pinto, Associate Professor, Department of Political Science, Columbia University

Santiago M. Pinto, Research Economist, Federal Reserve Bank of Richmond

Joseph L. Staats, Associate Professor, Department of Political Science, University of Minnesota Duluth

Michigan Studies in International Political Economy

SERIES EDITORS: Edward Mansfield, Lisa Martin, and William Clark

Michael J. Gilligan
Empowering Exporters: Reciprocity, Delegation, and Collective Action in American Trade Policy

Barry Eichengreen and Jeffry Frieden, Editors
Forging an Integrated Europe

Thomas H. Oatley
Monetary Politics: Exchange Rate Cooperation in the European Union

Robert Pahre
Leading Questions: How Hegemony Affects the International Political Economy

Andrew C. Sobel
State Institutions, Private Incentives, Global Capital

Roland Stephen
Vehicle of Influence: Building a European Car Market

William Bernhard
Banking on Reform: Political Parties and Central Bank Independence in the Industrial Democracies

William Roberts Clark
Capitalism, Not Globalism: Capital Mobility, Central Bank Independence, and the Political Control of the Economy

Edward D. Mansfield and Brian M. Pollins, Editors
Economic Interdependence and International Conflict: New Perspectives on an Enduring Debate

Kerry A. Chase
Trading Blocs: States, Firms, and Regions in the World Economy

David H. Bearce
Monetary Divergence: Domestic Policy Autonomy in the Post–Bretton Woods Era

Ka Zeng and Joshua Eastin
Greening China: The Benefits of Trade and Foreign Direct Investment

Yoram Z. Haftel
Regional Economic Institutions and Conflict Mitigation: Design, Implementation, and the Promise of Peace

Nathan M. Jensen, Glen Biglaiser, Quan Li, Edmund Malesky, Pablo M. Pinto, Santiago M. Pinto, and Joseph L. Staats
Politics and Foreign Direct Investment

Politics

AND

Foreign Direct Investment

Nathan M. Jensen,
Glen Biglaiser,
Quan Li,
Edmund Malesky,
Pablo M. Pinto,
Santiago M. Pinto, *and*
Joseph L. Staats

The University of Michigan Press · *Ann Arbor*

Published in the United States of America by
The University of Michigan Press
Printed and bound by CPI Group (UK) Ltd, Croydon, CR0 4YY

2015   2014   2013   2012   4   3   2   1

A CIP catalog record for this book is available from the British Library.

Library of Congress Cataloging-in-Publication Data

Politics and foreign direct investment / Nathan M. Jensen . . . [et al.].
        p. cm. — (Michigan studies in international political economy)
    Includes bibliographical references and index.
    ISBN 978-0-472-07176-0 (hardback) — ISBN 978-0-472-05176-2 (paper) —
ISBN 978-0-472-02837-5 (e-book)
    1. Investments, Foreign—Political aspects.   2. International business
enterprises—Political aspects.   I. Jensen, Nathan M. (Nathan Michael), 1975–

HG4538.P566   2012
332.67'3—dc23

                                                                         2012019742

The views expressed are those of the authors and not necessarily those of
the Federal Reserve Bank of Richmond or the Federal Reserve System.

Contents

Contents

Preface and Acknowledgments

THE INITIAL DISCUSSIONS about this project stemmed from a series of conferences at Washington University in St. Louis and Pennsylvania State University on the politics of foreign direct investment as well as presentations at the annual conferences of the American Political Science Association, Midwest Political Science Association, and International Studies Association. This book project is the culmination of work that has been influenced by the generous comments of numerous discussants, audience participants, and other colleagues. We wish to extend special thanks to Jeff Frieden, Peter Rosendorff, Marshall Garland, Dylan Saunders, and Tom Longoria for invaluable help on various stages of the book project. Greg Allen, Bob Corvin, David Klein, and Piotr Urbanski all provided excellent research assistance.

We acknowledge the financial support of the Weidenbaum Center on the Economy, Government, and Public Policy at Washington University in St. Louis for funding multiple conferences at Washington University and for research support to complete this book. The director of the Weidenbaum Center, Steve Smith, has provided personal feedback and guidance on this project. Gloria Lucy, Chris Moseley, and Melinda Warren all provided incredible staff support.

We would like to thank Melody Herr at the University of Michigan Press for her shepherding of this project through the review process. Her guidance not only made this project possible but ultimately pushed us to make it better.

The data on and analysis of expropriation events in chapter 2 draws on Quan Li, "Democracy, Autocracy, and Expropriation of Foreign Direct Investment," *Comparative Political Studies* 42, no. 8 (2009): 1098–1127. The section of that chapter on political risk insurance draws on Nathan Jensen, "Political Risk, Democratic Institutions, and Foreign Direct Investment," *Journal of Politics* 70, no. 4 (2008): 1040–52 (© 2008 Southern Political Science Association; reprinted with the permission of Cambridge University Press).

An earlier version of material appearing in chapter 3 comes from Glen Biglaiser and Joseph L. Staats, "Do Political Institutions Affect Foreign Direct Investment? A Survey of U.S. Corporations in Latin America," *Political Research Quarterly* 63, no. 3 (2010): 508–22 (reprinted with permission).

In chapter 4, the model presented in the appendix and the data analysis reported in the section "Allocation of FDI across Sectors: Empirical Evidence" draw on Pablo M. Pinto and Santiago M. Pinto, "The Politics of Investment: Partisanship and the Sectoral Allocation of Foreign Direct Investment," *Economics and Politics* 20, no. 2 (2008): 216–54 (© 2008; reprinted with the permission of John Wiley and Sons).

CHAPTER I

Introduction: Multinational Corporations and Governments

A MULTINATIONAL CORPORATION (MNC) organizes production of goods and services in more than one country, involving the transfer of assets or intermediate products within the investing enterprise and without any change in ownership.[1] Foreign direct investment (FDI) by an MNC is the purchase of physical assets or a significant amount of the ownership (stock) of a company in another country to gain a measure of management control. International production through MNCs and FDI has been increasing in volume and expanding in scope. It is widely viewed as one of the most salient aspects of globalization.

For the first four decades after the end of World War II, FDI was a phenomenon primarily associated with developed countries. Even today, the lion's share of FDI involves developed countries either from the investor side or as recipients of FDI. In 2007, 84.8 percent ($1,692 billion) of total worldwide FDI emanated from developed economies, and 68 percent ($1,248 billion) of the world total flowed into developed economies.[2]

One earlier reason for the significance of the developed world rested with the early, strong opposition of developing countries against MNCs. Developing countries, many newly emerging from harsh and bitter colonial periods, were wary of the excessive profits earned by MNCs, particularly in extractive resource industries, and fretted about the disproportionate financial power of foreign investors. Some leaders feared that openness to foreign capital flows would expose them to a new and more pernicious form of neocolonialism, a fear that was augmented by the fact that most MNCs were actually from former colonial masters. Consequently, many developing countries erected legal and financial barriers to FDI, especially in the early post–World War II era. Some investment still flowed to larger developing countries, including Mexico, Argentina, and Brazil, as MNCs saw opportunities to avoid tariff barriers and earn monopoly rents in large and protected domestic markets. However, most foreign investment flowed to industrialized states in Europe and North America and, in a more limited fashion, into Japan.

The attractiveness of developed markets for FDI provided an additional motivation for the relative neglect of foreign investment in developing countries. Unlike the political and economic instability characteristic of developing countries and the discouragement of foreign capital predicated on nationalistic policies, developed countries offered fairly stable political and economic conditions. The fall of fascist governments during World War II, the rise of economic integration via common markets, and political peace among developed democracies provided a wealth of opportunities for foreign investors to expand the market for their products. Developed countries also tended to encourage foreign capital flows through liberalization and incentive programs as part of an economic strategy to rebuild in the war's aftermath.

The pattern of FDI overwhelmingly favoring developed economies persisted through the early 1980s. However, many developing countries changed their mind-sets toward FDI in the 1980s, and this offered added opportunities for foreign investors. Mired in economic collapse after engaging in protectionist policies for more than thirty years, most developing countries, lacking capital to support economic growth and development, reversed policy direction. The economic strategy of import-substitution industrialization (ISI), which relied on protecting local firms and producing overpriced goods for the domestic market and prevailed for much of the post–World War II era, had run its course because of limited access to foreign currency to support protectionist policies. A debt crisis ensued in the 1980s, when many developing countries were not able to obtain loans without strict policy conditions imposed by lenders such as the International Monetary Fund (IMF). As a result of the capital shortages, developing countries, much like the developed world, began to understand the importance of attracting FDI. The positive benefits of FDI were brought home to developing countries by the experiences of Hong Kong and Singapore, which recorded rapid economic growth over several years through policies that not only encouraged foreign investment but also followed export-oriented strategies that represented the antitheses of the ISI approach especially popular in Latin America.

From the 1980s to the 2000s, foreign investors began to search for opportunities all around the world. Countries as diverse as Thailand, Chile, and Botswana became major FDI recipients. While developed countries today continue to receive a larger percentage of foreign capital flows, developing countries have witnessed tremendous capital expansion from foreign sources. Even with the global economic downturn in 2001 and the far worse economic crisis near the end of the first decade of the 2000s, FDI continues to play an active role in countries across the globe, developed as well as developing.

Thus, FDI and the economic power of MNCs have grown in significance throughout the world. According to the *World Investment Report* (UNCTAD 2008, xvi), the number of transnational corporation parent firms reached 63,000 in 2000 and 79,000 in 2007, associated with 690,000 and 790,000 foreign affiliates, respectively. Foreign affiliates worldwide now hire some 82 million employees (UNCTAD 2007, xvi). World FDI inflows reached $865 billion in 2007, which is about 16 percent of global gross domestic capital formation (UNCTAD 2009, 255). Gross product or the value added from international production accounts for about 11 percent of global gross domestic product (GDP) in 2007 (UNCTAD 2007, xvi).

The current strong increase in FDI remains a steady trend, with investments dispersed among all developed and most developing economies. The positive trend is particularly great for developing countries. The inward FDI stock of developing countries ($2.3 trillion) rose from about 13 percent of their GDP in 1980 to about a third of their GDP in 2002, almost twice the 19 percent for developed countries (UNCTAD 2003). Developing countries have attracted rising amounts of FDI inflows, from $316 billion in 2005, to $413 billion in 2006, to $500 billion in 2007—the highest level ever recorded and a 21 percent increase over 2006. In 2007, even the least developed countries (LDCs) set their record, attracting $13 billion worth of FDI. Quite remarkably, that year also saw FDI outflows from developing countries reaching the highest level ever—$253 billion (UNCTAD 2008, xv, 253).

The reasons for the impressive expansion in FDI inflows center largely on the potential benefits that MNCs bring with them, including additional capital formation, technology transfer, managerial know-how, access to international markets, productivity spillover, and economic growth. Foreign firms may also increase employment in the host country and mobilize local savings. Additionally, it has been argued that MNCs produce positive spillovers in terms of productivity, wages, and exports in the host countries, especially for those possessing an abundance of labor.[3] Empirical evidence also suggests that FDI helps to increase the host's level of democracy and reduces the likelihood of interstate military conflict.[4]

Despite the extraordinary growth and interest from developed and developing countries in attracting foreign capital, critics of MNCs are also abundant. In many countries, certain local businesses oppose foreign capital because MNCs are more productive and competitive and tend to pay higher wage rates than local firms, thereby threatening the survival of rival host firms (e.g., Görg and Strobl 2003; Aitken and Harrison 1999). Another long-standing criticism leveled against MNCs is that they are anticompetitive, creating monopoly or oligopoly market structures and causing distortions in the host country's political process (see, e.g., Bergsten, Horst, and Moran 1978; Graham 1996; Hymer 1976; Korten 2001; Moran 1978b; Vernon 1998). FDI also may increase firms' elasticity of demand for labor, raising the volatility of wages and employment and making workers feel less secure (Scheve and Slaughter 2004). At the aggregate level, FDI stocks, inflows, and financial openness are found to raise income inequality in host countries (Quinn 1997; Li and Reuveny 2003), which further marginalizes low-income groups.[5] Some also argue that FDI leads to deterioration in labor rights and in the labor movement (Klein 2000).

The dependency theory and antiglobalization activists further emphasize international investment as the mechanism through which the international capitalist order distorts the economies of developing countries.[6] Reliance on foreign capital perpetuates the low status of developing countries in the world hierarchy, which produces conflicts between the core and the periphery. For evidence, adherents to this view often point to many instances of the nationalization of foreign investment in various developing countries in the early years. More recent expropriations in Namibia, Venezuela, Russia, Bolivia, and elsewhere also appear to confirm that FDI could be a source of political tensions between states.

Perhaps as important as the debates centered on the economic merits of FDI in the developing world, there seems to be a crucial nexus between politics and FDI. During roughly the same time period that foreign capital dramatically expanded in developing states, a corresponding explosion of activity has taken place in the political realm. Since the 1980s, the world has witnessed a simultaneous movement toward democratization, with transitions erupting throughout the developing world. Regions as diverse as Africa, South and Southeast Asia, and Latin America have experienced the breakdown of authoritarian rule and the birth (or, in some cases, rebirth) of democratic institutions. The fall of the Soviet Union also precipitated democratic movements among the states in Eastern Europe, some of which would later join the European Union. These political and economic forces have interacted in multifaceted ways that may have reinforced the flow of FDI to developing economies. The logic of political stability and the ability of democratic governments to make the kind of credible policy commitments that prompted post–World War II investment in consolidated Western democracies could be at work here. Increasing democratization may, in fact, be yielding safer investor environments for MNCs.

The puzzle is that some countries have attracted great interest from MNCs while others have gained little fanfare from prospective investors. The disparities in these flows of foreign investment defy traditional explanations based on endowments, location, or sociocultural factors. In this book, we seek to answer why these variations in FDI inflows occur, postulating that politics plays a critical role in the decisions of investors to risk their hard-earned capital in overseas ventures. We push beyond the simple metrics currently available, to offer a nuanced treatment of how investors influenced by politics gauge political institutions and conditions and measure political risk.

Most treatments of the political economy of FDI have stopped with the analysis of the determinants of investment flows, accepting MNCs as passive actors in their new locations. Such analyses neglect the important impact that capital flows have on distributional politics, benefiting particular sectors over others and consequently shifting the terms of political debate in salient and predictable ways. Moreover, investors have proven to be active participants in the policy-making process as well, lobbying and informing decision makers in ways intended to protect their business interests and ease regulatory burdens. Once again, the constellation of political institutions helps shape these distributional effects and interactions with policy makers. Consequently, in the latter half of this volume, we turn our attention to the effects of FDI on political processes, paying careful attention to how institutions mediate the influence of MNCs on politics, reform choices, and regulatory decisions.

All in all, the controversies around MNCs only serve to further underscore the significance of the phenomenon. Therefore, studying the impact of politics on foreign capital and the influence of politics on MNCs has important theoretical and policy ramifications. It is fundamental that analysts provide an in-depth analysis of the interactions between FDI and politics, which we do in this book.

Push and Pull Factors and FDI

The importance of FDI has led to a vast body of literature to explain the determinants of foreign capital flows. Understanding patterns of FDI is not as simple as looking at capital endowments of countries or relative rates of return. FDI differs from other forms of capital flows, and so do its causes and consequences. Unlike portfolio flows, principally bonds and non-FDI equities, that tend to be shorter term and can often be moved by a stroke on a keyboard, FDI generally involves a longer-term investment. Hymer (1976) was among the first scholars to distinguish FDI from other forms of capital investment. The key insight is that explaining FDI determinants requires a more sophisticated theoretical framework than a simple comparison of country attractiveness for investment.

Despite the challenges with explaining FDI determinants, there is a consensus that foreign capital inflows result from both push and pull factors, identified, respectively, with conditions that are external and internal to the recipient countries (Calvo, Leiderman, and Reinhart 1993, 1996). The pull factors that draw in capital include economic and political conditions in the host country. As to economic conditions, investors are expected to prefer a large and growing market, access to raw materials, and low-cost/high-quality labor. Foreign investment may take place to supply large local markets, particularly when host countries impose high tariffs that create barriers to market access. MNCs also seek to lower transport costs by locating close to the eventual consumers. Access to raw materials is another reason to invest abroad, as firms may rely on natural resources available in the host country as inputs to produce their goods. Lastly, low-cost/high-quality labor is essential in a globalized world, where outsourcing and other steps are needed to compete effectively. Large domestic markets, resource access, and labor issues complement the recent internationalization of world production, reduction in transportation costs, and bilateral and multilateral agreements that have eased investment restrictions and lowered other regulatory barriers. The result has been a more promising investment climate (UNCTAD 2003; Büthe and Milner 2008).

From the political perspective, patterns of FDI can be explained by pull factors such as political stability, investment risk, predictable political institutions, and executive ideology. These pull factors are critical, as they may provide investors with credible assurances that their investments will be secure from contract renegotiation, government expropriation, and other detrimental policy changes. Historically, the lack of investment security was an important reason why MNCs grew relatively slowly up until the late nineteenth century. In an age of poor communication and transportation and where legal controls were likewise undeveloped, international investment faced large risks. To overcome the risks involved with international operations, the relatively minimal foreign investment in those days relied on familial or close personal connections. It was assumed that family members and close personal friends could be best trusted, especially when the businesses were far away in foreign lands.

Improvements in communication and transportation over the past century have centered more political attention on political and legal circumstances that affect investors. Factors that pull in prospective investors include such things as democratic government or authoritarian rule, which carry different potential benefits; rule of law and independent judiciaries to protect against unlawful violations of property rights; multiple veto players in the host governments that moderate policy volatility; and executive ideology that may exploit nationalism issues or may favor nationalization of industries and/or redistribution of property.

Emphasis on push factors suggests the importance of interest rates, imperfections in the credit market, and technological changes that encourage investors to set up facilities in a myriad of locations (Fernandez-Arias 1996). For example, telecommunication improvements have increased the ability of firms to integrate disparate production facilities around the world through real-time communication. This, in turn, has allowed firms to save costs on warehousing by shifting to just-in-time production networks, where inputs arrive at the factory floor within the day or sometimes even the hour that they are required for assembly. Examples of just-in-time networks abound, particularly in the electronics sector. Firms such as Apple and Dell use integrated production around the world to assemble goods including iPods and computers. As a result, firms can afford to locate nodes of their production network in the most efficient areas around the world, according to production costs and access to raw materials.

While research on push factors is extensive and important, our focus in this project is on the domestic, political pull factors of recipient countries, for two reasons. First, from a research perspective, the role of policy and institutional variables has not been as carefully conceptualized as the economic determinants of investment.[7] There is room for considerable improvement on how political risk is understood and how particular institutional configurations shape that risk. Second, from a policy perspective, there is very little host countries can do to alter the push determinants of investment, which are the product of international and technological forces beyond their reach. Since our ultimate goal is to understand why some countries have been able to capitalize and prosper from increasing global capital flows, we narrow our analytical lens on the political institutions and political interactions that shape the policy levers available to political leaders, to explain what makes a country an attractive location for FDI. The important role of political institutions and politics in affecting FDI flows has received far less attention and is far less nuanced in its theoretical predictions. In the next section of this chapter, we address this deficit by discussing the importance of regime type and the unpacking of political factors for a proper understanding of FDI.

Democracy, Political Institutions, and Risk

A recent line of research on the political economy of FDI has focused on the connection between investment outcomes and institutional design. Much of this literature assumes that regime type and investor risk are inextricably linked and, thus, that whether the government operates under democratic or authoritarian rule is an important determinant of FDI. Within this group of scholars focusing on political regime, some argue that autocracies are better hosts of multinationals (Huntington 1968; O'Donnell 1978; Oneal 1994; Tuman and Emmert 2004), because of the expected increased political risks associated with democracies. Much of the high democratic risk (and so-called benefits of authoritarian rule) falls into three categories: (1) policy instability, (2) the ability of competing interest groups to influence government policy, and (3) the redistributive bias of democracy.

First, it is assumed that policy instability is greater under democracy because of government turnovers from one party to another and politicking prior to elections (including priming the fiscal pump or even nationalizing firms). Policy instability under democracy creates an unpredictable policy environment that undermines investor confidence. Second, democracies may provide an outlet throughout which domestic firms disadvantaged by the possible entry of MNCs can push for policies that harm MNCs (Henisz 2002b). The trend toward ISI in much of the developing world from the 1940s to the 1970s, which protected finished goods produced by local firms from more efficient goods manufactured abroad, suggests that politicians are susceptible to local pressures. Third, the redistribution bias in democracy implies that because the median voter in a democratic country tends to come from the poorer section of a population, populist politicians who often serve the poor are likely to promote higher tax rates that adversely affect the business sector. Populist politicians may also support redistribution in favor of the poor and may back nationalistic tendencies, including asset expropriation, to gain political favor. In the end, regime type determines which groups are politically influential, and it will hence affect the incentives to expropriate or protect foreign investors according to the expected net benefit that direct investment has on the well-being of those actors.

Others, however, assert that democracies should receive more FDI because they actually lower political risk. Contrary to the argument of authoritarian advantage, political risk under democracy is lessened, according to this line of reasoning, because of four factors: (1) host policy is relatively stable and credible; (2) foreign firms are able to influence policy outcomes; (3) policy and politics are relatively open and transparent; and (4) because of reputation costs, political leaders are disinclined to expropriate multinational assets.

First, building on the work of Tsebelis (1995, 2002), scholars argue that democratic regimes promote policy stability because they have more veto players who are able to block bold policy changes that may have negative consequences to foreign investors (e.g., those that involve property rights violations) and that this enhances the credibility of government commitments to investors (North and Weingast 1989; Olson 1993, 2000). Regimes with multiple veto players ensure that radical policies are limited in both scope and number. Second, democratic institutions enable MNCs to lobby politicians for their favored policy choices. Moreover, many local firms that are suppliers for MNCs will also court politicians to support policies beneficial to MNCs (Garland and Biglaiser 2009). Third, the transparency of policy making under democracy reinforces the credibility of policy commitments and provides greater predictability for investors. Investors fear the unknown and prefer policy stability over uncertainty. Fourth, a democracy faces possibly high audience costs (i.e., punishment at the polls) when its government reneges on commitments to foreign investors or expropriates firms under circumstances where doing so tarnishes its reputation in the future for attracting FDI. The negative reputation with international investors can help to turn off the spigot of foreign capital, fomenting economic as well as political misfortune. The benefits associated with FDI thus create a restraint on democratic leaders and a more propitious environment for FDI (Jensen 2003, 2006; Li and Resnick 2003).

In chapter 2 of this book, we delve headfirst into the debate about how democratic institutions affect the risk environment for MNCs. We are aware of the bluntness of traditional institutional measures and devise a different tactic to improve our understanding of the effects of regime type on FDI inflows. Drawing on alternative sources of data pertaining to past acts of asset expropriation and the price of insurance contracts protecting against future acts of expropriation, we provide a novel contribution on how institutions affect political risk; in doing so, we sidestep many of the criticisms customarily leveled against using aggregate data to explain flows of FDI. We test how democracy affects political risk by retrospectively examining the relationship between democracy and expropriations of foreign investment and the effects that democratic institutions have on the pricing of risk insurance contracts covering future expropriations. Our general finding is that democracies reduce political risk for MNCs by being less likely to expropriate assets and that there are some democracies in which nationalization of foreign investments is not only possible but even likely to occur.

The debate about the connection between regime type and FDI has led to a wave of studies that question the value of such broad comparisons. Empirical results are mixed, so the controversy is not just theoretical. Institutions could be an intervening factor. A movement to and from democracy, for instance, may result in the (dis)enfranchisement of actors whose preferences vary over the policy dimension at stake (cf. Mayer 1984). Policy outcomes would thus reflect a change in the electorate or selectorate, the group of individuals with the ability in the political marketplace to choose the leadership in democratic and nondemocratic contexts. Moreover, some studies suggest that regime type makes little difference for FDI inflows (Biglaiser and DeRouen 2006; Crenshaw 1991). Rather than considering broad institutional measures such as regime type, more recent work looks at the component institutions that exist within the governmental structure.

Previous studies have shown the effects of local political institutions on FDI inflows. Some work, for example, documents the impact that federalism has for attracting FDI (Jensen and McGillivray 2005). Others note that particular aspects of electoral systems influence investor decisions, with candidate-centered systems raising interest from prospective MNCs (Garland and Biglaiser 2009). Still others suggest that institutional arrangements are key. Proponents of this line of reasoning assert that the number of political checks or veto players (within democratic or authoritarian regimes), the effectiveness of courts and adherence to rule of law, and property rights protection should generally lessen the risk of asset expropriation or contract renegotiation by host countries and thereby contribute to attracting foreign investors (Li and Resnick 2003; Biglaiser and Staats 2010). Such institutional arrangements provide investors with credible commitments that the government of the host country will not take unlawful actions or institute sweeping policy changes that increase investment risk or hinder profitability.

In chapter 3, we unbundle and test the effects of political institutions on FDI. We do so using both an original data set—assembled from a survey of chief executive officers (CEOs) of U.S. corporations with investments in Latin America—and aggregate data analysis of economic and political factors that the development literature offers as influencing FDI. The results we reach demonstrate the important role that strong political institutions can play in attracting investor interest. We find, in particular, that robust political institutions that incorporate key veto players into the process and include strong and effective courts, adherence to the rule of law, and property rights protection are key determinants of FDI. As we explain in chapter 3, these things all contribute to investment safety and prospects for economic gain, matters of crucial importance to investors. Complementing research by Biglaiser and Staats (2010), Garland and Biglaiser (2009), Jensen (2006), Li (2006a, 2006b), and Li and Resnick (2003), we argue that the FDI literature too often makes comparisons between regime types without giving due consideration to various factors embedded in regimes, including empowering different groups in the polity whose well-being could be affected by investment flows. This omission may help explain the inconsistent results that continue to dominate research on foreign investment.

Sectoral FDI and Partisan Politics

A second group of institutional explanations of FDI, based on constraints imposed on political decision makers, is rooted in the literature on transaction costs (Williamson 1979, 1983b, 1985). Some institutional scholars argue that investors worry about policy changes, especially once they have deployed their assets abroad. As noted earlier, host governments whose hands are institutionally tied can more credibly commit to investors. The prediction is that polities with more checks and balances in their political system (veto players), either through division of powers or parties in coalition governments, will provide better reassurance to foreign investors (Henisz and Williamson 1999; Henisz 2000, 2002b). These authors contend that veto players crystallize the status quo, making policies more stable, a condition that investors arguably prefer.

Despite its potential benefits to host countries, FDI is a source of intense political dispute around the globe. While praised by many, FDI was also intensely demonized during the post–World War II era, most particularly by scholars and intellectuals in developing countries (Moran 1978b; Kobrin 1987). To explain the disparate reaction toward FDI across countries and over time, some scholars have pointed toward the interests and preferences of political actors in host countries. One strand in this literature looks at the link between investment and politics through the prism of class conflict (e.g., Evans 1979; Evans and Gereffi 1982a, 1982b; Gereffi 1983). Most prominent in this literature is the argument of triple alliance, which asserts that host governments collude with domestic and foreign capital to exploit the popular sectors (Evans and Gereffi 1982b). Another class-based approach sees the preferences of workers as a function of both the degree of inclusiveness of the political regime and the prevailing developmental ideology. Proponents of this perspective argue that organized labor in countries with repressive political systems and populist ideology tends to perceive foreign investors as villains, whereas labor in democratic systems with a modernizing ideology perceive MNCs as partners (Guillen 2000).

Other explanations equate FDI with footloose capital that has the potential to create economic insecurity and/or income volatility, which workers dislike (Scheve and Slaughter 2001, 2004). But there are different forms of capital flows, which may play out differently in terms of the trade-off between income and volatility effects. Given that FDI, by definition, implies a flow of management responsibility that comes with the capital, it is less footloose than might be supposed and certainly less so than portfolio investment. Relative to financial capital flows typical of portfolio investment, the exit option of FDI is more limited because the markets for realization of a return on assets that would allow an MNC to leave a country are less developed than markets for securities. It is precisely this frictional factor that makes inflows of FDI preferable to other forms of investment for the host country, which is to say that the income effect associated with a capital inflow is not negated by the volatility effect associated with mobile capital (see Pinto 2004, 2005, 2013). As we argue in chapter 4, these high redeployment costs force investors to look for reassurance that they will not be taken advantage of once they have deployed their assets in a foreign venue.

Given that FDI is vulnerable to opportunistic behavior by host governments and that investors tend to look forward, the adoption of investor-friendly policies alone might not be enough to lure investors in. They face a classic problem of consistency over time (Kydland and Prescott 1977; Calvo 1978). The likelihood that governments will eventually exploit them reduces foreign investors' propensity to invest. Certain kinds of capital are relatively mobile and show high elasticity to policies of host countries, including taxes, because investors are able to withdraw without major effort or cost. In such scenarios, governments are engaged in the problem of a "race to the bottom": when they act noncooperatively, governments end up imposing an inefficiently low tax rate on capital. By contrast, immobile types of foreign investment, which are often sector specific, become inelastic to unfavorable policies and differential tax rates immediately after investment takes place, rendering them virtual hostages of host governments. Investors holding sector-specific assets with high costs of redeployment are exposed to opportunistic behavior by host governments. Foreign investors have two options to reduce the risk of this type of opportunistic behavior: they can pay a redeployment cost and leave the country after government intentions become apparent, or they can withhold investment altogether. Both conditions are economically inefficient and politically sensitive. Higher levels of location-specific assets involved in an investment project give more salience to the dilemma of opportunism by host governments, which is at the center of the literature on the obsolescing bargain (discussed in more detail later in this chapter). As a result, the determinants of FDI and MNC activity are tied to local conditions, and their consequences are likely to vary with type of firm and investment strategies (see Pinto and Pinto 2008, 2011).

Foreign investors have to contend with a number of factors, pertaining to probable return on investment and investment risk, that convince them whether and in what amounts to invest in any given country. These are the pull factors (previously discussed) that attract outside investment into a country. The host country has control over these factors to the extent that it can reduce investment risk through fortifying political and legal institutions and adhering to the rule of law, all things that give investors some assurance that their investments will be protected and given the opportunity to flourish. In addition or alternatively, they can increase the probable rate of return on investments through various policy incentives that (among other things) lessen tax and regulatory burdens. Each country has to decide for itself how to go about enhancing the pull factors, but strategies directed at reducing risk are most difficult to accomplish and take time to effectuate, so we would expect many or most developing countries to devote considerable attention to policies directed at increasing the rate of return on investments as a means of pulling in FDI.

We need to realize, however, that FDI is a means to an end, not the end itself. One end that FDI serves is arguably economic growth and development in the host country. The argument that there is a connection between FDI and growth and development is not without controversy, but it is certainly the conventional wisdom among international donor agencies and the major players in the developed world, and the majority of development scholars support this idea as well.[8] Yet we would be mistaken if we assume that economic growth and development is the only end in the minds of policy makers in the host country when deciding how much and what type of FDI they wish to pull into the country and what measures they want to utilize in doing so. Domestic politics also enter into the equation. Policy makers in the host country have to consider the needs and demands of their core constituents before deciding on policies conducive to attracting FDI. In chapter 4, we show that the focus of these policies will depend, to a great degree, on the partisan nature of the government in power, principally whether the government receives its greatest support from labor or capital interests.

Not all FDI is alike in terms of the effects on labor or capital. A host country's economic conditions are important in this regard, as is the particular economic sector within which FDI operates and whether the FDI requires significant capital or is labor intensive. Depending on local conditions and the productive sector, some forms of FDI will complement the local labor pool and either not diminish employment or even increase it. This is precisely the calculation made by the autoworkers union in Argentina in the early 1990s, as they put their political weight behind the Menem administration's attempt to promote investment by foreign car manufacturers. The union had experienced firsthand the deleterious effect of the investment policies adopted during the military government's experimentation with naive liberalization in the 1970s.[9] In other cases, however, FDI will supplant the labor pool and lead to diminished employment, at least in the short run. Economists may argue that the long-run benefits of industrial upgrading outweigh the short-run labor dislocations, but politicians in the host country who depend on labor for support will be hard pressed to make this argument to their core constituents. Along the same lines, some forms of FDI in certain sectors will compete with and overwhelm local firms. This may benefit consumers in the form of lower prices and pave the way for future growth spurred on by technology spillovers, but it will not sit well with local investors, and a government that depends on their support will be severely constrained in the policies that it can or is willing to implement.

Complicating the foregoing is the fact that governments change over time, especially those that operate under democratic auspices. A government today that favors labor may be gone tomorrow, replaced by a government that favors capital. Yet a future government that favors capital will be constrained by policies put in place by a government that backs labor, and because of institutional inertial factors of the sort discussed in chapter 3, it will not always be able to make major changes preferred by core constituents. Challenging our appreciation of the connection between the partisan politics in a host country and FDI is the fact that the development literature has largely ignored this part of the FDI equation. Because we do not have a robust theoretical exposition of the intersection between partisan politics and FDI, we have little in the way of empirical investigation. Chapter 4 addresses the former deficit through a formal model and empirically tests some of the implications of this model using FDI data that is disaggregated by sector.

MNCs and the Obsolescing Bargain

Thus far, we have examined how economic, institutional, partisan political, and firm-specific factors influence FDI, without overtly addressing the complex relationship between politics and FDI. As previously discussed, most studies of FDI in political science focus on how politics affects the risk environment for multinationals. These scholars, either explicitly or implicitly, build on the obsolescing bargain theory (OBT) of Raymond Vernon by assuming that investors have limited influence on the investment environment *ex post*, because the sunk costs associated with start-up shift the bargaining power to the host government (Vernon 1971, 1980). For example, a petroleum firm that has already committed substantial resources to site inspection and research or a manufacturing firm that has already hired staff and imported production equipment is less likely to walk away than a firm that has yet to commit financial resources to a particular project. This is not to say that foreign investors lose all bargaining power; the argument is that through strategic interaction, their power is *ex ante*. To attract foreign investment, developing and transition countries need to make the institutional changes investors desire and to offer a credible commitment that these institutions will remain in place; otherwise they will lose to their neighbors in the race of investment attraction (Schneider and Frey 1985; Weingast 1993a, 1993b; Knack and Keefer 1995; World Bank 1997; Henisz and Williamson 1999). All bargaining over the regulatory regime, policy changes, and institutional structures is essentially concluded before investors ever break ground.

OBT was reinforced by early studies of business strategy concluding that MNCs had no opportunities to influence policies of host governments (Green and Korth 1974; Penrose 1987; Robock 1971). Political factors and policies of economic reform therefore came to be seen as just more variables to be added to the long lists in analysts' existing economic models of FDI determinants. The International Political Economy paradigm building from OBT has three significant weaknesses that have handcuffed research on the political implications of investment flows.

First, political scientists have expanded the scope of OBT far beyond the initial parameters for which it was intended (Pinto and Pinto 2011). Second, international investment has changed a great deal since the inception of OBT thirty-five years ago. Finally, studies of the impact of economic reform on economic attraction have overlooked the enormous energy that MNCs have invested in lobbying for economic reform in the transition countries and the successes lobbying has garnered.

The basic intuition of OBT begins with two actors: a host government and an MNC. The host government has valuable natural resources that it is unable to exploit because of a lack of financial resources, technological capacity, or marketing prowess. To overcome this problem, the host government seeks to lure a technologically advanced MNC from a developed economy to extract the natural resources, though the government knows that it is at a serious bargaining disadvantage relative to the corporation. A current situation in Cambodia provides a telling example. Tremendous oil deposits were discovered off the coast of Sihanoukville, but these are extraordinarily deep in a difficult-to-access seabed. No domestic Cambodian firm is capable of mining these deposits alone, because the industry lacks the exploration and drilling technology for the hard-to-reach deposit. Consequently, the Cambodian government has put out a tender for foreign firms interested in access to the oil. Because the oil will remain untouched without the foreign expertise, Cambodian officials hold the weaker opening hand in their negotiations with the foreign firm that has the winning bid. The MNC can always choose not to invest, in which case Cambodia will essentially waste the tremendous wealth that sits hundreds of yards off its coastline.

In its initial interaction before an investment commitment, the MNC remains relatively mobile; it can invest wherever resources exist. To induce the firm to take on the risk of investing in the economy, a host government like the Cambodian leadership will offer a range of concessions such as tax holidays and regulatory change, thereby setting the stage for the MNC to earn lucrative profits. Once the investment has had a few successful years of operations, however, the risk to the firm that was present at the inception diminishes, and the host country may begin to perceive as inappropriate the high returns realized by the MNC. Meanwhile, the MNC's valuable technology has already been transferred or is available in some form on the open market, and gaps in management skills between foreigners and locals have declined (Kobrin 1987). In the Cambodian example, for instance, local contractors working with Exxon or Shell will soon learn how to operate expensive new drills and high-tech exploration software through their interactions with the MNCs. Once they gain enough expertise, they may be able to convince national leadership that they could go it alone, importing needed equipment but managing the investment project themselves. As a result, profits from these investments would be retained locally, perhaps even by entrepreneurs connected to the leadership. As an alternative or additional scenario, national priorities may have changed, with new political leaders entering power and facing pressure from voters to alter their perceptions of economic development. The distributional effects of FDI previously discussed can play a key role in these shifting political alliances. Meanwhile, the MNC will have already invested tremendous capital into a profitable project that it certainly wants to continue running (Jenkins 1986).

The increased pressure on the host government to raise demands on the investor and the ex-post immobility of the MNC create a situation where the attractive agreement first carved out by the MNC will inevitably "obsolesce" (Vernon 1980). Theoretically, obsolescence can take the form of renegotiated contracts, higher taxes, expropriation of assets, or seizure of the income stream of the firm (Gatignon and Anderson 1998; Williamson 1996; Kobrin 1984; Jensen 2003). As Vernon (1980, 47) elegantly puts it, "Almost from the moment that signatures have dried on the document, powerful forces go to work that render the agreements obsolete in the eyes of the government." The bargaining advantage now rests with the host country.

After Vernon's articulation of OBT, two changes were made in the way political scientists understood investment decisions. Bargaining over investment contracts was a one-shot game, so foreigners could only hope to influence the initial details of the contract; they would have little impact on local institutions or policies. Because of the substantial costs of ex-post contract infringement, foreign investors were much less likely to invest in sizable amounts where the risk of obsolescence and policy uncertainty were greatest (Dixit and Pindyck 1994; Rajan and Marwah 1998). As a result, MNCs relied on overt signals of a country's ex-ante credibility, such as whether it was a democracy (Jensen 2003; Li and Resnick 2003) or had plausible checks on the powers of key decision makers (Henisz and Williamson 1999; Henisz 2000). From an analytical perspective, this discovery meant that interesting insights were conceivably more likely to be gleaned from studying not what happened after direct investment had taken place but how investors chose where they were going to invest in the first place.

The focus on the obsolescing bargain has brought attention to the ex-ante decisions of firms, generating a rich set of theoretical and empirical models. Yet it would be unwise to conclude generally that foreign firms have no influence over host governments after investments are in place. OBT is premised on the ex-post immobility of firms (Pinto and Pinto 2011). It is quite clear that Vernon only had investors in natural resources in mind when he first articulated the theory. This is understandable. Mineral extractors can only invest where the minerals are and suffer very large up-front expenditures that would be very difficult to recover in the event that they became unhappy with some government policy and wanted to leave or if their property was expropriated.

Other types of firms, however, are not constrained in this way. Many investors are less limited by geographical constraints on inputs and, due to more complicated production chains, are much less exposed to the ex-post changes in the national bargain. It would be quite easy for an investor in the garment industry, for example, to shut down a factory, sell off or move sewing equipment to another country, and leave the country at the first sign that an initial agreement had gone sour. Manufacturers thus hold a great deal of ex-post bargaining power. Kobrin (1987) showed that direct foreign investment in the manufacturing industry and export-oriented investment were less vulnerable to such tactics by host countries, but the lessons derived from this have been largely ignored. These days, services related to technology and software production are similarly mobile and less prey to predatory governments, which is why American entrepreneur Steve Keil chose to move his software company Sciant from Bulgaria to Vietnam, reckoning he would face lower production costs and a less obtrusive government in the nominally communist regime (*Economist* 2005).

Not only are manufactures more mobile, but economic theory implies that weak institutions in the host country might actually be an incentive for investment, rather than a deterrent. Ceteris paribus, manufactures should prefer direct contractual relationships with overseas suppliers, provided they can enforce quality in the production (Fung et al. 2002). Under these conditions, foreign investment becomes a means of protecting property when a regime cannot; that is, FDI in manufacturing should theoretically be correlated with weaker property rights, not stronger ones, and the same may be true of the service sector as well. Knowing that investors in the manufacturing and service sector may invest as a means of protecting property rights, it makes sense that once on the ground, they would begin to lobby local officials for legal changes that would better protect their investments.

Second, Vernon only described the relationship between an individual investor and a government; he likely would have conceded that coalitions of foreign investors could use their aggregate bargaining strength to fend off expropriation by a predatory state or to lobby for change in the host government's institutions and policies, especially if they were large contributors to employment or revenue in the economy. Economists and political scientists studying U.S. economic policy have noted the important influence of business lobbying on policy choices (Brasher and Lowery 2006; Grossman and Helpman 1994; Grossman and Helpman 2002; Gawande and Bandyyopadhyay 2002). These findings, however, have not had much influence in the analysis of FDI in developing and transition countries, where it is possible that aggregate bargaining strength would be even stronger.

Third, international investment has changed a great deal since the inception of OBT thirty-five years ago. MNCs in all sectors have learned to hedge their entries into risky environments through incremental implementation of capital and transfer pricing, which mollify the shift in bargaining power to the host government (Jensen 2008).

Thus, building on Vernon's work has helped generate a deeper understanding of relations between firms and governments, yet a full understanding of this dynamic requires us to explain both ex-ante and ex-post relations and bargaining. Strategy analysts have long understood that no contract is ironclad and that the political risk faced by MNCs has to be actively managed (Henisz and Zelner 2003). Consequently, the strategy field has devoted great attention to how MNCs can mitigate the bargaining advantages of host governments through strategic alliances with local partners (Boddewyn and Brewer 1994; Eden and Molot 2002), broad alliances with other investors (Stopford and Strange 1991), staged entry and incentive alignment with local actors (Henisz and Delios 2004), the use of home governments and international organizations to spearhead discussions (Ramamurti 2001), and the tactical allocation of proprietary technology and international finance (Luo, Shenkar, and Nyaw 2002). The general consensus in the literature on business strategy is that MNCs have become quite adept at functioning politically within host countries and that the obsolescing bargain is of limited utility today as a theoretical framework (Hillman and Hitt 1999; Eden, Lenway, and Schuler 2005; Wint 2005).

Despite these three clear constraints on the generalizability of OBT, a number of political scientists rely on the argument as a starting point for their analyses of foreign investment. In these analyses, they often use total investment flows or stocks, which has exacerbated the gap between their studies and the original notion of the obsolescing bargain, by conflating different types of investment to which OBT was never meant to apply. Studying total FDI also ignores the presence in Vernon's original model of negotiations between individual firms and host countries. Finally, studying total flows augments the endogeneity problem, because coalitions of investors are more powerful lobbyists than individual firms.

In the chapters that follow, we examine both the ex-ante and ex-post influence of firms. Chapters 2 and 3 focus on the ex-ante relationship, specifically on how political institutions affect the risk environment. In chapter 4, we explore how partisanship affects the incentives of governments to promote specific types of investment. Thus, while chapters 2 and 3 examine what constrains predatory governments, chapter 4 addresses the circumstances under which host governments and firms will or will not have similar incentives, as well as the fact that different incentives will still be present when foreign investment faces high relocation costs. In the next section of this opening chapter, we highlight the final contribution of our book, the exploration of how firms can influence policy change.

The Effect of FDI on Economic Reform

As noted in the previous sections, multinationals have the ability to influence politics in a number of issue areas, from taxation to regulation. These stakes are extremely high in countries undergoing economic reform, where multinationals both respond to reform and help shape the policies that lead to economic reform.

Rigorous models of the determinants of FDI in transition and developing countries demonstrate that factors such as infrastructure, agglomeration, access to raw materials, human capital, and labor costs play the substantively largest roles in attracting investment (Diechman et al. 2003; Resmini 2000; Navaretti and Venables 2004; Biglaiser and DeRouen 2007). Knowing that investors are primarily attracted by structural and market factors opens up new avenues for research; namely, how do investors influence the political process once they are there? Lewis (2005) colorfully depicts a wide variety of successful lobbying efforts by MNCs, including Fiat, Daewoo, and General Motors, which took stakes in Eastern Europe in 1991, prior to any serious progress on efforts toward economic reform. Along the same lines, when Volkswagen decided to buy Czechoslovakia's Skoda car plant in 1992, there was not yet any law on privatization, so legal principles on privatization and FDI regulation were developed in consultation between the firm and the government (Lewis 2005, 115).

As stressed by John Hewko, a former lawyer with Baker and McKenzie in the Ukraine and Russia who often worked closely with foreign investors, most companies that have committed resources to transition states understood, before embarking on their investment, that the legislative and legal systems were inadequate. They were more interested in capitalizing on existing opportunities and believed that their specific concerns would be addressed through subsequent discussions with policy makers (Hewko 2002–3, 79). Hewko (2002–3) identifies three distinct mechanisms by which investors, lured to a country by structural and market conditions, serve as agents for economic policy reform. These mechanisms closely track the causal logics described by Simmons, Dobbins, and Garret (2006) in their review of the literature on policy diffusion across national borders.

First, investors are important providers of information to politicians in transition countries. No economic policy reform can ever be completed in one sweeping action; it is a process of continual revision and adjustment. Each piece of commercial legislation must be revised on the occasion that it proves inadequate to deal with the progressively more complex business environment. Because of their experience in other environments, foreign investors are critical in identifying these shortcomings and communicating them to policy makers and bureaucrats. Laws often lag behind the actual transactions taking place, such as the use of derivatives in the Czech Republic, and it falls upon foreign investors to explain these complex mechanisms and the need for new laws to address them (Hewko 2002–3). Prakash and Potoski (2007) offer empirical evidence that such a process took place with the spread of ISO 14001 management systems across developing countries.

Along these same lines, foreign investors can offer critical information to inexperienced legislators about similar laws in other countries and can impart basic lessons on the day-to-day functioning of a market economy. Luo (2001) argues that to ensure that the foreign enterprise will continue its contributions to the country over the long term through reinvestment or technology upgrading, it is likely that national governments will adopt a cooperative stance and be responsive to a foreign firm's opinion about any new regulation affecting its business conditions. Certainly, policy makers will not see investor-provided information as unvarnished. Understanding that MNCs, like all advocates, have their own agendas, policy makers will weigh the policy suggestions of MNCs against alternatives provided by other domestic actors. What distinguishes countries with substantial FDI from those without, however, is that policy makers hear and consider information from the MNCs at all.

Second, if politicians do not willingly seek out the advice of investors in these areas, investors may be forced to lobby for the changes in legislation that will affect their operations. Olarreaga (1999) models this lobbying process formally, demonstrating that the entry of foreign investment into an economy eventually leads to greater trade liberalization. Foreign lobbying efforts often are abetted by alliances with domestic investors or regional governments who may have better access to policy makers than does the foreign investor (Kennedy 2007; Malesky 2008), as Gillespie (2006) shows was the case regarding commercial law in Vietnam and as Pyle (2006) demonstrated with regard to business associations in Russia.

Third, existing investors can use coercion. Moderate forms of coercion include offering access to company-specific financial and technical endowments, local charitable giving, and preferential access to proprietary technology (Eden and Molot 2002; Moon and Lado 2000; Ramamurti 2001). Less moderate coercion involves threatening to leave if legal and institutional changes are not made. In addition to the immediate loss of revenue and employment, investors closing up shop send a powerful signal to future investors interested in the country. As Hewko (2002, 17) notes, "Whereas an inadequate legal system is often not a decisive factor in attracting FDI, the lack of legislative and institutional reform is a significant barrier to retaining such investment. Even the most entrepreneurial foreign investors have a limit as to the type and level of systematic difficulties that they are willing to endure."

Dixit and Pindyk (1994) demonstrate that this third mechanism can be costly for firms, which is why they argue that firms wait for diminished uncertainty before investing. Yet the high cost of walking away from a large project makes the signal to other investors credible. Not only can the threat of exiting investors provide an incentive for new reforms, but their bargaining power also provides a check against backsliding of reform. Governments are less likely to backtrack on reform initiatives when they risk upsetting a powerful group of investors (Pyle 2006). Testing this theory, Campos and Horvath (2006) find that the presence of a large stock of foreign investment leads to significantly fewer reversals of privatization projects.

To these three mechanisms, Lewis (2005) adds a fourth: that the economic might of foreign investors can help free captured local politicians from the grips of entrenched interests, described by Hellman (1998) as the trap of partial reform. When there is a large presence of foreign investors, their combined power on key issues offers an external check on entrenched interests. Desbordes and Vauday (2007) use data from business environment surveys to test this hypothesis, finding that foreign firms are more likely than domestic firms to believe that they can influence the local regulatory environment of their host country. Among the forty-eight developing countries they study, perceived influence of enterprises in foreign investment is highest in Eastern Europe and Central Asia, where regulatory institutions are most malleable.

Addressing endogeneity bias through an instrumental variables analysis, Malesky (2009) tests these arguments by studying the impact of exogenously determined FDI on policies of economic reform in transition states. He finds persuasive evidence that stocks of FDI are positively correlated with reform progress in subsequent years. In short, OBT does not preclude the ability of existing investors to lobby for and succeed in shaping reform choices and new regulations that are advantageous to them.

In chapter 5 of this book, we revisit and build on the analysis of Malesky (2009). Demonstrating a statistical relationship between FDI and subsequent reform choices is only the first step. The next logical question is, under what conditions is MNC lobbying most effective? In chapter 5, we study differences in political institutions that have been shown to affect lobbying, finding that the most important factor is the competitiveness of participation and, consequently, the diversity of opinions in the polity with which MNCs compete. Interestingly, constraints on executive decision making do not appear to mediate FDI influence. Knowing the effect of particular institutions on the success of postinvestment lobbying has important implications for how we understand the regulatory choices of developing economies and feeds back into our discussion of FDI attractiveness. Investors may not just choose locations based on the ex-ante credible commitment provided by sets of institutions; rather, they may choose institutions where they perceive themselves as having the greatest post-investment influence on policy choices (Henisz and Delios 2004).

The influence of MNCs on policy is not only mediated by institutions; it may also be conditioned by the policy arena the investor wants changed. In the final section of chapter 5, we disaggregate economic reform into specific policy dimensions, finding that investors have the strongest influence on the liberalization of trade and prices, large privatization, and competition policy but fail in their efforts to expedite reform in the banking and financial sector.

Politics and Influence

This introductory chapter has explored the broad parameters of relationship between MNCs and governments, but in so doing, it has raised more questions than answers. Despite the excellent work on the political economy of FDI, there is much that we still do not understand. In the remaining chapters or this book, we forge deeper into this complex relationship, contributing further to our current knowledge of both political risk and political influence.

In the next two chapters, we explore the political factors that affect the risk environment for multinational investors. In chapter 2, we examine how democratic institutions affect this risk environment. Our key contribution here is empirical. To test how democracy impacts political risk, we delve into the effect of regime type on past expropriations of foreign investment and into how democratic institutions influence the pricing of risk insurance contracts protecting against future expropriations. The general finding is that democratic institutions reduce political risk for multinationals, yet this finding is complex and not deterministic. Democracies are less likely to expropriate, yet there is clear evidence that expropriation is not only possible but even likely in some democracies.

Chapter 3 builds on chapter 2 by looking further into the ways in which politics impacts the risk environment. In chapter 3, we unpack regime type to show how political institutions affect FDI. Rather than relying solely on aggregate country-level data, as has been true of so much previous work conducted in this area, we use a survey questionnaire administered to CEOs of U.S. firms with investments in Latin America, to assist in understanding the determinants of FDI. In both the survey and aggregate data analysis that we conduct, we consistently find that political institutions matter to foreign investors. Strong and effective courts, adherence to the rule of law, and property rights protection are especially important. We maintain that this seems to be so in large part because investors, who want to reduce their investment risk, see courts and fair and effective enforcement of laws as means of lowering their risk and protecting their firm's assets. We also suggest that foreign investors may prefer investing in countries with these hallmark institutions because they see such conditions as conducive to political stability (a matter of no small importance to investors) and because strong and effective courts can be effective instruments for upholding private property rights, enforcing commercial contracts, and avoiding arbitrary and abrupt swings in public policies, which can be inimical to business interests.

In chapter 4, we provide a bridge between studies of political risk introduced in chapters 2 and 3 and literatures on political influence. Going beyond the earlier contributions in this book, chapter 4 provides novel theoretical insights into the relationship between multinationals and politics. The main insight in chapter 4 is that FDI can have different impacts on domestic economies based on the type of investment. Our central insight in this chapter is that the type of investment affects the incentives of domestic politicians. Leftist governments privilege investments in industries that have positive spillovers for local labor, while rightist governments will attempt to attract FDI into sectors that have positive spillovers for domestic capital. Once we account for the political determinants of FDI flows, we are better able to assess the direction and extent of the expected economic and political consequences of those investment flows.

In chapter 5, we study differences in political institutions that have been shown to affect lobbying, finding that the most important factor is the competitiveness of participation and, consequently, the diversity of opinions in the polity with which MNCs compete. We show empirically, using data from 26 countries in economic transition, that investors have a more difficult time influencing key decision makers when their views on regulatory reforms must do battle with other perspectives in free and fair electoral competition. Interestingly, it appears that the constraints on executive decision making are more important for investment attraction than is postinvestment influence. The influence of FDI on the policy process does not appear to be mediated by checks and balances or coalition politics. Furthermore, we show that some policy arenas are more subject to investor persuasion than others. Both of these insights are important for our ability to predict the directions of economic reform in developing and transition countries.

Chapter 6 concludes the book by revisiting the main theoretical insights offered throughout the work and identifying areas for future research. Given the importance of FDI as a source of economic growth and development, understanding the politics of foreign capital flows will surely continue to draw increased attention in the future.

CHAPTER 2

Democracy and the Political Risk of Expropriation for International Business

AS OUTLINED IN CHAPTER 1, political risk is a central concern for foreign direct investors, especially when they invest in developing countries. Many scholars in international business, economics, and political science have employed some type of composite indicator of political instability or risk to assess the impact of political risk on international business.[1] At the same time, many other scholars attempting to understand the determinants of foreign direct investment have found that political institutions influence investment and entry-mode decisions of international businesses by shaping investor perception of political risk in the host environment.[2] Very rarely, though, do those investigating FDI offer a direct evaluation of the link between political institutions and political risk. This chapter fills this important gap by studying how political regime type, a central feature of political institutions, influences not only the perception of risk in the minds of investors but also actual risk, the most extreme form of which is manifested when the host government expropriates investor assets.

The research presented in this chapter has important implications for international business, because FDI is, by its very nature, structurally vulnerable to the risk of property rights violations by the host government. As outlined in the previous chapter, FDI is characterized by cross-border jurisdiction and ex-post illiquidity, both of which pose difficulties for foreign investors (see, e.g., Frieden 1994; Vernon 1971). Because direct investment is foreign in the host country, cross-border jurisdiction becomes inevitable

27

inasmuch as local affiliates of MNCs are subject to the host's laws and regulations. The host government, by its sovereign nature, monopolizes the coercive power to define and enforce property rights within its own territory. Neither the legal status of expropriation nor the standard of compensation for expropriation has been clearly established in international law, giving further discretion to the government (Thomas and Worrall 1994; Easton and Gersovitz 1983). The host country often is not held legally accountable to any other higher authority when it breaks its promise to protect foreign assets, and the host-MNC contract is incomplete because it cannot anticipate all contingencies. The government may resort to intervening circumstances (e.g., war or economic crisis) as a basis to renege on its agreement with the MNC ex post. Hence, the host government's ex-ante promise to protect foreign assets lacks credibility. Added to this difficulty, FDI is inherently illiquid ex post, compared to other forms of investment, due to the long time horizon needed to realize profitable returns on direct investment and because assets cannot be moved easily out of the host country. Because of all these factors, FDI is intrinsically vulnerable to the risk of property rights violation by the host government.

Therefore, uncovering the link between political institutions and political risk allows us to move closer to understanding the root cause of property rights violations than would be possible by merely focusing on some aggregate indicator of political instability. By better understanding what causes property rights violations, our effort also helps to inform the research on the link between political institutions and flows of FDI. The new knowledge may even facilitate better management of political risk by international businesses, particularly in the developing world.

We need to add, at this juncture, that there has been a considerable amount of research on how bilateral investment treaties (BITs) may affect political risk.[3] Bilateral investment treaties, which often provide for arbitration of disputes between the host government and investors from the other country, may reduce political risk, but the empirical evidence is quite mixed.[4] This book, however, focuses on the link between domestic political factors and foreign investment, and we leave for future research the question of how international agreements may come into play

In this chapter, we directly study the links between regime type and political risk both theoretically and empirically. While political risk can encompass a number of political activities affecting firms, we focus on the risk of expropriation and identify various theoretical mechanisms by which democracy may raise or lower the risk of expropriation against multinationals. We examine and evaluate empirically the net impact of democracy on both actual expropriations and the perceived risk of expropriation, an empirical innovation over previous research that has focused on either actual expropriations (e.g., Li 2009) or risk perceptions (e.g., Jensen 2008) but not both. To our knowledge, ours is the first analysis of the two simultaneously.

Our primary findings can be summarized as follows: Democratic countries engage in fewer actual expropriation acts than nondemocracies, and political risk insurers perceive them as posing less of such a risk, as reflected in how political risk insurance contracts are structured and specified. These effects are largely attributable to the fact that highly democratic countries have more institutional veto players than do less democratic ones. But it is clear that democratic countries do engage in actual expropriation occasionally, and we identify certain types of democratic countries as presenting relatively high expropriation risks.

The first section of this chapter discusses how regime type theoretically affects political risk for international business. The second section presents three sets of empirical analysis and evidence, with subsections based on actual expropriation data, data on perceived expropriation risk, and a reevaluation of the findings in the previous two subsections within the context of statistical modeling to ensure their robustness. While the materials in this subsection are technical in nature, the main findings are consistent with those in the highly accessible earlier subsections. Readers who are not familiar with statistical modeling may skip the technical materials without loss of comprehension of the central message and findings of this chapter. The last section of this chapter summarizes our main findings and discusses their implications.

Political Institutions and Political Risk

How do political institutions affect political risk? One may identify conflicting theories that advocate either a positive or a negative impact of democracy on political risk. In this section, we briefly discuss these arguments on how democratic institutions can decrease or increase political risks for multinational investors.

Democracy Decreases Political Risk

Democracy can influence political risk in a number of ways. Scholars who argue that democracy reduces political risk have focused on three specific mechanisms: (1) the stability and credibility of host policy, (2) the ability of firms to influence policy outcomes, and (3) how reputation costs affect leaders' incentives to expropriate multinational assets.[5]

Drawing on the work of Tsebelis (1995, 2002), some scholars argue that democratic regimes can lead to policy stability because they have larger numbers of veto players that have the ability to block policy change. When the number of veto players is large and their preferences are heterogeneous, policy change is difficult. In the case of government commitment to private property, increasing the number of veto players who have stakes in property rights violations helps prevent the state's opportunistic behaviors and improves the credibility of government commitment (North and Weingast 1989; Olson 1993, 2000; Li 2009). The existence of multiple veto players with diverse preferences prevents any individual veto player from single-handedly changing the status quo, thereby reducing state depredation against business. Hence, democratic institutions often lead to a status-quo bias in policy, which reduces the ability of leaders to enact sweeping policy changes that could harm multinationals. Meanwhile, greater checks and balances in democracies prevent the state from predatory rent seeking, making its commitment to private property credible and reducing expropriation risks for investors. Thus multinationals can enter into these foreign markets with better assurance that their policies will not change dramatically after entry and that their property rights will be protected.

The second mechanism linking political regime type to political risk is that democratic institutions provide formal avenues for investors, foreign and domestic, to influence the policy-making process. This gives foreign firms the ability to affect legislation before it is passed and to observe the legislative process and anticipate changes in policy.[6] Such transparency in the process clearly has a positive impact on multinational investors' ability to both predict and mitigate political risks. This is not to say that firms cannot lobby or influence politicians in authoritarian regimes. Rather, the process of influencing policy in democratic regimes is more formal, transparent, and predictable.

One political economy argument helpful to our discussion is Ehrlich's (2007, 2008) access point theory. Ehrlich (2007, 577) argues that increasing the number of access points, defined as "any *relevant* policymaker who is also either *independent* or serves a *distinct* political constituency," increases the ability of firms to effectively lobby for protection. We do not directly address firm lobbying in this chapter, but chapters 4 and 5 examine firm influence over politics.

The final mechanism linking political regime and political risk is the issue of reputation. When a government engages in a contract dispute, expropriates foreign assets, or enacts other policies that harm MNCs, there are serious reputation costs. Politicians that enact policies that harm firms are faced with lower levels of future investment.[7] As argued by Jensen (2003, 2006), democratic leaders can suffer "audience costs" by reneging on commitments with foreign investors. Audience costs are the costs generated through the domestic political process, where politicians are punished at the polls for having a poor reputation with investors. Even if expropriations are politically popular in the short run, voters may ultimately have an incentive to replace political leaders with tarnished reputations, because of resulting negative economic consequences. Thus, if voters do not credibly commit to reelecting a politician after an expropriation, forward-looking individual leaders will have less incentive to expropriate.[8] In the end, these reputation costs reduce the incentives for expropriation in democratic regimes.

Democracy Increases Political Risk

Although democratic institutions can, in theory, clearly decrease political risk for MNCs, aspects of democratic institutions may often raise political risk for multinationals. This may occur through three main mechanisms: (1) policy instability, (2) the ability of competing interest groups to influence government policy, and (3) the redistributive bias of democracy.

Democratic institutions can lead to unstable policies, either due to regularized government turnovers via elections or through problems of time-inconsistent preferences of politicians (Rodrik 1991). The former claim is relatively self-evident, because democratic politics ensures regular changes in government, thus causing policy swings between different ruling parties of conflicting ideologies. Yet the latter claim requires clarification. It has been highlighted in the literature on political business cycles that incumbent governments tend to manipulate monetary and fiscal policy prior to elections for electoral gains.[9] Incumbent politicians may also make policy changes that tie the hands of future governments (e.g., by increasing government debt), even if these policies lead to poor macroeconomic outcomes (Persson and Svensson 1989; Alesina and Tabellini 1990). Li (2009) shows that relative to autocracies, democracies have more frequent leadership turnovers, which reduce leaders' time horizons and encourage expropriation behaviors. Thus, while democratic institutions often are noted to lead to policy stability, influential scholarship has shown that an individual politician's preferences for electoral survival can lead to policy positions that could harm investors.[10]

The second mechanism linking democracy and higher political risk relates to the ability of competing interest groups to influence government policy. Although democratic systems provide multinationals with formal mechanisms to influence policy, this also opens the door for domestic actors to push for policies that harm MNCs (e.g., Li and Resnick 2003). Domestic firms may be disadvantaged relative to MNCs in access to investment capital, management expertise, technology, and international markets, but local firms likely have a deeper knowledge of local markets and domestic politics. This can put foreign firms at a disadvantage relative to domestic firms. Authors of influential works, such as Henisz (2002b), have argued that one motivation for foreign firms to enter into joint ventures with domestic firms is to utilize their political influence on government. Yet Henisz also illustrates that local partners may either protect foreign investors or push for policies that harm foreign investors.[11]

Consequently, democratic institutions allow government policies to be responsive to the preferences of various firms and voters. In cases where the preferences of MNCs overlap with domestic firms and voters or, alternately, when MNCs can influence politicians through lobbying or campaign contributions, democratic institutions lead to policies that favor MNCs. However, when these societal groups have competing preferences, democratic governments may accommodate interests opposing the multinationals and their supporters, adopting more stringent antitrust regulations affecting foreign investors and offering less generous financial incentives to them (Li and Resnick 2003; Li 2006a; Pinto and Pinto 2008, 2011; Pinto 2013). In these situations, foreign investors may experience a rise in political risk.

The third mechanism by which democracy may raise political risk concerns the so-called redistribution bias in democracy. This bias has been studied in depth in the literature on taxation and growth (see, e.g., Alesina and Rodrik 1994; Persson and Tabellini 1994a, 1994b). The idea is that because the median voter in democracy tends to be from the poorer section of a population, the voter has an incentive to use his or her political power to promote a higher tax rate and obtain redistribution in favor of the poor.[12] When economic conditions are dire and nationalist feelings are high, democratic governments often face strong populist, redistributive pressures to do something. Multinationals are likely targets of such redistribution bias, because expropriating the assets of multinationals can be a politically attractive and expedient strategy for politicians in such circumstances. This is especially plausible when the incumbent government has a leftist ideology.[13] One may conveniently allude to the recent expropriations of the assets of foreign oil and natural gas companies in several Latin American countries as a case in point.

These conflicting theoretical claims over the impact of democracy on political risk highlight the need for rigorous empirical analysis. Theoretically, one could expect that in terms of the net impact, democracy may either increase or decrease political risk. But there is very little empirical work that directly evaluates the impact of regime type on political risk. In the next section, we seek to sort out this relationship by looking at how democracy relates to actual expropriation behaviors of host countries and expropriation risk insurance ratings.

Empirical Analysis

Our empirical analysis consists of three subsections analyzing the relationship between regime type and political risk. One subsection focuses on actual expropriation events, and another studies the perceived expropriation risk data that political risk insurers use to structure and specify political risk insurance contracts. Both subsections employ cross-tabulations and graphs to provide exploratory analysis accessible to as wide a readership as possible. The final subsection repeats the analyses in the two previous subsections but employs sophisticated statistical modeling to ensure that our findings are robust and not statistical artifacts.

Past Expropriations

Asset expropriation is arguably the most extreme type of political risk that international businesses have to confront in developing countries. International business scholars have studied how a variety of other factors influence host expropriations, such as enterprise- or industry-specific factors, government capabilities and time horizon, national economic conditions, and temporal characteristics.[14] Expropriation events were rampant in the late 1960s and early 1970s, started to decline precipitously after 1976, and almost completely vanished in the late 1980s and early 1990s (Kobrin 1984; Minor 1994).

A spate of recent expropriations, however, has demonstrated the continuing relevance of this particular type of political risk for international businesses. For example, the Namibian government issued expropriation orders to 18 white commercial farmers in 2005. Venezuelan president Hugo Chavez seized two oil fields from two foreign oil firms, France's Total and Italy's Eni, in April 2006. Bolivian president Evo Morales decreed the nationalization of the country's natural gas industry on May 1, 2006. At a news conference on December 20, 2005, in La Paz, two days after winning the presidential election, Morales announced, "Many of these contracts signed by various governments are illegal and unconstitutional. It is not possible that our natural resources continue to be looted, exploited illegally, and as the lawyers say, these contracts are legally void and must be adjusted" (Associated Press, December 21, 2005).

As these recent events demonstrate, FDI remains vulnerable and exposed to the risk of expropriation. In fact, expropriation as a business risk has never ceased to impose economic costs, for foreign investors have always had to insure against such risk. The spread of international production around the globe may create more opportunities for host countries to expropriate multinational assets. Since host countries have the authority to expropriate, their domestic politics have an obvious impact on its use.

What does the actual expropriation data tell us about the relationship between regime type and expropriation? Before presenting the evidence, we should first define the concepts and their measures. According to Dahl's (1971, 1998) conception, representative democracy is a political regime that allows free and fair elections of the executive and legislative offices; the right of citizens to vote and compete for public office; and institutional guarantees for the freedom of association and expression, as provided through such means as an independent judiciary and the absence of censorship. In contrast, autocracy does not allow competitive elections and is often associated with the existence of a single leader or small ruling clique, weak political mobilization, and legal limitation on pluralism (Linz 2000).

For measurement, we use two popular indicators of regime type, one discrete and the other continuous. The discrete measure is based on the minimalist definition of democracy by Alvarez et al. (1996) and Przeworski et al. (1996, 2000); that is, for a country to be considered a democracy, the minimalist definition requires both the executive and the legislature to be elected, that there be more than one party, and that the incumbent have some chance of losing an election. Otherwise, a country is treated as an autocracy. Alternately, scholars often consider democracy to be a continuum and employ an alternative measure to indicate the level of democracy. This is the widely used composite indicator of regime type from Polity IV (Marshall and Jaggers 2008), computed as the difference between the 10-point democracy index (DEMOC) and the 10-point autocracy index (AUTOC). It ranges from –10 to +10, with larger values indicating higher levels of democracy. We employ both the discrete and continuous indicators of democracy in our analysis.

Following Kobrin (1980, 1984) and Minor (1994), expropriation refers to the forced divestment of equity ownership of a foreign direct investor.[15] Such divestment is involuntary (i.e., against the will of the owners and/or managers of the enterprise) and entails divestment of equity ownership that is across national borders and involves loss of managerial control. An expropriation act is an event that applies to all of those firms in the same industry (typically a three-digit Standard Industrial Classification code) in a country year.[16] According to Kobrin (1980, 1984) and Minor (1994), expropriation acts against foreign multinationals were committed by 79 developing countries from 1960 to 1992.[17]

Table 2.1 presents the findings from an exploratory analysis by classifying expropriation acts across regime types in terms of the total number of events, the number of regime years, the number of regime years per expropriation act, the minimum and maximum numbers of events, and variance within regime type. This is based on the discrete measure of democracy for 65 developing countries over 30 years (1960–90). Because of missing data on democracy, we lose 52 expropriation acts and 14 countries.

As shown in table 2.1, among the 523 expropriation acts in 65 countries between 1960 and 1990, democratic governments committed only 97, comprising less than 20 percent of the total, while autocracies committed the remaining 426.[18] Because the period witnessed more autocratic regime years (1,403) than democratic ones (439), however, a more accurate comparison is computed for the number of regime years per act. It takes, on average, 4.5 years for a democracy to perpetrate one expropriation act and

3.3 years for an autocracy to do so. It is clear that even using this more accurate measure, democracies remain less appropriative than autocracies.

It is also worth noting that, as table 2.1 demonstrates, both democracy and autocracy exhibit large variations in expropriation activities. Between autocracy and democracy, the ranges in the count of expropriation acts are 0–25 and 0–16, respectively, while the sample variances are 1.47 and 1.04, respectively. These statistical variations are the subject of more sophisticated statistical modeling later in this chapter, which confirms the general conclusion of table 2.1.

Figure 2.1 illustrates the distribution of expropriation acts along the different levels of democracy, to verify if the patterns in table 2.1 remain robust under the alternative, continuous measure of democracy. Since the continuous indicator of democracy has a wider coverage, figure 2.1 ends up using a larger sample for the same period (1960–90), including 76 developing countries and covering 570 acts of expropriation. As shown, most expropriation events occur near the end of full autocracy (from –5 to –10), with many fewer expropriations near the end of full democracy. But as in table 2.1, there are nonetheless a significant number of expropriation events near the end of democracy. The largest spike of expropriation acts near the end of full democracy occurs at the level of +6 of the democracy measure. It is safe to conclude that these patterns are consistent with the findings in table 2.1.

Overall, the exploratory evidence presented in both table 2.1 and figure 2.1 suggests several tentative findings. First, democracy is, generally speaking, less appropriative than nondemocracy, hence imposing less expropriation risk on international businesses. This finding is consistent with the argument that democracy decreases political risk. Second, democracy also engages in a significant number of expropriation acts. This clearly suggests

TABLE 2.1. Expropriation Acts and Regime Type (65 countries, 1960–90)

	Autocracy	Democracy	Whole Sample
Number of expropriations	426	97	523
Number of regime years	1,403	439	1,842
Number of regime years per expropriation act	3.3	4.5	3.5
Minimum	0	0	0
Maximum	25	16	25
Variance	1.47	1.04	1.36

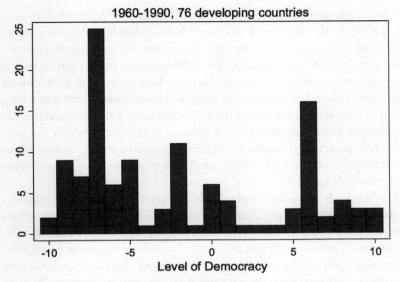

Fig. 2.1. Annual expropriations acts and democracy

that there may be a grain of truth to the expectation that democracy may, in certain circumstances, increase expropriation risk for international businesses. Hence, to gauge the net impact of regime type on expropriation requires more comprehensive statistical modeling.

The Future Risk of Expropriation

In the previous section, we provided clear, though tentative, evidence on how democratic institutions affect actual expropriation events. There are, however, two limitations to this analysis. First, in some, though not all, cases, scholars have built their theories of democracy and expropriation by observing past acts of expropriation. For example, mass nationalization in Cuba led to changes in thinking about how unconstrained authoritarian regimes increase risks for firms. Yet empirical work often uses this same data on nationalization to both build and test theory. Ideally, scholarly research should test theory on data that is independent of the theory-building process.

Second, with dramatic changes in the world economy over the past decades, is the past still a best predictor of the future? Many social scientists (including the authors of this book) believe that history is very informative and that many of the domestic factors that influence politicians remain quite similar and relevant. Yet differences in the structure of the international system and changing ideas on how to operate an economy clearly affect the relations between firms and politicians. There was a long period of time around the end of the 1980s and early 1990s when actual expropriations essentially disappeared (Minor 1994), even though the perceived risk of expropriation for foreign investors did not drop to zero. Thus past expropriations may have little predictive power in explaining current and future political risk.

We believe it is important to take this skepticism seriously. In this subsection, we examine the preliminary evidence for how political institutions affect the future risk of expropriations. This may seem like a daunting task, but insurance providers do just that in the business of assessing, predicting, and pricing risks. In the pricing of auto insurance, for example, insurance companies take into account past information such as accident history, coupled with current factors such as age and location, to assess the probability of a policyholder being involved in an accident. Knowing how insurance companies assess political risk when underwriting policies for international clients, which we endeavor to explain in this section, gives an insight into the decision-making calculus of foreign direct investors, and data used by these underwriters help us make our own determination of the connection between political risk and FDI.

A large and complex insurance industry has emerged to help multinationals mitigate political risk by purchasing insurance contracts. While there are some companies that specialize in providing political risk insurance, such as Sovereign, many of the major providers are part of a broader insurance industry, including Lloyd's of London, Chubb, and AIG. Among the underwriters in this broad spectrum are those affiliated with governments, such as Export Development Canada and the U.S. government's political risk insurer, Overseas Private Investment Corporation (OPIC); multilateral institutions, such as the World Bank's political risk insurance provider, Multilateral Investment Guarantee Agency (MIGA); and a slew of newly privatized export credit agencies. All of these organizations offer political risk insurance for multinational investors.

Political risk insurance is distinct from other types of property insurance in that it is designed to insure against specific political events. The political risk insurance industry typically categorizes these political risks into three broad categories: (1) war and political violence, (2) expropriation/ breach of contract, and (3) transfer risk. War and political violence risks are associated with the direct or indirect impact of political violence, such as civil war, uprisings, or some types of terrorist attack. The political violence covered by insurance can be directly targeted at the firm or simply can occur in the country at such levels as to make multinational operations unprofitable. The second type of risk, expropriation risk, covers direct nationalization and expropriation of assets, along with breach of contracts between the firm and government. Finally, transfer risk encompasses the risk of governments restricting capital flows in ways that harm MNCs, usually during a financial crisis.

One of the largest providers of political risk insurance to emerging markets is the World Bank's MIGA.[19] Its mandate is to provide investment insurance and investment promotion to developing countries. From 1990 to 2000, MIGA issued 473 political risk insurance contracts totaling $7.1 billion (West and Tarazona 2001). These contracts helped facilitate $36 billion in FDI to some of the most risky countries.

Another major provider is the U.S. government's political risk insurer, OPIC. In 2007, OPIC provided political risk insurance or financing for 150 projects in 49 countries, including beverage bottling in Afghanistan, airport construction in Ecuador, oil and gas exploration in Egypt, a university in Lebanon, power generation in Pakistan, housing construction in Tanzania, banking in Turkey, and a shopping center in the Ukraine (OPIC 2007). Political acts have affected OPIC-insured investments on a number of occasions. From 1971 to 2008, OPIC paid 286 claims totaling $969.6 million.[20] Some of these were claims based on nationwide expropriations, such as claims of expropriated U.S. investments in Iran and Vietnam in the 1970s. In other cases, OPIC paid claims for single events, some as major as an expropriation claim for $217 million by MidAmerican Energy Holdings against the government of Indonesia.

Risk insurers, both public and private, have paid major claims in recent years. In the power sector alone, claims have been made on the imposition of capital controls in Argentina, the cancellation of power projects in India and Indonesia, and investment disputes in Venezuela and China (Martin 2004). These disputes are not just concentrated in investments in mining, gas, oil, and infrastructure. According to a survey of past OPIC claims, firms that purchased risk insurance and brought claims to OPIC spanned across a number of industries, including services, manufacturing, banking, and agriculture. Among the 279 OPIC claims during 1971–2004, there were only 30 claims from oil, gas, and mining industries and 10 claims from infrastructure investments (O'Sullivan 2005).

Although political violence risks have received a tremendous amount of attention recently, expropriation remains the event that is most damaging for firms. Of all the dollars paid out by OPIC from 1970 to 1978, 96 percent of the claims were for expropriation. From 1991 to 2004, even after including the major financial crises that triggered a number of transfer claims, 84 percent of the settlement amounts of OPIC claims were for expropriations (O'Sullivan 2005, 31). The Organization for Economic Co-operation and Development (OECD) notes that "disputes on direct expropriation—mainly related to nationalization that marked the 70s and 80s—have been replaced by disputes related to foreign investment regulation and *indirect expropriation*" (OECD 2004, 2). Although risk insurance solves some of the risk problems for multinationals, it does not cover all types of political risk. Coverage can be prohibitively expensive and usually applies to only 90 percent of the investment.[21] The U.S. government political risk insurer (OPIC) provides rough guidelines on coverage rates. For investments in the oil and gas industry, a production facility would pay 1.35 percent to 1.6 percent of the value of the assets per year for coverage against expropriation, and full coverage (expropriation, inconvertibility, political violence, etc.) would cost 3.4 percent of the value of the assets per year. These are only baseline prices for the coverage, and rates can go higher based on country and type of operation.[22] Most providers also require firms filing claims to hand over the asset to the provider.[23] In such cases, a firm filing a nationalization claim essentially gives the asset to the risk insurer in exchange for the claim.

As explained earlier, our goal here is not to explain the limitations of the risk insurance industry. Rather, we believe that the actuarial work done in this industry provides useful information to social scientists attempting to understand the factors that contribute to political risk. The political risk insurance industry hires teams of analysts to conduct both quantitative and qualitative risk analysis that is used for pricing insurance contracts and relied on by some location consultancies to evaluate political risk when making recommendations to their clients.[24] This data is especially useful in our context.

First, it provides detailed information on the exact type of risk that we wish to investigate. Most past studies have dealt with this issue indirectly, focusing on FDI flows and linking this to political risk. In this chapter, we address our inquiry more directly, using data on actual expropriations and political risk insurance ratings on expropriation. Second, this insurance data looks forward, as risk insurance contracts usually cover 15 years into the future. Thus this data is an excellent complement to the analysis of past expropriations. Third, this data represents the perceptions of political risk insurers. The perceptions of insurers and, by implication, those of their investor clients are central to explaining how institutions affect FDI. To the extent that business decision-making hinges on the perceived level of risk, the perceptions of insurers and their investor clients, regardless of whether these perceptions are biased or not, play an important role in determining which countries receive investment and the amount of investment in each case. Equally important, we believe these perception-based measures of risk are an excellent complement to the measure of actual expropriation acts.

The data presented in this study comes from ONDD, the Belgian Export Credit Agency, which provides both export credit and political risk insurance.[25] The ONDD is one of the few political risk insurance providers that make their data publicly available (via their website), and the data provided by ONDD is especially useful because it contains disaggregated ratings by type of risk—expropriation/breach of contract, political violence, and transfer risk. We believe that this data is broadly representative of political risk ratings by other agencies.[26]

The ONDD rates countries at least once a year, using both a qualitative and quantitative methodology to assign each country a risk rating. This rating represents an assessment of risk over the 15 years of insurance coverage offered by the ONDD and, thus, is used to generate the prices charged for political risk insurance. Although prices can vary based on project attributes, this risk rating is the core data used to price the country-level risk and, therefore, offers an ideal measure of political risk for purposes of this chapter.

The ONDD risk insurance rating groups countries into seven categories of risk. The countries with lowest risk are coded 1, while those with highest risk are coded 7. In table 2.2, we present the seven categories of the ONDD expropriation risk ratings for 153 countries in 2004, including some representative countries and a count of the number of countries per category. While a large number of countries (39) have the lowest expropriation risk, this group contains mostly high-income OECD countries.

What explains the cross-national pattern of the perceived expropriation risk in table 2.2? Of the 39 countries with the lowest expropriation risk, 24 of these achieve the highest level of democracy (+10). There are only two major outliers in this group, including Singapore (Polity score of –2) and Bahrain (Polity score of –7), both of which are nondemocratic but in the lowest risk category. The pattern is even more striking when we look at countries in the sample with the highest democracy scores. Only 32 countries in the world achieve a +10 in the Polity score, and 75 percent of these countries are in the lowest risk category. The remaining eight democratic countries have risk ratings of 2, 3, or 4. These higher-risk democratic countries include Israel (3), Mongolia (3), Trinidad and Tobago (3), Uruguay (3), Papua New Guinea (4), and Mauritius (4), most of which are not long-established, mature democracies.

These patterns also hold when we look at other levels of democracy. Authoritarian regimes are largely clustered at the highest risk levels, while semidemocratic regimes tend to fall in the middle of the spectrum. Overall, the patterns of expropriation risk ratings are consistent with our findings based on actual expropriation data. Democracies are, on average, associated with less expropriation risk than nondemocracies, but some democratic governments may be perceived to have high expropriation risks.

Statistical Models of Expropriation

Our data analyses in the previous two subsections emphasize accessibility and their exploratory nature, thus avoiding highly technical statistical tests. But the simplicity of those analyses, in not providing rigorous statistical tests of the theoretical expectations and controlling for confounding

TABLE 2.2.   ONDD Expropriation Risk Rating Categories (153 countries, 2004)

1 Lowest Risk	2	3	4	5	6	7 Highest Risk
Australia	Botswana	Argentina	Angola	Republic	Belarus	Iraq
Belgium	Bulgaria	China	Colombia	of the	Côte d'Ivoire	Somalia
Latvia	Estonia	India	Kenya	Congo	Cuba	Zimbabwe
Singapore	Mexico	Peru	Russia	Libya	Haiti	
United States	Tunisia	Turkey	Vietnam	Indonesia	Iran	
				Nigeria		
				Venezuela		
$N = 39$	$N = 15$	$N = 24$	$N = 40$	$N = 22$	$N = 10$	$N = 3$

forces, has the potential to render results that are artifacts of confounding factors or to disguise what is, in reality, random noise in the data. For example, one may argue that the findings in the previous two subsections could have resulted from the failure to consider the role of economic development. It is well known that economic development encourages and promotes democracy and, at the same time, typically correlates with better rule of law and, by implication, less expropriation risk.[27] An analysis of the relationship between democracy and political risk without controlling for the level of economic development could thus be misleading. Hence, in this subsection, we present two statistical tests of the impact of democracy, first on actual expropriation events and then on perceived expropriation risk.

Modeling Actual Expropriation Events

Our statistical model of the effect of democracy on actual expropriation is based on a sample of 63 countries[28] from 1960 to 1990. According to the data of Kobrin (1980, 1984) and Minor (1994), during that period, 79 countries committed at least one expropriation act that fits our earlier noted definition. Sixteen of the 79 countries dropped out of our sample in statistical analysis, due to missing data on the independent variables.

In addition, the analysis excludes those countries that never experienced any expropriation, because they may follow a qualitatively different causal process; pooling the two types of countries may lead to biased estimates. These excluded countries are mainly of two types. The first type includes over 20 traditional OECD countries. They are excluded from analysis for two primary reasons. First, OECD countries are much more developed and have better rule of law than those in our sample. None of these OECD countries has been reported in the news sources to have committed the type of actual expropriations we study here. Hence, it is reasonable to expect that the expropriation process (or the lack thereof) in these countries differs qualitatively from that in our sample countries. Second, as Blonigen and Wang (2004) show convincingly in their analysis, FDI activities in highly developed and less developed economies follow different patterns and should be studied separately. Since expropriations are often driven by the attributes of FDI assets (e.g., oil sector), government expropriations are likely to differ between these two types of countries as well.[29]

The second type of countries excluded from analysis consists of long-established socialist economies, such as the Soviet Union, other East Euro-

pean countries, Cuba, China, and Vietnam. These countries largely restricted FDI from entering their economies in the sample period. The oc-
casional foreign investment in these economies was often favored and protected by the governments. The complete or almost complete absence of
foreign capital makes its expropriation an unlikely proposition.

The dependent variable of the statistical model is the annual number of
expropriation acts in a given country. The key independent variables are
the discrete indicator of democracy and the continuous indicator of the
level of democracy we employed previously.

We control for three types of confounding factors that can influence expropriation. The first set of control variables is economic, including GDP
per capita, its squared term, and economic growth. All the economic variables are lagged one year to control for possible reverse causality. As argued
by Jodice (1980), the effect of GDP per capita on expropriation is expected
to be curvilinear, rising at the low level of economic development and declining after passing a certain threshold. To model the curvilinear relationship requires us to include GDP per capita and its squared term. Economic
growth, measured by the annual growth rate of per capita income, reflects
the overall economic conditions in a country. It reflects the impact of economic dislocations and recessions and correlates with currency and banking crises. Low economic growth encourages more expropriation acts.

The second set of control variables, including the lagged dependent
variable, duration dependence variables, and the expropriation history of a
country, concerns the time-series nature of expropriations and other unob-
served factors. The lagged dependent variable serves to control for the previous period behavior and other potentially relevant variables absent from
the model. In addition, since the mid-1970s, host expropriations showed a
decline across countries (Kobrin 1984; Minor 1994), albeit with variations
among them. To control for the duration dependence in countries for years
without expropriation, we include in the regression the nonexpropriation
year counter and three cubic spline variables (see Beck, Katz, and Tucker
1998). Finally, investors are forward looking and avoid host countries that
often expropriated foreign assets in the past. The amount of FDI available
for expropriation in such countries would be less than in those without the
reputation of expropriation. Hence, some countries expropriate less not
because they prefer not to but because they have already seized most of
what is available. In the absence of FDI stock data for the early years, we
use the number of past expropriation acts in a country until the previous

year to control for the effect of spoiled reputation and strategic behaviors by forward-looking investors. This variable should have a negative sign.

The third set of control variables are other political factors, including regime durability, left-right party orientation of the chief executive, and veto players. First, the short time horizon of leaders may motivate expropriations of foreign assets for political gains (Li 2009), and political instability and regime transition may affect the time horizon of leaders. If such effect is not controlled for, the estimated impact of democracy may be confounded by the missing variable. To capture the effect of political instability and regime change, we use the measure of regime durability from Polity IV. It is the number of years since the most recent regime change, defined by a three-point change in the Polity score over a period of three years or less, the end of the transition period defined by the lack of stable political institutions, or the year 1900, whichever comes last. The first year during which a new (postchange) polity is established is coded as the baseline "year zero" (value = 0), and each subsequent year adds one point to the value of the variable. Regime durability should discourage expropriations.

Second, as noted, the leftist ideology of the chief executive, favoring labor interests and state interventions in the economy, may encourage more expropriations of foreign assets, whereas right governments representing business elites should be less likely to expropriate foreign investments (e.g., Hawkins, Mintz, and Provissiero 1976), but some scholars (Kobrin 1980, 1984; Lipson 1985) suggest that ideologically motivated expropriations either became concentrated in a few countries (e.g., Algeria, Angola, Chile, Ethiopia, Indonesia, Mozambique, Peru, Tanzania, Uganda, and Zambia) from 1960 to 1979 or largely declined after 1960. The left government is coded 1 if the chief executive's party is communist, socialist, social democratic, or left-wing; it is coded 0 otherwise. The right government is coded 1 if the chief executive's party is conservative, Christian democratic, or right-wing; it is coded 0 otherwise (Beck et al. 2001). The reference category for both variables is the centrist executive or executives that are not clearly left- or right-leaning. Since the expectation is that left governments should be qualitatively different from right governments in terms of expropriation behaviors, we will conduct an equality test of the coefficients of the two variables.

Third, to measure the impact of veto players, we use Henisz's (2002a, 2002b) political constraint index (POLCON III) (Henisz 2010). The index uses information on (1) the number of independent branches of government (including executive, lower, and upper legislative chambers) with veto power over policy change, (2) the degree of alignment across branches of government based on party composition of each branch, and (3) the degree of preference heterogeneity within each legislative branch. For the index, each additional veto point not only has a positive but diminishing effect on the level of constraints on policy change but also causes the homogeneity (or heterogeneity) of party preferences within an opposition (or aligned) branch of government to raise the level of constraints.[30] Veto players should discourage expropriations. Since democracies typically have more veto players than nondemocracies, this variable should allow us to test whether the constraining effect of democracy on expropriations is driven by the presence of more veto players or not.

In chapter 3, we incorporate judicial institutions into our analysis, through the use of Henisz's POLCON IV index. This choice of variables is driven by theory. In this chapter, we control for how veto players affect our findings on the relationship between democracy and risks; in chapter 3, we focus on a more nuanced test of political institutions, ultimately isolating judicial institutions from other political institutions. It is worth noting, though, that our statistical results in this chapter are not sensitive to which version of the POLCON index we use in analysis.

Because the dependent variable is an event count, ordinary least square (OLS) estimates can be inefficient, inconsistent, and biased (Long 1997). While Poisson regression is often used to model event count, it imposes the restrictive assumption that the conditional mean equals the conditional variance. This assumption does not hold even by eyeballing the values of the unconditional means and variance of the dependent variable (not reported due to space). Negative binomial regression addresses this problem by including an overdispersion parameter, allowing the conditional variance to exceed the conditional mean (Cameron and Trivedi 1998). Given the pooled design of the data, we apply the negative binomial fixed effects model used by Hausman, Hall, and Griliches (1984). The model has the advantage of allowing for the individual-specific fixed effect and overdispersion parameter by conditioning them out of the likelihood function. The disadvantage of the model is that it does not work like a typical fixed effects estimator and fails to eliminate completely the individual-specific time-invariant heterogeneity (Allison and Waterman 2002).

Table 2.3 presents our statistical findings. Model 1 employs the level of democracy; Model 2 uses the discrete indicator of democracy; Model 3 tests whether the effect of democracy is driven by the presence of many veto players in the polity; and Model 4 tests the effect of regime type after controlling for the difference between left and right governments.

Across the models in table 2.3, the control variables have effects that are consistent with the expectations in the literature. The effect of real GDP per capita is positive and statistically different from zero, while that of its squared term is negative and statistically different from zero. As income rises, the number of expropriation acts first increases and then declines. Economic growth has a statistically significant negative effect on expropriation. Under favorable national economic conditions, the host is less likely to expropriate foreign investment. But economic slowdown induces more acts of expropriation.

The effect of expropriation history is statistically different from zero

TABLE 2.3. Democracy and Actual Expropriation Acts

	Model 1	Model 2	Model 3	Model 4
Level of Democracy	−0.0476***		−0.0180	−0.0479***
	(0.0166)		(0.0203)	(0.0169)
Democracy		−0.4173*		
		(0.2397)		
Veto Player			−1.7936**	
			(0.7337)	
Left Executive				0.2592
				(0.2368)
Right Executive				−0.4548
				(0.3702)
Regime Durability	−0.0146*	−0.0140*	−0.0134*	−0.0146*
	(0.0077)	(0.0077)	(0.0078)	(0.0077)
GDP per Capita	0.0005***	0.0005**	0.0006***	0.0005***
	(0.0002)	(0.0002)	(0.0002)	(0.0002)
GDP per Capita Squared	−4.0925e-08*	−3.9029e-08*	−5.3122e-08**	−3.8721e-08
	(2.3289e-08)	(2.3404e-08)	(2.4602e-08)	(2.4042e-08)
Growth Rate	−0.0210**	−0.0198**	−0.0215**	−0.0205**
	(0.0093)	(0.0093)	(0.0092)	(0.0094)
Expropriation History	−0.0677***	−0.0640***	−0.0713***	−0.0691***
	(0.0123)	(0.0121)	(0.0122)	(0.0145)
Lagged Dependent Variable	0.1186***	0.1194***	0.1203***	0.1111***
	(0.0274)	(0.0269)	(0.0274)	(0.0278)
Constant	−1.0933***	−0.8078***	−0.9230***	−1.1093***
	(0.3004)	(0.2838)	(0.3127)	(0.3045)
Observations	1,769	1,758	1,748	1,769

Note: Negative binomial fixed effects estimator, with standard errors in parentheses. Nonexpropriations years and three cubic splines not reported.

Two–tailed test: * significant at 10%; ** significant at 5%; *** significant at 1%.

and negative. This is consistent with the expectation that investors avoid countries that are known to have expropriated in the past, giving them fewer expropriation opportunities in the future. The lagged dependent variable has a statistically significant positive effect, suggesting that countries that did not expropriate the previous year are less likely to do so this year.

Regime durability has a statistically significant negative effect across all four models. This indicates that political stability and durable regimes discourage expropriations of foreign investments. The veto player variable has a statistically significant negative effect in Model 3, showing that countries with more veto players are less likely to expropriate foreign assets. In Model 4, while the positive effect of the left executive and the negative effect of the right executive are not statistically different from the centrist executive or executives that are not clearly left- or right-leaning, an equality chi-squared test between the left and right variables would indicate that their coefficients are statistically different. This suggests that left governments are more likely to expropriate foreign investments than right governments.

These findings give us confidence in the strength of our model of expropriation behaviors. Now, moving to the effect of democracy, the results are consistent with the theoretical expectations. Model 1 indicates that more democratic countries engage in fewer expropriation acts than less democratic ones. Model 2 shows that democracies expropriate less frequently than autocracies. Hence, the effect of regime type on actual expropriations is not sensitive to whether we use a continuous measure or a discrete indicator of democracy.

Model 3 indicates that the effect of democracy is no longer statistically different from zero when the effect of veto player is controlled for. This demonstrates that the effect of democracy on expropriation is largely driven by the fact that more democratic countries tend to impose more constraints on public policy-making, including expropriations, than do less democratic ones. Finally, in Model 4, the effect of democracy remains negative and statistically different from zero even when we control for the partisan difference between left and right governments. The constraining effect of democracy on expropriation is not affected by the partisan difference of the executive.

Overall, democracy tends to reduce the number of expropriation acts against foreign investors. This effect is not sensitive to how we measure regime type, to the partisan bias of the chief executive, or to other economic causes of expropriations.[31] It is also worth noting that the beneficial effect of democracy largely derives from the presence of greater political constraints over the government in more democratic countries. To the extent that the democracy variable does not dominate the explanatory power of the models, democracy does not correlate "perfectly" with the absence of expropriation events. These results clearly support our findings in the previous two subsections.

Modeling Perceived Expropriation Risk

Our empirical analysis of the effect of democracy on perceived expropriation risk includes as many as 134 countries, where mostly very small countries are dropped from the analysis due to data availability.[32] The dependent variable is the ordinal measure of the disaggregated ONDD expropriation risk price category for 2004, which is used by insurance agents to determine the pricing for a 15-year forward-looking political risk insurance contract. This measure ranges from 1 to 7 (lowest risk to highest risk). The key independent variables are the discrete indicator of democracy and the continuous indicator of the level of democracy we employed previously.

The control variables build on the regressions in the previous section, including regime durability, the level of development (GDP per capita and GDP per capital squared), economic growth, and regional dummy variables.[33] Since a country fixed effect model is not possible for a cross-sectional data set, regional dummy variables are included to mitigate region-specific effects. It is also worth noting that given the cross-sectional nature of the data set, we could not control for the lagged dependent variable, a counter of past expropriations, or the duration dependence cubic splines like in the actual expropriation model.

Table 2.4 presents our statistical results. The first model (Model 1) includes the level of democracy using the –10 to +10 Polity IV measure (*Level of Democracy*) and our control variables. We find that democratic institutions lead to a statistically significant reduction in political risk. These results are surprisingly robust under a number of specifications. This includes excluding the OECD countries from the sample, dropping the extreme cases of political risk, adding measures for natural resource endowments, and using alternative measures of political regimes. In Model 2, we substituted the Polity measure of democracy with the discrete measure of political regimes. This measure, coded 0 for dictatorships and 1 for democracies, yields substantively similar results.[34] Unlike in the actual expropriation analysis, we did not find GDP per capita squared as statistically significant, which is not surprising given the limited variations in the small cross-sectional sample.

In Models 3 and 4, we further examine the robustness of our results. In Model 3, we include the Henisz measure of veto players. Democracy is robust at the 0.10 level to the inclusion of veto players, but given the high correlation between veto players and democracy as well as the limited variations in the veto player variable in the small cross-sectional sample, we hesitate to conclude that the veto players are not associated with lower levels of perceived political risk.

In Model 4, we include dummy variables for the partisanship of the executive. Note that this is a cross section that drops half of the observations of the previous models due to missing data. Even though we feel that the limited number of observations does not allow us to draw any clear con-

TABLE 2.4. Democracy and Political Risk Ratings

	Model 1	Model 2	Model 3	Model 4
Level of Democracy	−0.0759***		−0.0628*	−0.107***
	(0.0256)		(0.0332)	(0.0388)
Democracy		−0.7346***		
		(0.2559)		
Veto Player			−0.5270	
			(0.7983)	
Left Executive				0.7736
				(0.6020)
Right Executive				1.324*
				(0.6977)
Regime Durability	−0.012**	−0.0092*	−0.012**	−0.0165
	(0.006)	(0.0052)	(0.0056)	(0.0105)
GDP per Capita	0.1798	0.3286	0.3219	−0.4063
	(0.9085)	(0.8662)	(0.9454)	(1.3189)
GDP per Capita Squared	−0.0602	−0.0729	−0.0692	−0.0266
	(0.0606)	(0.0579)	(0.0632)	(0.0887)
Growth Rate	−0.0398	−0.0477	−0.0436	−0.0202
	(0.0309)	(0.0323)	(0.0313)	(0.0413)
Observations	133	135	132	72
Pseudo R^2	0.3414	0.3284	0.3420	0.4566

Note: The dependent variable in all regressions is the ONDD political risk rating for expropriation/breach of contract risks. Ordered probit with robust (Huber–White) standard errors in parentheses.

Two–tailed test: * significant at 10%; ** significant at 5%; *** significant at 1%.

clusions on the relationship between partisanship and political risk, the effect of democracy is robust to the inclusion of dummy variables for left and right governments.

We estimated changes in predicted values for each category of political risk from Model 1 of table 2.4.[35] Holding all other control variables at their mean, we estimate a move from an authoritarian regime to a democratic regime (–10 to +10 in the policy score) on changes in political risk ratings. A move from –10 to +10 increases the probability of being in the lowest risk category by 22.35 percent and increases the probability of being in one of the three lowest categories by 52.5 percent. Thus democratic institutions have an enormous impact on political risk.

Conclusion

How do domestic political institutions affect expropriations against multinationals? While recent events reaffirm the relevance of this question, it has received little theoretical and empirical scrutiny in international business, economics, and political science. We identify theoretical mechanisms by which democracy could increase or decrease political risk for international businesses, and we offer, for the first time, large-N empirical analyses that examine the impact of democracy on both actual expropriation behaviors and expropriation risk insurance ratings. Our evidence demonstrates that both democracies and autocracies expropriate foreign investment but that democracies do so less frequently. Based on our analysis of the larger sample of actual expropriations, the democratic advantage in better property rights protection for foreign investors appears largely driven by the presence of more veto players and political constraints in democratic countries.

Our research has implications for studies of rule of law, property rights, investment behaviors, and privatization reforms. In recent years, the rule of law has attracted wide attention because it affects the success of economic transition, democratic transition and consolidation, and the effects of democracy on growth. Some theoretical research and little empirical analysis focus on the link between regime type and political risk. In this chapter, we fill this gap by directly analyzing the relationship between regime type and political risk.

In the literature on how politics influences investment behaviors, some scholars argue that one reason why democracies attract investment, both domestic and foreign, is that they offer better property rights protection (e.g., Feng 2001; Li and Resnick 2003; Li 2006a; Jensen 2003). The analysis in this chapter provides direct empirical support for these arguments by showing that democracies expropriate less often.

This analysis has implications for the prospect of privatization reforms in many less-developed and transitional economies. Many scholars (e.g., Spiller 1995; Schmidt 2000) argue that for those reforms to succeed, governments must be committed not to expropriate later on the assets and returns of successful private firms. Since foreign investors have purchased much of the privatized assets, this analysis informs us that democratic governments' commitment to the privatization reform process is likely to be more credible. The prospect of privatization reform is more promising in democracy.

Identifying these regime effects on political risk is the first step in understanding how politics affects the business environment. In the next chapter, we dig more deeply into how politics affects political risk, by conducting a survey of multinational investors. Thus, while the current chapter focuses on acts of expropriation and risk insurance ratings, the following chapter explores at the microlevel how the types of institution affect the risk environment for multinationals.

CHAPTER 3

Institutional Determinants of Foreign Direct Investment in the Developing World

THE PAST TWO DECADES have seen a revival of both democracy and foreign direct investment in the developing world. The similar time frame has led many political economy scholars to argue that simultaneous political reform and growth of foreign investment are no mere coincidence and that democratization actually promotes increased FDI in the developing world.[1] Beyond minimal notions of what it takes to be a democracy, there is also an argument that effective courts and adherence to the rule of law promote a climate conducive to domestic and foreign investment.[2]

In the previous chapter, we examined how democratic institutions affect the risk environment for multinational investors. Our empirical analysis finds that democratic countries are associated with fewer acts of expropriation and that investments in democracies pay considerably less for insurance contracts covering expropriation and breach of contract. While our evidence in the previous chapter suggests that democracies should be effective in attracting FDI, not all scholars concur about the benefits of democracy for FDI. Some studies find that authoritarian regimes are more attractive to foreign investors[3] or that regime type makes little difference for FDI inflows.[4] Other researchers claim that economic factors, including macroeconomic conditions and market-oriented reforms, are the most important FDI determinants.[5] Still others suggest that security issues (e.g., good relations between the host and home country) and geographic proximity to the home country of the investor are key considerations for explaining investment flows.[6]

Understudied in the existing literature is the effect that political institutions within democracy can have on investment decisions of individual firms. Most previous studies use large data sets from the World Bank, the International Monetary Fund, and other sources to arrive at their conclusions. Missing from these studies, however, is information from the actual decision makers—the foreign investors themselves. While imputing the motivations of investors based on broad economic and political measures is justified when there is nothing else available, it seems that a better understanding of investor motivations is to go directly to the source.

This study attempts to reap the benefits from both large-N studies and more direct measures of investor preferences. While chapter 2 points to a broad relationship between democratic institutions and political risk, we dig deeper in this chapter into how institutions affect the risk environment for multinational investors. First, we investigate investor motivations by querying investors about their investment priorities. In doing so, we rely in large measure on a survey including questions related to political, economic, and geographic factors, administered by Biglaiser and Staats (2010) to chief executive officers of U.S. firms with operations in Latin America, to understand what influences CEO investment decisions.[7] Latin America is an ideal setting to survey FDI determinants: not only has the region shed many of the authoritarian orientations that plagued it during the 1940s through the 1970s, but FDI inflows vary across the region, which enriches country comparisons (Garland and Biglaiser 2009; Blonigen and Wang 2004). Second, to test the validity of the survey results, we carried out a large-N panel data analysis of 138 developing countries as well as an analysis of Latin American countries exclusively, to gauge the importance of political institutions, including the courts and rule of law.

Confirming findings in work by Biglaiser and DeRouen (2006), Feng (2001), Li and Resnick (2003), Globerman and Shapiro (2002), Grosse (1997, 148), Crenshaw (1991), and Tuman and Emmert (2004), the survey and panel data indicate that property rights protection through democratic institutions, including strong and effective courts that help bring about adherence to the rule of law, weighed most heavily relative to other factors in whether to increase investments in any given country. In contrast, factors not directly tied to investment risk, such as general economic conditions and respect for human rights, civil liberties, and political rights appeared to play a less pivotal role. Similarly, good relations with the United States and proximity of the investment venue to corporate headquarters were found to have less influence on FDI inflows.

It is not surprising that foreign investors appear most concerned with factors relating to protection of property rights. As highlighted in chapter 2, there are often high sunk costs associated with overseas investments. Investors are usually in a dominant position when host countries are courting them, but once they "sink" large amounts of capital, the advantage turns to the host country, in what Vernon (1998, 65) refers to as the "obsolescing bargain." Concerns about property rights are relevant especially in Latin America, a region long known for appropriating foreign assets.[8]

The survey findings, supplemented by aggregate data analysis, hold implications on the determinants of FDI. First, confirming the findings of chapter 2 as well as work by Jensen (2006, 2008), Li (2006a, 2006b, 2009) and Li and Resnick (2003), the results suggest that regime type alone is less important than factors more directly tied to investment risk. While the survey indicated that democracy is moderately important for investor decisions, such a consideration paled in comparison to investment safety. Although democracy potentially affects investment safety through political checks and balances, adherence to the rule of law, and efficient and effective court systems, such protections are not necessarily embedded in a democratic regime.

Second, the findings contribute to the debate on the effect of good governance and property rights on foreign investor preferences. Building on North (1990) and de Soto (2000), who claim that stable property rights are critical for economic growth and development, our results show that foreign investors similarly favor secure property rights. Third, recent discussions and, in some instances, actions related to expropriation or contract renegotiations in Namibia, Russia, South Africa, Thailand, Zambia, and Zimbabwe have reawakened investor fears, circumstances that show the importance of our study to developing areas beyond Latin America.

Fourth, our results suggest the value of survey research to understand the dynamics of FDI. Many FDI studies have relied solely on data from the World Bank and the IMF because of their breadth in terms of countries, years, and potential determinants. While the data sets are highly beneficial for scholars working on political economy questions, there are limitations with such data. In the case of FDI, survey work is helpful to uncover the calculi decision makers actually use. Our use of both large-N data and survey work helps to open the foreign capital black box.

This chapter is divided into five sections. We first discuss the determinants of FDI and develop hypotheses to assess investor decisions. We then present issues of model specification and the results for the survey and panel data of developing countries. After this, we provide an explanation for the results. Next, we focus on the importance of judicial institutions and rule of law for attracting FDI inflows. using survey and panel data from Latin American countries, before we conclude this chapter.

Determinants of FDI in Latin America

As outlined in the first chapter of this book, FDI, defined as private capital flows that provide a parent firm with at least 10 percent control over an enterprise outside the home country, has a legacy dating back at least hundreds of years. Global FDI fell in the early 1900s, only to take off in the mid-1950s, with U.S. firms at the forefront. As FDI expanded in the early post–World War II years, much of the investment flowed to developed countries, as many in the developing world questioned the merits of allowing in foreign ventures. Indeed, in the 1930s through the 1970s, nationalist governments in Latin America frequently expropriated the assets of U.S. multinational corporations within their territory, converting these firms into state-owned enterprises.[9] Since the 1980s, most Latin American countries have attempted to attract FDI. As figure 3.1 illustrates, for the 17 most-often studied countries in Latin America, U.S. FDI inflows grew in the mid- to late 1980s and took off in the mid-1990s (Bureau of Economic Analysis 2007). However, there is wide variation among recipients of U.S. FDI inflows in Latin America (Garland and Biglaiser 2009).

The cross-national variation has stimulated a large literature on FDI determinants, with researchers often reaching very different conclusions. The FDI literature is divided into five broad categories: (1) macroeconomic conditions and the characteristics of the host country; (2) economic reforms; (3) good governance, including democratization and political risk; (4) property rights protection; and (5) security and geographic considerations. Some research shows that macroeconomic conditions provide differing incentives for foreign investors. For example, rising per capita GDP, high rates of domestic growth, and large GDP indicate an attractive do-

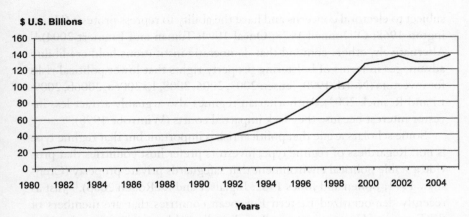

Fig. 3.1. Total U.S. FDI in Latin America, 1980–2004 (current U.S.$)

mestic market for investors (Brewer 1993; Crenshaw 1991; Grosse 1997, 145). In addition, certain characteristics of host countries, such as literacy and education, are expected to catalyze FDI based on the need for skilled labor (Mankiw, Romer, and Weil 1992).

Economic reforms including trade and tax liberalization, minimal government regulation, and limited state ownership of industries, along with support for private enterprise, also affect the decision making of prospective investors.[10] Trade liberalization is critical for firms interested in outsourcing goods in host countries for export or to unbundle goods into multiple stages of production for cost savings (McKeown 1999; Agarwal, Gubitz, and Nunnenkamp 1992). Tax liberalization is also important for firms wanting to lighten their tax burden or to receive tax subsidies that create added incentives to invest abroad (Root and Ahmed 1978; Bajpai and Sachs 2000). Similarly, minimal government regulation and domestic sectors that support private enterprise suggest that foreign businesses will face few challenges from more nationalistic interests in host countries (Gastanaga, Nugent, and Pashamova 1998, 1310–12).

In contrast to economic explanations, factors related to good governance, including regime type and risk considerations, also may influence FDI. In the development literature, there is a big debate about the effects of regime type on investment. Some authors posit that authoritarian regimes are most likely to inspire investor confidence because they are less subject to electoral concerns and have the ability to repress protests (Huntington 1968; O'Donnell 1978; Oneal 1994; Tuman and Emmert 2004).[11] Alternatively, others contend that democratic institutions hold credibility advantages in terms of bolstering property rights that lower political risks for investors (North 1990; Jensen 2003, 2006, 2008; Li 2006a, 2006b, 2009; Li and Resnick 2003). Authoritarian regimes also arguably attract less investor interest because they lack impartial courts (Wintrobe 1998).

Some scholars argue that political risk is important but that regime type is not. Regardless of regime type, investors prefer host countries that provide a stable political environment that safeguards private property (Crenshaw 1991; Bollen and Jones 1982; Biglaiser and DeRouen 2006).[12] Just as recently democratized Eastern European countries that are members of the European Union are generally politically stable, so, too, are authoritarian countries such as Singapore and China. Political corruption also arguably lessens FDI inflows: corrupt governments increase the costs of setting up plants or extractive operations, and there is no guarantee that the governments will not expect higher future payouts from MNCs.[13]

Lastly, security concerns and geographic proximity are expected to affect investor interest. Given the history of U.S.-Latin American relations that range from direct warfare to trade agreements and alliances,[14] investors most likely feel more secure investing in countries with good relations with the U.S. government. Good relations suggest that the country might be careful not to alienate the U.S. firm (Biglaiser and DeRouen 2007; Jones and Kane 2005).[15] In addition, investors prefer host countries that get along with their neighbors, reducing the likelihood of conflict spreading between borders and disrupting manufacturing facilities or extractive operations.

Method and Results

We estimate the effect of political, economic, and security and geographic variables on FDI in Latin America by utilizing data obtained by Biglaiser and Staats (2010) from a survey of U.S. MNCs that have invested in at least one Latin American country over the past five years. Our goal is to understand why firms chose to invest in some Latin American countries over others. The survey consists of 23 two-part questions that attempt to cover all determinants mentioned in the literature. The survey was sent out in three stages (starting in November 2006 and ending in May 2007), addressed to the CEOs of U.S. firms identified as having operations in Latin America (Uniworld Business Publications 2005).[16] The assumption was that the CEOs would know the issues most important to the firm when making investment decisions or would have quick access to those with such knowledge lower in the corporate hierarchy. As Hoffman and Gopinath (1994, 626) note, "Although the responsibility for setting the strategic direction of a firm usually rests with the entire management team, CEOs play a major leadership role in the process."

In preparing to administer the survey, Biglaiser and Staats (2010) compiled an initial list of 886 corporations. However, they eliminated 133 firms after discovering duplicate entries under different names or determining that a firm had been acquired by or merged with another business, was no longer in business, was a shell corporation controlled by some other entity, had recently undergone a CEO change, or did not have investments in Latin America. They mailed surveys to the remaining 753 firms. The post office returned 44 of the surveys as undeliverable, and the researchers received 66 completed surveys, a return rate of 9.3 percent. This may seem low, but a number of published works using corporate surveys report similar response rates (Martínez, Esperança, and de la Torre 2005, 13 percent; Pearce and Zahra 1991, 14 percent).[17] Indeed, research published by the World Bank based on a 2002 survey to MNCs received a response rate of 6 percent (MIGA 2002, 3). The reason rates of return are of interest is because of possible return bias error. The higher the rate of return is, the less effect differences between responders and the target population can have on the results. Thus, where the rate of return is low, it is incumbent on the investigator to show that the characteristics of responders are not substantively different from those of the target population (Curtin, Presser, and Singer 2000, 413; Groves, Presser, and Dipko 2004, 4; Keeter et al. 2000; Merkle and Edelman 2002).

The problem for many surveys is that pertinent characteristics of the target population are unknown, so that it is not possible to gauge how closely responders approximate the population. This is especially problematic for surveys conducted of general populations where great variation is assumed. Our survey is of corporate CEOs with investments in Latin America, of whom we can assume there is much less diversity of relevant features than would be the case with a general population survey. Nevertheless, we have published sources to compare our survey participants with the target population, and we do so to alleviate concerns with return bias error.

Table 3.1 compares target population companies with our responding firms in terms of type of industry, revenue, revenue growth, market capitalization (for public firms), and balance between public and private firms. The relatively modest differences between the responding corporations and the larger population of U.S. firms with regard to each characteristic give us confidence that the responding firms are reasonably representative of all firms. Yet there are differences, so we wanted to determine more definitively whether these differences could affect responses on any given survey question.

We start by looking at differences in the Standard Industrialization Classification of the responding corporations as compared to the population. Since there is little difference with regard to manufacturing corporations, and inasmuch as manufacturing corporations comprise more than 50 percent of the corporations, we created a dummy variable coded 1 for manufacturing corporations and 0 for all other corporations. We then compared scores between the two variables on each of the 23 survey questions, and there were only three where the difference was statistically significant at even $p < .10$. These three—government regulation, taxation, and government ownership of enterprises—had minor differences, in each case showing higher scores in amounts of only .44, .34, and .48, respectively, on

TABLE 3.1. Survey–Population Comparisons

Standard Industrial Classification	Survey Respondents, Percentage by SIC	All Corporations, Percentage by SIC
Agriculture, Forestry, Fishing	0.0	0.4
Mining	4.8	2.8
Construction	0.0	1.1
Manufacturing	54.8	53.8
Transportation, Communication, Electric, Gas, and Sanitary Services	8.1	6.1
Wholesale Trade	12.9	7.0
Retail Trade	0.0	2.4
Finance, Insurance, Real Estate	8.1	4.7
Services	11.3	21.6
Average (median) 2006 Corporate Revenue	$6.92 ($1.97) billion	$10.96 ($2.23) billion
Average (median) Individual Corporation Sales Growth 2005–6	11.99 (8.62)%	11.11 (8.61)%
Percentage of Public Corporations	65.6%	69.2%
Average (median) Market Capitalization of Public Corporations	$9.44 ($2.21) billion	$14.34 ($2.51) billion

a 1–6 scale. We note that there are substantially less service corporations among our survey responders than in the total population. One could argue that service corporations are less risk adverse than other corporations because of the inherent portability of this type of investment and that having fewer of these types of corporations among our responders would bias our results in favor of more concern about taking on risk. This is not borne out by closer inspection of our results, however. On each of the items most associated with investor risk (Questions 2, 6, 7, and 8, collectively referred to later in this chapter as Factor 1), the mean scores are lower (meaning more importance is attached to them) for service corporations than for all other types of corporations.[18]

We also considered the differences in mean and median revenue and market capitalization between survey respondents and the target population. Because the target population has higher revenue and market capitalization, we created a subset of our respondents with higher levels of revenue and market capitalization essentially equal to the target population. When we compare the response scores for each survey question between all respondents and the subset, the differences are trivial and in no case met even a $p < .20$ standard. We also ran Pearson and Spearman correlations on 2006 revenue growth and the responses to each survey question, and none are significant at a $p < .20$ level, bringing added confidence in our survey results.

It is useful to look at the representativeness of our survey respondents as compared to the total population in terms of the countries in which they have invested. This is important because companies with investments in countries with histories or current conditions suggesting property risk may be sensitive to investment threats to a degree not shared by the general population of investors. We therefore want to make sure that our survey respondents have investments in the range of countries in Latin America roughly comparable to all investors. We present such a comparison between our survey respondents and the general population of investors in table 3.2. As can be seen, our survey investors have their investment in the same general mix of countries as the general population—Mexico, Brazil, and Argentina being at the high end; Venezuela, Chile, and Colombia in the middle; and the remainder of the countries at the low end. Among countries that have some history of expropriation (e.g., Bolivia, Ecuador, Nicaragua, and Venezuela), only Nicaragua and Bolivia show anything that is more than a trivial difference between survey respondents and the general population. Even as to these countries, we see little that gives us concern. First, the differences are likely only statistical anomalies resulting from the small number of survey respondents that have investments in these two countries. Second, because of the small percentage of survey participants with investments there, any systematic error arising from those investors would be minuscule in terms of the overall results that we have reported.

Based on the tests, we conclude that between our survey respondents and the totality of target corporations, there are no significant differences that would affect response choices. The fact that CEOs are busy with corporate affairs appears to explain the low rate of return.

Each CEO was asked to indicate separately the level of importance assigned by that corporation to the 23 survey factors when deciding during the past five years to either increase investment in any given country or to invest in a country for the first time. The possible answers were (1) "extremely important," (2) "very important," (3) "moderately important," (4) "of little importance," (5) "of almost no importance," (6) "of no importance/not considered." We quantified the responses by assigning numbers to each response in the same order already presented—that is, with the greatest importance receiving a 1 and the least importance a 6. Statistics for

TABLE 3.2. Survey–Population Comparison by Countries where Invested

Percentage of Companies with Investments in Each Country	Survey	Population
Argentina	10.98	12.65
Bolivia	2.44	1.23
Brazil	15.45	21.24
Chile	8.13	5.11
Colombia	5.69	6.95
Costa Rica	4.47	2.76
Ecuador	2.85	2.73
El Salvador	2.85	1.61
Guatemala	3.66	2.38
Honduras	2.85	1.26
Mexico	19.92	24.35
Nicaragua	2.44	0.79
Panama	2.85	1.56
Paraguay	2.03	0.79
Peru	4.47	4.37
Uruguay	1.22	2.08
Venezuela	7.72	8.13

the responses to each question are contained in table 3.3. The table shows that only 52 of the corporations responding indicated that they had made an investment in a country for the first time during the past five years. Additionally, the scores they assigned to first-time investments in a country are not much different from those relating to decisions to increase existing investments. To be certain of the inconsequence of any difference in scores, we ran difference of means tests comparing scores for increases in investments and new investments for each question. The differences were far from statistical significance in almost all instances, and none reached even a $p < .30$ level. While we realize that deciding to invest somewhere for the first time is a separate process from deciding to increase investment, investors in the survey apparently consider the same factors in making their decisions. For this reason, we only discuss the results for existing investments.

From table 3.3, we see considerable between-factor variation, ranging from a highest importance mean score of 1.59 for "rule of law" to a least importance score of 3.95 for "geographical proximity." This variability gives us assurance that the participating corporations took seriously the task of separately considering each item on the survey. Another way to check for discernment evidenced in the responses is to look at inter-item correlations. Responses that do not correlate at all, especially between theoretically related items, would cause us to suspect randomness in the answers. We conducted Pearson correlations of all items on the survey and found a mixture of relationships between items. Correlations between 137 items are statistically significant to the $p \leq .05$, while 116 are not statistically significant to this level. Of the ones that are statistically significant, the strength of the correlations range from .80 for "rule of law" and "recognition of property rights" to .24 for "effective and efficient court system" and "upheld and recognized political rights." Again, this gives us assurance in the responses returned by the firms.

Refining the Variables

To this point, we have treated all the questions on the survey as if they were individual variables, each of them separately affecting (or not) the investment decisions of U.S. firms. However, among the many questions asked on the survey, there are general categories or factors within which one might fit multiple responses. Indeed, the literature on FDI suggests as

TABLE 3.3. Determinants of FDI Survey Results (ranked in order of importance)

Factor	Increase/New Investment	Rank	Mean	St. Dev.	Min	Max	N
Adhered to the rule of law	Increase	1	1.59	.82	1	5	63
	New	1	1.50	.92	1	6	52
Recognized and upheld private property rights (e.g., enforcement of contracts and absence of government expropriation)	Increase	2	1.76	.84	1	5	63
	New	2	1.65	.97	1	6	52
Had a relatively high level of political stability	Increase	3	2.10	.80	1	6	63
	New	3	2.02	.83	1	6	52
Had a relatively efficient and effective court system	Increase	4	2.19	.78	1	5	63
	New	4	2.19	.91	1	6	52
Had relatively low levels of government restrictions on investments and capital flows	Increase	5	2.38	.76	1	4	60
	New	5	2.29	.81	1	4	51
Recognized and upheld basic human rights, such as freedom from arbitrary arrest, detention, imprisonment, or torture	Increase	6	2.43	1.07	1	6	63
	New	7	2.40	1.19	1	6	52
Had a relatively low level of government corruption	Increase	7	2.52	.82	1	6	62
	New	6	2.31	.65	1	4	51
Recognized and upheld basic civil liberties, such as freedom of speech, association, press, and religion	Increase	8	2.76	1.05	1	6	62
	New	10	2.73	1.12	1	6	52
Had a relatively strong democracy	Increase	8	2.76	1.10	1	6	63
	New	9	2.71	1.05	1	6	52
Had relatively low levels of taxation	Increase	10	2.84	.61	1	4	61
	New	11	2.81	.60	2	4	52

Had relatively high official support for markets and private enterprise	Increase	11	2.87	1.05	1	6	62
	New	8	2.69	.97	1	6	51
Recognized and upheld political rights, such as the right to vote and run for office	Increase	12	2.90	1.03	1	6	63
	New	12	2.85	1.13	1	6	52
Had relatively high levels of literacy and education	Increase	13	3.00	.83	2	5	62
	New	15	2.98	.93	1	5	51
Had relatively low levels of government regulation of business operations	Increase	14	3.02	.85	1	6	61
	New	13	2.88	.82	1	5	51
Had relatively good relations with the government of the United States	Increase	15	3.03	1.16	1	6	63
	New	17	3.17	1.22	1	6	52
Had relatively low tariffs	Increase	16	3.06	1.07	1	6	62
	New	14	2.92	.91	1	5	51
Had relatively high recent economic growth	Increase	17	3.28	.95	2	6	61
	New	16	3.16	1.00	1	6	50
Had relatively good relations with neighboring countries	Increase	18	3.40	.99	1	6	63
	New	18	3.48	1.08	2	6	52
Had relatively high overall wealth (e.g., gross domestic product)	Increase	19	3.59	1.09	2	6	61
	New	19	3.56	.99	2	6	50
Had relatively low levels of government-owned enterprises	Increase	20	3.75	.98	1	6	61
	New	20	3.73	.90	1	6	51
Had relatively high level of average income (e.g., gross domestic product per capita)	Increase	21	3.89	.98	2	6	61
	New	21	3.78	1.02	2	6	50
Had relatively high degree of income equality between classes	Increase	22	3.90	.76	3	6	62
	New	22	3.88	1.01	2	6	51
Had relatively close geographical proximity to your American offices/facilities	Increase	23	3.95	1.57	1	6	63
	New	23	4.17	1.42	1	6	52

much, dividing the foreign investment determinants into the five broad categories mentioned earlier. Building on these five broad categories, we can envision seven factors within which to place the individual survey questions. We indicate these seven categories, including the labels we have given them and the survey questions that comprise them, in table 3.4.[19] We conducted factor analyses of each of the seven categories and confirmed to our satisfaction the correctness of the groupings within each factor.[20]

TABLE 3.4. FDI Survey Factors

Factor Number	Factors	Survey Questions Included in Factor
1	Protection of Property Rights	Adhered to the rule of law
		Recognized and upheld private property rights (e.g., enforcement of contracts and absence of government expropriation)
		Had a relatively efficient and effective court system
		Had a relatively high level of political stability
2	Regime Type/ Liberal Democracy	Had a relatively strong democracy
		Recognized and upheld basic civil liberties, such as freedom of speech, association, press, and religion
		Recognized and upheld basic human rights, such as freedom from arbitrary arrest, detention, imprisonment, or torture
		Recognized and upheld political rights, such as the right to vote and run for office
3	Regulation/Corruption	Had a relatively low level of government corruption
		Had relatively low levels of government regulation of business operations
4	Regional Trade	Had relatively high official support for markets and private enterprise
		Had relatively good relations with neighboring countries
5	Control over Investments	Had relatively low levels of government restrictions on investments and capital flows
		Had relatively good relations with the government of the United States
		Had relatively close geographical proximity to your American offices/facilities
6	Neo-Liberal Reform	Had relative low levels of taxation
		Had relatively low tariffs
		Had relatively low levels of government–owned enterprises
7	Economic/Country Conditions	Had relatively high recent economic growth
		Had relatively high overall wealth (e.g., gross domestic product)
		Had relatively high level of average income (e.g., gross domestic product per capita)
		Had relatively high degree of income equality between classes

To quantify the factors just discussed, we summed the responses from each corporation for each question within any given factor, took the average sum for each corporation, and calculated the mean score of all average scores within that factor. Table 3.5 shows the results of this process, along with margins of error calculated for each factor.

Among the extracted factors, protection of property rights is the most important factor for investment decisions. Figure 3.2 shows the placement of each factor in relation to all others, and we see that there are big gaps between the protection of property rights (Factor 1) and all other factors. Particularly noteworthy is the distance between protection of property rights and regime type/liberal democracy (Factor 2). The lower placement of Factor 2 is consistent with theoretical arguments in the political economy literature that claim that a primary determinant of FDI, not democracy itself, is the strength of democratic institutions (Jensen 2006, 2008; Li 2006a, 2006b, 2009; Li and Resnick 2003). This also reinforces the findings from chapter 2 where checks on the executive are the mechanism limiting political risk. Our results suggest that investors want assurances that democracy alone cannot provide.[21] This does not cause us to conclude, however, that democracy is of little or no importance to investors. After all, the 2.72 score for Factor 2 places it between "moderately important" and "very important." In addition, it is likely that investor preferences as to Factors 1 and 2 are not separable.[22] After all, it is difficult to conceive of the

TABLE 3.5.   Factor Scores

Factor Number	Factor	Rank	Mean	St. Dev.	N	Margin of Error (95% confidence level)
1	Protection of Property Rights	1	1.91	0.66	63	+/− 0.16 (8.5%)
2	Regime Type/ Liberal Democracy	2	2.72	0.91	62	+/− 0.23 (8.3%)
3	Regulation/ Corruption	3	2.77	0.73	61	+/− 0.18 (6.6%)
4	Regional Trade	4	3.15	0.86	62	+/− 0.21 (6.8%)
5	Control over Investments	5	3.16	0.88	60	+/− 0.22 (7.0%)
6	Neo-Liberal Reform	6	3.22	0.70	60	+/− 0.18 (5.5%)
7	Economic/Country Conditions	7	3.68	0.78	60	+/− 0.20 (5.4%)

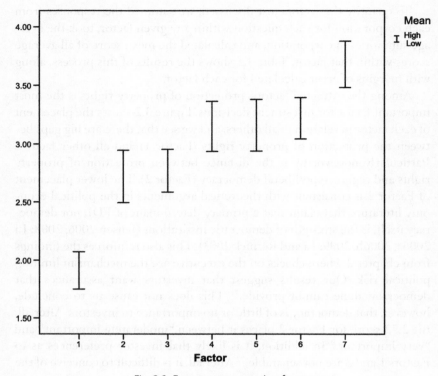

Fig. 3.2. Factor scores margin of error

items contained in Factor 1 as existing in any type of known regime other than a democracy.

Also important is the relatively limited significance investors seem to place on economic conditions. The literature has reached varying conclusions on the effects of economic conditions on FDI inflows. For example, while Li and Resnick (2003) observe that large markets and economic growth in the host country increase FDI inflows, Jensen (2003) finds, in some models, that economic growth actually lessens FDI inflows. Similarly, Biglaiser and DeRouen (2006) find that most economic conditions are not statistically significant FDI determinants and that GDP per capita even has a significant negative effect on investment. Part of the explanation for the inconsistency in findings is that investor interests have changed over time. Unlike past instances when firms set up plants to tariff jump in order to sell to overseas domestic markets, most U.S. firms today are interested in outsourcing facilities to host countries that manufacture goods for reexport to the U.S. market. Consumer markets in host countries are not the driving force for investment flows. Thus political factors related to investment stability, not democracy alone or economic factors, appear to catalyze foreign investors' decisions.

Panel Data Testing of Political Institutions

We also conducted an aggregate analysis of FDI determinants to test the validity of our survey results. The survey findings suggest that CEOs prefer countries that provide investment safety linked to adherence to rule of law, upholding of private property rights, use of a relatively efficient and effective court system, and promotion of high levels of political stability. These are hallmarks of democratic countries, as robust political institutions impose checks on policy makers and administrators. Under such circumstances, political actors cannot easily engage in arbitrary and abrupt policy changes inimical to private ownership or mandate transfer of wealth from one segment of society to another or from the private to the public sector (Durham 1999; Henisz 2000, 2004). Moreover, the executive branch does not dominate a compliant legislature, and independent courts are able to put the brakes on excesses of either or both of the other two branches. A government operating under such constraints is able to credibly commit not to interfere with property rights (North 1990; Weingast 1993b; Henisz 2000, 2004), something that CEOs in our survey claim is important.[23] While chapter 2 quantified the impact of institutions on political risk, this test examines how risk affects FDI inflows.

To test empirically the effects of political constraints among many other possible determinants, we construct a cross-sectional data set for 113 developing countries from 1976 to 2007.[24] Use of pooled data to study FDI is quite common in the political science literature, as is evidenced by Li and Resnick (2003), Jensen (2003), and Biglaiser and DeRouen (2006), among many others. We employ an OLS regression with panel-corrected standard errors as recommended by Beck and Katz (1995). Results from a Hausman test suggest that we need to model for country-specific fixed effects, and we do so by creating dummy variables for each country. We also created dummy variables to reflect investment occurring during or after the Cold War; during the worldwide recession of the 1980s; and during 2003, the lagged year following the 9/11 attacks. Our dependent variable is net FDI inflows as a percentage of GDP, a measure commonly used in the literature (Jensen 2003, 2006; Biglaiser and DeRouen 2006).

We use Henisz's (2010) political constraint index (POLCON V), which looks at the number and effective strength of policy veto points among the institutional actors within a country, as the main explanatory factor. In effect, we are using political constraints as a proxy for property rights protection and assuming that investors do likewise. In the POLCON V measure, a country with a unicameral legislature would have less political constraints than one with a bicameral legislature (all else being equal). Similarly, a federal system would have more constraints than a unitary system, as would a system with independent courts as compared to a country where courts are dominated by other branches. A divided government also has more constraints than one where a single party controls both the legislature and the executive branch. We adopt this measure to determine the robustness of constrained democratic institutions as a determinant of FDI.

In addition to POLCON V, we include many economic and political controls commonly identified in the literature as critical for attracting FDI. Among economic factors, we use GDP logged, GDP per capita, GDP growth, trade openness, capital liberalization, current account balance, and natural resource stocks.[25] For the political factors, we include conflict, terror, and executive ideology.[26] Positive economic conditions, capital openness, and abundant resource stocks are predicted to increase FDI inflows, while political factors such as high conflict, terror, or leftist executives are likely to fuel risk, lessening investor interest. However, as Pinto and Pinto (2008) note, partisanship affects FDI, as pro-labor governments are expected to encourage FDI inflows that complement labor in production, while pro-capital governments are likely to promote foreign investment that substitutes capital for labor. We use economic data from the World Bank (2008), except for capital liberalization (Chinn and Ito 2008) and resource flows (Epstein et al. 2006). The conflict measure comes from Marshall (2009), and the political terror scale is taken from the average of the Amnesty International and State Department scores reported by Gibney (see Montero 2008, 68n13). We use data from Beck et al. (2001) to measure executive ideology. We score 1 for executives that are associated with leftist ideology and 0 for executives more identified with the center or right. We lag all independent variables by a year, since economic and political developments take time to affect policy outcomes. We also include a lagged dependent variable on the right-hand side, as previous experience with FDI likely affects future MNC decisions.

We report model estimations in table 3.6. Many of the economic controls (trade openness, GDP growth, and capital liberalization) are positive and in the expected causal direction. Political factors such as executive ideology and terror are also positive and significant, which suggests that leftist leaders may not always discourage FDI (as found in Pinto 2004 and 2013)—something we also discover in chapter 4—and that political abuses may actually attract some forms of FDI. More important, POLCON V is positive and significant, which helps to affirm our survey results about the vital role political institutions play in affecting FDI inflows.

Survey and Panel Data Results

Results from both the survey and the panel data reflect the strength of political institutions generally found in democracies that promote investment safety. Why is investment security important for developing countries, especially in Latin America? As mentioned earlier, Latin America has a long history of asset appropriation. Between the 1930s and 1970s, the largest countries in the region—including Argentina, Brazil, Chile, Mexico, and Venezuela—engaged in extensive expropriations (Biglaiser and DeRouen 2006, 68). These countries, regardless of regime type, ignored property rights and provided limited compensation to British and U.S. MNCs, who controlled the main exports and infrastructure in much of the region.

Recent actions taken against MNCs operating in Venezuela, Ecuador, and Bolivia reinforce investor concern. Venezuelan president Hugo Chávez, who has used foreign ownership as a rallying cry to mobilize nationalistic support, imposed new contract terms on foreign oil companies (*Economist* 2007c). Bolivian president Evo Morales nationalized a tin smelter and attempted to expropriate his country's natural gas industry, only to later sign tougher contracts with MNCs (*Economist* 2007a). Ecuador's president Alfredo Palacio confiscated Occidental Petroleum in 2006. Given Latin America's history, it comes as little revelation that enforcing property rights are important to foreign investors.

The return of Sandinista Daniel Ortega as Nicaragua's president in 2007 further underscores the importance of political risk factors. Prior to his election, Nicaragua witnessed increased outsourcing opportunities following the signing of the Central American Free Trade Agreement (CAFTA) in 2004, which provides concessions for Nicaraguan garments into the U.S. market. Because of CAFTA, free trade zones expanded in the country. The proximity of Nicaragua to the U.S. relative to East Asia and China also bolstered investment in the finishing of garments. In the fashion industry, where jean styles (e.g., holes in the garment or modifications in the size or shape of pockets) change frequently, the ability to manufac-

TABLE 3.6. Determinants of FDI in the Developing World, 1976–2007

Independent/Control Variables	
Dependent Variable (lagged)	.547***
	(.070)
GDP log	2.219**
	(.888)
GDP per Capita	.000
	(.000)
Trade Openness	.010*
	(.005)
GDP Growth	.015
	(.011)
Capital Liberalization	.234***
	(.059)
Current Account Balance	.007
	(.013)
Natural Resource Stocks	−3.530***
	(.841)
Executive Ideology	.288
	(.191)
Conflict	−.005
	(.027)
Terror	.142*
	(.075)
POLCONV	.432*
	(.259)
N	2,165
R^2	.438
Wald χ^2	494.73
Prob > χ^2	.000

Note: All independent/control variables are lagged by one year. Coefficients are fixed-effects estimations. Numbers in parentheses are panel-corrected standard errors.

Two-tailed test: * significant at 10%; ** significant at 5%; *** significant at 1%.

ture and ship products in less than a month's time creates advantages for companies operating close to the United States (España 2007; Vaughn 2007). However, the election of President Ortega increased risk fears.

According to personal interviews that Biglaiser and Staats (2010) conducted in Managua with U.S. investors, Nicaraguan business and labor officials, and the former president of Nicaragua's Central Bank and finance minister in the Bolaños (2002–6) government, uncertainty is the perception among investors (Arana 2007; España 2007; Vaughn 2007). No one has forgotten the property appropriations by the Sandinista government in the 1980s. Ortega's close ties with Venezuela's Chávez[27] and his meeting with Iranian president Mahmoud Ahmadinejad immediately after taking office have unnerved prospective U.S. investors even more (*Economist* 2007b). It is not because of his leftist ideology that investors fear Ortega. Such leftist presidents as Brazil's Luiz Inacio Lula da Silva and Chile's Michelle Bachelet have attracted FDI. Indeed, as shown in table 3.6, we found that leftist executives may actually promote FDI inflows. Instead, the few political constraints on Ortega make investors apprehensive. Political institutions significantly impact investor perceptions about investment security.

Judicial Institutions and FDI

We now turn our attention from the strength of democratic political institutions generally and put specific focus on the importance of judicial institutions and the promotion of the rule of law in encouraging foreign investment. The survey results suggest that strong and effective courts are an important consideration for investors. In this section, we offer additional theoretical detail about why the courts and rule of law receive great interest from investors. We also examine time-series panel data targeted at judicial performance, to assess if our survey results conform to other data.

The Effects of Judicial Performance and Rule of Law on FDI

The relevance of effective legal institutions is well documented in the political economy literature. Running parallel with protection from governmental predation and large swings in public policies is the concern whether the host country will uphold investor property titles and enforce contracts entered into in private commercial transactions. Effective and fair courts provide a convenient and relatively low-cost venue for providing this assurance (North 1990, 34, 58). According to Olson (1993, 572), there "is typically no reliable contract enforcement unless there is an impartial court system that can call upon the coercive power of the state to require individuals to honor contracts they have made." While foreign investors commonly insist that contracts contain arbitration clauses allowing them to work around less-than-reliable court systems, having to rely on such systems means adding to commercial transactions a layer of expense that investors will in many instances want to avoid if possible.[28]

Moreover, since arbitration agreements and awards are not self-enforcing, an aggrieved party must typically go to court anyway to force the other side to submit to arbitration and must thereupon return to court and resort to court proceedings to collect on an arbitration award. In addition, while certain types of regimes (e.g., China) have bureaucratic institutions other than courts for enforcing commercial obligations (Clarke 2003), such arrangements have given way in most of the developing world, including Latin America, to neoliberal market reforms that reject close governmental supervision over private transactions.

In addition to protecting property rights and enforcing contracts, foreign investors ultimately seek to earn profits on their investments. When making investment decisions, some foreign investors presumably also take into account whether the economy is on a path for long-term growth and prosperity that provide ample domestic markets. The degree to which an economy expands depends largely on the level of aggregate private investment. What can government do to encourage aggregate investment and thereby spur economic growth? The answer is that what works at the individual investor level also works at the aggregate level; that is, government can give credible assurances that it will uphold the rule of law and protect property rights. As North and Weingast (1989, 803) maintain, "For economic growth to occur the sovereign or government must not merely establish the relevant set of rights, but must make a credible commitment to them." The problem investors confront is that current government policies conducive to economic growth and development may not last, that future politicians may be tempted to change course for personal advantage or political gain that harms business interests (Brunetti, Kisunko, and Weder 1997, 10–11). Outright corruption arguably is a concern, but so are the possibilities that government will impose high business taxes to finance social welfare initiatives or will strictly regulate business operations to satisfy populist demands.

In the face of such concerns, government brings credibility to its commitments by delegating to courts the authority to force current and future governments to conduct themselves in accordance with the law (Landes and Posner 1975, 882; North and Weingast 1989, 819; Brunetti and Weder 1999, 2). This does not guarantee that current policies will persist or that government will totally refrain from enacting policies harmful to business or the economy generally.[29] However, courts can require government to follow established legal procedures when it wants to change items affecting business interests, such as giving advance notice of proposed changes, conducting public hearings, making formal findings, getting legislation passed, or even amending the constitution. This court-enforced "constitutionalization" of rights[30] makes change more difficult and costly, which supports investor confidence in the stability of policies (Henisz 2000; Jensen 2003; Li 2006a, 2006b).[31]

Strong courts and adherence to the rule of law also contribute to political stability, an issue distinct from policy stability, although changes in political regime can obviously lead to changes in policy. Political stability is a matter of serious concern for foreign investors (Pinto and Pinto 2011). Two theoretical strands are in play here, insurance policy theory and a variation of the credible commitment theory discussed in the previous section. Insurance policy theory suggests that opposing political forces operating under competitive conditions are motivated to install strong and independent courts, especially those with the power of judicial review, to enforce a democratic bargain between the governing party and its challengers. Because of competitive balance, even a governing party must contemplate the possibility of someday entering the opposition. The idea is that it is better for those currently governing to give up prerogatives while in office as the price to pay to avoid having seriously diminished rights in the future when out of power (Ginsburg 2003, 73, 78; Finkel 2004, 2005; Chavez 2004).[32] Commitment theory also comes into play in the form of an agreement between all political participants, backed by the courts, to continue playing the democratic game rather than defect to extralegal regime change and/or potentially unstable authoritarian rule (Ginsburg 2003, 73, 78). Thus strong courts contribute to political stability, which, in turn, encourages FDI by providing a climate of predictability for investors (Crenshaw 1991; Bollen and Jones 1982; Rummel and Heenan 1978).

Finally, foreign investors consider the state of lawfulness existing in the host country. An investor incurs costs when it posts senior officials and technical employees to countries where crime and corruption are rampant and personal safety is at stake. The employer may have to take extraordinary steps to ensure the overall security of its employees, both on the job and off, and it often has to pay higher salaries to compensate employees for the danger and unpleasantness of the situation. In the mid-1990s, for instance, when Intel considered where to locate its first plant in Latin America, management considered whether expatriate employees would be happy living in the country selected and whether the country posed a security risk to them (Nelson 1999, 5). Strong courts are part of the arsenal that fights against crime and the unpleasantness that it brings to everyone in the host country, including the workforce supported by foreign investment.[33]

Based on the expected advantages of judicial strength and adherence to the rule of law for attracting FDI, it comes as little surprise that our survey results affirm investor interests in the courts and rule-of-law protections. The recent experiences of Nicaragua reinforce the survey findings that weak judicial independence and deficient rule-of-law procedures negatively affect investor decisions. In interviews conducted in 2007 with members of the business and financial community, many raised concerns about judicial and legal procedures. Mario Arana, a former finance minister and president of Nicaragua's Central Bank, remarked that Nicaragua's judiciary lacks independence, which provides little comfort that the courts will protect investors from government predation (Arana 2007). Scott Vaughn, owner of a U.S. garment factory operating in Nicaragua, went a step further, contending that the Sandinistas now control the court system and that labor thus wins every case (Vaughn 2007). Because of the lack of integrity in Nicaragua's courts (where there are problems with bribe taking and other forms of corruption), many businesses often forgo recovery entirely or settle out of court for values very much below what they believe they are entitled to recover (Staats, Bowler, and Hiskey 2005). Moreover, as is true in other Latin American countries, many firms include arbitration clauses in their contracts so that they have a form of protection not possible through the courts (Zamora 2007). Not unexpectedly, investors are wary of expanding their businesses, and Nicaragua has attracted few new firms. The survey's findings and interviews suggest that the lack of judicial independence and rule-of-law procedures, compounded by Ortega's history, produced much uncertainty that affects FDI.

Earlier interviews conducted by one of the authors of this volume

(Staats) in Argentina, Chile, and Uruguay similarly show that the local business community and foreign investors typically forgo using unreliable and inefficient local court systems to enforce contracts and resolve commercial disputes, preferring instead to use more expensive and reliable arbitration procedures (Whitelaw 2003; Jorquera 2003; Klein 2003). As a prominent business attorney stated, "Because of long delays, the worst-case scenario for a business is to be involved in litigation in the civil court system" (Vial 2003).

The decision by Intel to locate its first Latin American microprocessor plant in Costa Rica and not in other countries in the region also bolsters claims about the importance of judicial strength and adherence to the rule of law. As mentioned earlier, in the mid-1990s, Intel explored placing a plant in Latin America. Intel had a host of criteria for the possible location, including availability of technical personnel and engineers, labor unions and labor regulation, transportation infrastructure and costs, availability and reliability of the electrical power supply, and government tax incentives (Nelson 1999, 5). Intel narrowed the list to four countries: Costa Rica, Brazil, Chile, and Mexico. In 1996, the company chose Costa Rica, in part because of the country's respect for rule of law and the courts. Indeed, in ruling out Mexico, Intel's site selection team worried that Mexican government officials would ignore labor laws and make exceptions for Intel. As Nelson (1999, 15) writes, "If the rules were not clear-cut, objective, and adhered to in a straightforward manner, then this created an unpredictable, nontransparent environment." Costa Rica's reputation for carrying out policies in a transparent, legal way that did not depend on who served as the next president gave Costa Rica a leg up on the others.

Aggregate Data Analysis of Courts and FDI

To validate the survey results and what Costa Rican and fieldwork findings tell us, we again turn to time-series panel data, this time specifically targeted at judicial performance. Since we surveyed only U.S. corporations, we begin this time-series analysis by looking at U.S. FDI in Latin America rather than FDI from all countries. This has the dual advantage of allowing us to test the validity of the survey results and, if successful in doing so, to provide additional evidence pointing toward legal system performance and rule of law as determinants of U.S. FDI. We will then look at global (not just U.S.) FDI to Latin America, to determine whether the results obtained from our study of U.S. firms are generalizable to investors from other regions of the world.

As we did in the previous panel data, we use, as our metric in both cases, net FDI inflows as a percentage of GDP, but this time we cover the period 1996–2007. We selected 1996 as our starting point because we have reliable lagged judicial data beginning then and because by the 1990s (similar to the period when we conducted our survey), most countries had completed the transition to minimal forms of democratic rule and followed more export-oriented economic strategies. We obtained data for U.S. FDI from the Bureau of Economic Analysis, which is also used in previous work (Biglaiser and DeRouen 2007; Tuman and Emmert 2004).[34] We obtained global FDI data from the World Bank (2008).

Our independent variable, referred to in our model as "judicial performance," comes from the measure of "legal structure and security of property rights" contained in the Economic Freedom of the World (EFW) report published by the Fraser Institute. The EFW report is now published annually, but until 2000, reports were only issued every five years, the last in 1995.[35] We use a linear interpolation equation to calculate values for the missing years between 1995 and 1999 (see Montero 2008, 68n12).

Our other independent and control variables consist of the same factors that we used in our previous model (e.g., lagged dependent variable on the right-hand side, the natural log of GDP,[36] GDP per capita, GDP growth, trade openness, capital liberalization, current account balance, conflict, natural resource stocks, and executive ideology), except we also include a measure for corruption from the *International Country Risk Guide (ICRG)*.[37] Corruption is rated on the *ICRG*'s 0–6 scale, with 6 indicating the least corrupt country (*ICRG* 2007). We again lag all independent variables by a year, for the reasons stated previously.

We report model estimations for U.S. FDI and global FDI in table 3.7. Without looking any further, most economic and political controls are not consistently significant for both U.S. FDI and global FDI models. Among economic variables, only capital liberalization and previous experience with FDI are significant in both U.S. and global FDI models. Trade openness and current account balance are significant only in the global FDI model. Most economic controls are not significant FDI determinants

We find a similar scenario with the political variables. Although executive ideology and terror appear to have important effects on U.S. FDI, the effects of such factors are not significant in the global FDI model. Other political controls that include corruption and political conflict seem insignificant in either model, and POLCON V is only significant for global FDI. However, and most important for our purposes, judicial performance is positive and significant in both models. The findings that judicial performance is positive and significant help to validate our survey results about the role that judicial institutions and rule of law play in attracting FDI.

TABLE 3.7.   Aggregate Models of Determinants of FDI in Latin America, 1996–2007

Independent/Control Variables	U.S. FDI	Global FDI
Dependent Variable (lagged)	−.080	.192
	(.172)	(.147)
GDP log	−2.644	3.238
	(4.053)	(7.737)
GDP per Capita	−.000	.000
	(.000)	(.001)
Trade Openness	−.012	.045**
	(.016)	(.020)
GDP Growth	.024	.011
	(.023)	(.034)
Capital Liberalization	−.158	−.355**
	(.106)	(.155)
Current Account Balance	.005	−.075
	(.029)	(.052)
Natural Resource Stocks	30.612	−41.061
	(42.896)	(82.853)
Executive Ideology	.425*	−.105
	(.238)	(.408)
Conflict	−.046	.055
	(.153)	(.280)
Terror	−.483*	.138
	(.266)	(.311)
Corruption	.007	.094
	(.177)	(.176)
POLCONV	−.708	4.858***
	(.681)	(1.612)
Judicial Performance	.372***	.695***
	(.143)	(.234)
N	141	145
R^2	.326	.833
Wald χ^2	1,335.08	522.82
Prob > χ^2	.000	.000

Note: All independent/control variables are lagged by one year. Coefficients are fixed-effects estimations. Numbers in parentheses are panel-corrected standard errors.

Two-tailed test: * significant at 10%; ** significant at 5%; *** significant at 1%.

Conclusion

As noted in the introduction of this chapter, FDI has grown as a pivotal source of foreign capital for the developing world and especially for Latin America. For more than two decades, Latin American countries have relied on FDI as the largest source of foreign capital. However, there are variations in the amounts of FDI received, with some countries attracting significant investor interest while others gain much less attention. In chapter 2, we argued that political regimes affect levels of political risk. Our goal in this chapter has been to understand the determinants of FDI and particularly to address issues related to the effects of political institutions on foreign capital inflows.

Based on the survey of U.S. foreign investors and the complementary large-N data studies, we discover that regime type is a useful first step in understanding FDI, but it requires unpacking. The results suggest that political institutions and not necessarily just regime type influence investor decisions. Specifically, institutions that support property rights enforcement, adherence to the rule of law, and effective courts bolster investor confidence. Most other political and economic determinants are not consistently significant in the survey or the large-N models.

The findings in this and the previous chapter reinforce the benefits of disaggregation. Much too often, comparisons are made between regime types without giving sufficient consideration to factors embedded in regimes, which could help explain why some authoritarian governments attract significant FDI while others do not. The same is true for democracies and their appeal to investors. Chapter 2 found that executive constraints are the primary factor linking regimes to risk. This chapter focuses more directly on judicial institutions and the rule of law. While democracies often are associated with the good-governance political institutions that affect investment risk, such protections are not necessarily embedded in a democratic regime. It is important to pinpoint the specific factors that influence investor decisions. Our work is a first step toward uncovering the decision-making calculi used by foreign investors. Hopefully, our study will stimulate future scholarship beyond Latin America, particularly as expropriation threats and changes in contract terms are drawing increased interest and use by sovereign governments across the developing world. More important, given that political institutions generally found under democratic rule provide credible commitments that insure investment safety and contribute to investor confidence, the results hopefully will prompt developing countries not only to support democracy but also to uphold institutions that enhance political openness and greater freedoms in their countries.

The next chapter builds on this research agenda. While chapters 2 and 3 have explored how institutions affect the risk environment for investors, the following chapter examines the complex interactions between FDI and partisan governments. In chapter 4, we delve deeper into the preferences of governments and how left and right governments have different preferences on the types of firms that they will try to attract. Thus, while chapters 2 and 3 have begun to unpack institutions, the following chapter starts by disaggregating the types of investments and the preferences of governments as a function of the expected distributive consequences of foreign investment flows.

CHAPTER 4

Partisan Governments and the Distributive Effects of Foreign Direct Investment

CONTINUING WITH THE ARGUMENT that political institutions and politics affect foreign investment, we present, in this chapter, a political economy explanation of the causes and consequences of foreign direct investment, focusing on the expected distributive effects of direct investment flows. The empirical literature reports that the consequences of FDI are likely to vary in different economic and political environments. The framework presented here, which builds on the work of Pinto and Pinto (2008), aims at explaining this dynamic.

Motivation

Ample anecdotal evidence from OECD countries identifies an association between the orientation of the ruling coalition and the pattern of allocation of foreign investment across industries in host countries. This association has been documented by Pinto and Pinto (2008) and is reproduced in table 4.1.

As a graphical illustration of this pattern, figure 4.1 reproduces a comparison of the average ratio of FDI inflows into the United Kingdom to GDP, disaggregated by sectors. The top graph in figure 4.1 suggests that there are differences between the average sectoral inflows under the Conservative cabinet led by John Major (1991–96) and the average sectoral performance under Labour rule (1997–2003). A similar pattern is observed in

TABLE 4.1. FDI Inflows and Government Political Orientation: Regressions by Sectors

Industry Code	Left	Real GDP (per capita)	Openness	Population (millions)	Constant	Obs.	Countries	R^2
1	0.0029 (0.0110)	0.0017 (0.0036)	0.0011* (0.0006)	0.0002 (0.0005)	−0.0224 (0.0791)	249	21	0.175
2	0.3591** (0.1543)	0.0773 (0.0520)	0.0156* (0.0092)	−0.0211** (0.0083)	−1.482 (1.1527)	271	21	0.280
3	0.3065*** (0.0791)	−0.0262 (0.0265)	0.0092** (0.0046)	−0.0173*** (0.0053)	0.7598 (0.5467)	280	23	0.404
4	0.0813 (0.1272)	0.0033 (0.0344)	0.0093* (0.0049)	−0.0125 (0.0105)	−0.1457 (0.7179)	220	23	0.291
5	0.7963 (1.3968)	0.158 (0.3152)	0.0306 (0.0457)	−0.1049 (0.1172)	−2.8113 (6.8114)	209	22	0.158
6	0.4318* (0.2284)	0.0638 (0.0592)	0.0297** (0.0137)	−0.0148 (0.0162)	−1.9186 (1.3009)	224	22	0.471
7	0.155 (0.2132)	0.1273*** (0.0446)	0.0322*** (0.0114)	0.0062 (0.0109)	−4.7107** (2.0412)	200	20	0.343
8	0.3533*** (0.1293)	−0.0122 (0.0333)	−0.008 (0.0072)	−0.0076 (0.0110)	−0.3975 (1.0082)	166	18	0.534
9	0.356* (0.2066)	0.1565 (0.1709)	0.0194 (0.0138)	−0.0507 (0.0382)	−2.5914 (3.3463)	123	18	0.390
10	−0.0733*** (0.0256)	−0.0021 (0.0082)	−0.0024* (0.0015)	−0.0056*** (0.0015)	0.1811 (0.1745)	278	23	0.364
11	0.1776 (0.1156)	0.0727 (0.0447)	0.039*** (0.0101)	−0.0114 (0.0075)	−1.1418 (0.9592)	326	23	0.379
12	−0.0145 (0.0880)	−0.0231* (0.0136)	0.004 (0.0041)	0.0106** (0.0054)	0.6198* (0.3325)	148	19	0.155
13	−0.0667* (0.0398)	0.0053 (0.0133)	−0.0054 (0.0033)	−0.0031 (0.0020)	0.6563 (0.6179)	196	18	0.531
14	0.911* (0.4844)	0.6229*** (0.2290)	0.0459* (0.0247)	−0.1157*** (0.0430)	−13.069*** (4.2292)	137	17	0.465
15	1.496*** (0.4321)	0.4363** (0.2114)	0.0965*** (0.0329)	−0.1156*** (0.0314)	−8.2864* (4.2416)	342	24	0.943
16	−0.0436 (0.0643)	0.1526*** (0.0431)	0.0217*** (0.0058)	−0.0278** (0.0113)	2.471 (2.2152)	109	18	0.768
17	−0.0588 (1.0898)	0.4501 (0.9774)	−0.1083 (0.1222)	−0.6815*** (0.2449)	148.71*** (50.9780)	109	18	0.471

Source: Pinto and Pinto 2008, 241–42.

Note: Industry codes are described in table 4.2. All regressions include country and year dummies. Heteroskedastic panel corrected standard errors in parentheses.

Two-tailed test: * significant at 10%; ** significant at 5%; *** significant at 1%.

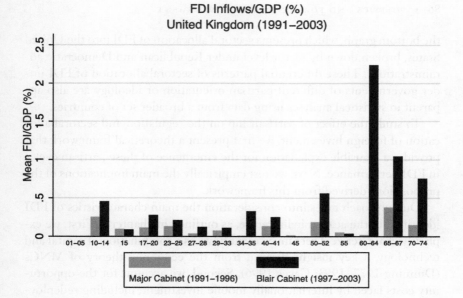

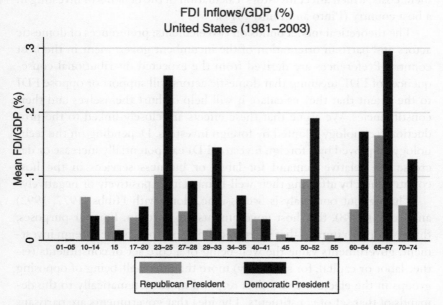

Fig. 4.1. Average FDI/GDP by industrial sector—United Kingdom (1991–2003) and United States (1981–2003). ISIC codes: 01–05, Agriculture and fishing; 10–14, Mining and quarrying; 15, Food; 17–20, Textile, leather, footwear, and wood; 23–25, Petroleum, chemical, rubber; 27–28, Basic metals and metal products; 29–33, Machinery and equipment; 34–35, Vehicles and transportation equipment; 40–41, Electricity, gas, and water; 45, Construction; 50–52, Trade and repairs; 55, Hotels and restaurants; 60–64, Transports, storage, and communication; 65–67, Financial intermediation; 70–74, Real estate and business activities. (Data from Pinto and Pinto 2008, 219–20.)

the bottom graph, which presents sectoral allocation of FDI into the United States, broken down by sector level under Republican and Democratic administrations. These differential patterns of sectoral allocation of FDI under governments of different partisan orientation or ideology are also apparent in statistical analyses using data from a broader set of countries.

To study the effect of partisanship on the regulation and sectoral allocation of foreign investment, we first present a theoretical framework that provides a plausible explanation for the emergence of these partisan cycles in FDI performance. Next, we test empirically the main implications of the propositions derived from this framework.

Our approach takes into consideration the main characteristics of FDI identified in the academic literature, as outlined in chapter 1. First, we explicitly characterize direct investment flows as a combination of capital and technology, a key insight derived from the economic theory of MNCs (Dunning 1977, 1993; Caves 1996). Second, we account for the opportunity costs faced by internationally mobile investment, including redeployment costs, which affect investors' calculation of the benefits of investing in a host country (Pinto and Pinto 2011).

The theoretical model builds on two elements: preferences of domestic actors and partisan orientation of the incumbent government in the host country. Preferences are derived from the expected distributional consequences of FDI, meaning that domestic actors will support or oppose FDI to the extent that they calculate it will help or hurt themselves and their constituencies. We argue that these effects are closely linked to the production technology adopted by foreign investors. Depending on the technology employed by a foreign investor, FDI can potentially increase or decrease the relative demand for labor or business services in the host country, thereby affecting their well-being, either positively or negatively.

Throughout our analysis, we assume, along with Hibbs (1977, 1992) and Tufte (1978), that host governments are partisan. For our purposes, this assumption implies that when deciding how to regulate foreign investment, governments value the well-being of a core set of constituents (either labor or capital, for simplicity) more than the well-being of opposing groups in the electorate and thus respond more systematically to the demands of that set of constituents. The idea that governments are partisans is pervasive in the comparative and international political economy literature. Our framework is, however, a novel extension of this idea to the academic literature on the political economy of investment.

Combining preferences and partisanship, we argue that the political links between the incumbent government and its core constituents—whose material well-being is affected by the inflow and outflow of internationally mobile investment—determines the incumbent's incentives to supply policies that benefit those groups. The outcome is a differential regulatory environment toward foreign investment that depends on the government's partisan orientation in the host country, resulting in different patterns of sectoral FDI allocation. The theoretical framework establishes the scope conditions under which these outcomes should be expected.

Next, we perform an empirical analysis and obtain results consistent with the model. In particular, we show that there is, in fact, a differential pattern of sectoral allocation of FDI under governments of different partisan orientation. Additionally, the statistical evidence suggests that the effect of investment on wages also varies with partisanship in the host country, in line with the assumptions and propositions from the model.

Moving beyond the predictions from our model, we speculate that the mode of entry of foreign capital into different sectors of the host country also responds to partisan cycles. For instance, governments of the right would encourage foreign investors to introduce production technologies that help increase the returns to domestic businesses—that is, those technologies that either increase the demand for the services of domestic capital owners or save on labor costs. Along this line of reasoning, we argue that domestic business interests would strictly prefer technology transfer agreements to investment capital inflows.[1] In sum, to the extent that they respond strategically to conditions in host countries, the activity of MNC affiliates is likely to covary with the degree of organization and influence of labor and capital in host countries and with the firm's ability to adapt to political change (see Hanson, Mataloni, and Slaughter 2001).[2]

Related Literature

Our research fills several gaps in the literature. First, while there has been extensive work on the effects of policy decisions (in trade and tax policy in particular) on aggregate FDI flows (Feldstein, Hines, and Hubbard 1995; Hines 2001), the link between partisanship and investment performance has not been duly explored in the extant studies.

Second, recent contributions to the literature on the politics of investment (surveyed in chapter 1) look at the role of policy and political stability on investment decisions and assume that investors put emphasis on minimizing ex-post expropriation risk. Under this approach, one would expect FDI to strategically flow to countries that appear to be politically and institutionally stable and whose economies are well managed.[3] While these are sensible explanations, we propose theoretical and empirical extensions. In terms of theory, these arguments treat host governments as passive actors. Empirically, the literature leaves a large part of the variance in FDI regulation and performance unexplained.

Third, while recent academic work has analyzed the effect of politics on investment decisions within an individual industry (see, e.g., Levy and Spiller 1994; Henisz and Zelner 2001; Henisz 2002b), research on the political determinants of the allocation of foreign investment across multiple sectors is scant.

Fourth, earlier models of "tariff-jumping" FDI are built around a similar distributive rationale as the one employed in our analysis. For instance, Bhagwati, Dinopoulos, and Wang (1992, 188) argue that among those actors supporting the position of foreign investors, we are likely to find business groups brought into joint ventures with foreign investors, labor unions that experience employment gains, and local communities that benefit from the location of the foreign affiliate's facility. Grossman and Helpman (1996) describe a different political cleavage around endogenous investment policy, one that pits "domestic firms wanting investment restrictions" against "workers with industry-specific skills wanting free entry by multinationals" (220). A similar rationale is found in more recent analyses on the politics of investment promotion, one of which argues that "attracting multinationals may benefit specific constituencies from whom politicians derive support" (Hanson 2001, 23). Yet the source and direction of the distributive consequences of FDI remains underdeveloped in that literature.

Finally, our focus on partisan motivations breaks new ground. While Dutt and Mitra (2005) and Milner and Judkins (2004) show that ideology and partisanship (whether left- or right-leaning) are good predictors of countries' (and parties') trade policy orientation,[4] the analysis of partisan motivations in terms of FDI is hardly present in the existing scholarly literature.[5]

In the ensuing sections, we first present an informal treatment of the central elements of our theory. Next, we present some preliminary empirical evidence consistent with the implications from the theoretical argument. Finally, we briefly discuss a couple extensions of the theoretical analysis.

The Political Economy of Sectoral FDI Regulation

In this section, we present and discuss briefly the formal framework of analysis used to examine the effect of partisanship on the regulation and sectoral allocation of foreign investment.[6]

The Economic Environment

We develop a game-theoretic model aimed at capturing the strategic interactions between host governments, foreign investors, and domestic political agents. The model considers a host country that operates in a small open economy, populated by two groups of individuals: workers and business owners (or owners of domestic capital). Economic agents are engaged in productive activities. Each domestic actor derives utility directly from the income the actor receives for his or her participation in the market (or factor returns) and from government transfers.

The economy consists of several productive sectors; output in each sector is a function of domestic capital, foreign capital, and labor. While domestic capital is assumed to be sector specific, labor is mobile across sectors.[7] This assumption emphasizes the idea that within the country, the cost of moving across sectors is higher for capital than for labor.[8] Moreover, labor mobility assures that wages are equalized across sectors.[9] Foreign capital can enter either sector and operate as a complement to or substitute for labor or domestic capital, depending on the production technology chosen for the local affiliate.[10]

The host government regulates investment flows through a tax on internationally mobile capital. In the formal version of our argument, we assume that the tax falls entirely on foreign investment and that the government can impose different tax rates on capital operating in different sectors. Implicitly, the latter assumption implies that the host government can discriminate between capital that is internationally mobile (foreign) and capital that cannot move beyond the national borders (domestic).[11] The tax revenue collected in this way by the host government is used to finance a lump-sum transfer targeted to the domestic political groups.

The model assumes that events take place sequentially. In the first stage, the government chooses taxes for each sector and the distribution of government output that would be optimal given the government's partisan orientation. In the second stage, labor and foreign investors decide in which sector to operate after observing the tax rates adopted by the government in the first stage. We find the subgame perfect Nash equilibrium of the game using backward induction; that is, we solve for the labor and capital allocation in the second stage and then derive the partisan government's solution in the first stage.

The regulatory environment chosen by the host country influences the decisions of foreign investors and ultimately affects domestic factors of production. To the extent that FDI results in a flow of capital, it is likely to have an impact on the host country's production and national income. It is precisely through their effect in production that investment inflows are likely to have distributive consequences: they have the potential to affect the return to domestic factors of production. We claim that the direction of the distributive consequences—who benefits and who hurts—is associated with the characteristics of the specific investment project.

In our stylized framework, the distributive consequences depend on the technology that the investor chooses for its affiliate. The technological choice determines which domestic factors would benefit from the entry and expansion of the activity of the MNC: those factors, labor or capital, that complement FDI in production will experience an increase in the demand for their services and, consequently, a rise in their returns. By contrast, factors of production that FDI substitutes for will suffer, since their relative demand and factor returns are likely to fall.[12]

In sum, changes in foreign capital flows have an impact on the relative demand of domestic factors of production, affecting their returns. Foreign investment can enter the host economy as either a complement to or substitute for labor and capital, depending on the available technology to the foreign firm. As a result, different types of foreign investment are expected to have different distributive consequences.

The Political Environment

Domestic factor returns are affected by investment flows, which are, in turn, affected by policies; and those policies are ultimately the result of a political process that aggregates the preferences of domestic economic agents. At the first stage of our model, we characterize this political process in terms of the links between a partisan government and specific groups in the polity.[13]

In our theoretical framework, partisan motivations are introduced by assuming that governments place a higher value on the welfare of a group of political actors—their core constituents. Those constituencies are likely to vary depending on the government's type, or partisan orientation.[14] We assume that partisanship can vary along two extreme types, pro-labor and pro-capital, depending on the relative weight they place on the well-being of workers or businesses, respectively. We label the pro-labor party as the "left" and the pro-business party as the "right." Left-leaning governments will enact policies that favor owners of labor, and right-leaning government will adopt policies that favor capital.

There is good reason to believe that left-leaning parties will be more receptive to labor's demands, while right-leaning parties will favor owners of domestic capital: governments on the left side of the political spectrum tend to cater to labor for political support and, consequently, place more emphasis on issues such as unemployment and income redistribution. Right-leaning parties tend to be more business oriented, assign high priority to price and stability, and usually clash with labor on issues such as income redistribution, as previously discussed.[15]

Given that foreign investment is likely to shift the income of domestic owners of factors of production up or down depending on the type of FDI, we should expect workers and business owners to organize politically and rally behind the issue of regulating the inflow of direct investment. This would result in a cleavage around the politics of FDI that pits workers and business owners against each other. Whether each of these groups adopts a pro- or anti-FDI stance depends on the type of technology associated with the specific investment activity. Workers would support policies aimed at encouraging FDI that complements labor in production, while local capitalists would oppose. Business owners would support FDI that substitutes for labor, whereas workers would oppose.

Main Results

Combining the expected distributive consequences of FDI with the government's partisan motivations (both discussed in previous subsections), the following theoretical results can be established.

First, left-leaning parties—those that cater to workers—will adopt policies that encourage the inflow of foreign investment in sectors where labor is complemented by FDI, that is, sectors where the entry of foreign capital increases wages. Second, left-leaning governments will discourage foreign investment in sectors where foreign capital substitutes for labor in production. Finally, when foreign capital inflows benefit domestic capital owners, right-leaning governments—those that cater to domestic business interests—would enact policies that selectively promote the entry of foreign capital.[16]

Accordingly, the previous results would be consistent with the following pattern of tax rates on foreign capital across sectors. First, tax rates decided by pro-labor governments would be relatively lower (than the corresponding tax rates chosen by pro-capital governments) in sectors where labor and foreign capital are complements. Second, pro-labor governments would impose relatively higher tax rates (than pro-capital governments) in sectors where labor and foreign capital are substitutes. Finally, to the extent that FDI benefits domestic capitalists in certain sectors, pro-capital governments would impose lower tax rates on foreign capital entering into those sectors.[17]

Together with the results from the first stage, we can predict a differential pattern of sectoral allocation of foreign investment as the partisan orientation of the host government changes.

Allocation of FDI across Sectors: Empirical Evidence

In the previous sections, we concluded that to the extent that foreign investment has the potential to affect the relative demand of domestic factors of production, that governments are partisan, and that their policy interventions can affect economic outcomes, we should expect regular cycles in economic performance that can be mapped onto changes in partisanship of the incumbent government. We now move to exploring the empirical content of this conclusion.

Using data on FDI inflows disaggregated at the industry level, obtained from the OECD's International Direct Investment Statistics database, we test two indirect implications derived from this framework. First, if foreign investment is a complement to labor in some sectors and to capital in other sectors, governments with different ideologies would selectively stimulate or deter the entry of foreign capital into different sectors. Hence, we would expect an association between government partisanship and sectoral allocation of FDI inflows. Second, if FDI inflows are endogenous to the political process, the effects on the return to factors of production in the host country should differ under governments of different partisan orientations. We would, for instance, expect FDI inflows to have a positive effect on wages under pro-labor governments but not under pro-business incumbents.

In this section, we present some evidence indicating that the pattern of FDI allocation across sectors is systematically different for governments with different political ideology, which is consistent with (but not a direct test of) our theory. Next, we claim that these patterns might be explained by the fact that left-leaning governments would be inclined to promote measures that stimulate the entry of foreign capital into those sectors that generate an increase in average wages.

Political Ideology and FDI Allocation across Sectors

We begin by running the following regression for each sector i:

$$FDI_{ijt}/Investment_{jt} = \alpha_{0i} + \alpha_{1i} Left_{jt} + \theta_i' X_{ijt} + \varepsilon_{ijt}. \tag{1}$$

The subscripts i, j, and t denote, respectively, sector i, country j, and time t. The dependent variable is net inflow of FDI in sector i as a proportion of total investment in country j.[18] This normalization of the dependent variable aims at capturing the differential effect that politics has on FDI as opposed to the effect on overall investment.[19] Ideally we would normalize sectoral inflows to investment in sector i, yet we could not obtain data disaggregated at this level.[20]

Left is a dummy variable indicating whether a left-leaning party is in government in country j at time t, and X is a vector of control variables.[21] Following the political science, economics, and international business literature on the determinants of FDI (Markusen 1998a, 1998b; Markusen and Maskus 1999a, 1999b; Oneal 1994; Jensen 2003; Li and Resnick 2003), control variables include real GDP per capita, to account for level of development and relative endowment of capital; trade openness, which may create incentives or disincentives to invest in the host country, depending on the type of investment and product; population, to account for market size; and a battery of country and year dummies that allow us to control for country-specific and slow-moving variables that are likely to affect the incentives to invest in the host country (e.g., natural resource endowments, educational attainment, legal system and property rights protection, and other institutional features of the host) and for temporal shocks that could affect investment across countries.[22]

Controlling for the determinants of FDI, a value of α_{1i} significantly different from zero suggests that sector i receives higher FDI flows (as a proportion of domestic investment) when left governments are in power, relative to countries and governments of other partisan orientation/political ideologies.[23] Table 4.2 provides a list of the sectors employed in the analysis.[24]

Following equation 1, we perform a pooled regression for each sector separately. The estimates are presented in table 4.1. Two results are worth emphasizing. First, the pattern of FDI allocation systematically differs across countries or governments with different partisan orientation.[25] The results suggest that when the party in government is categorized as left, FDI predominantly flows into the primary sector 2 (mining and quarrying); into the manufacturing sectors 3 (food products), 6 (metal and mechanical products), and 8 (vehicles and transport equipment); and into the service sectors 9 (electricity, gas, and water), 14 (telecommunications), and 15 (financial intermediation), relative to right and center governments.[26]

TABLE 4.2.   Codes for Industrial Sectors Used in Empirical Analysis

Number	Description	ISIC Code
1	Agriculture and fishing	01–05
2	Mining and quarrying	10–14
3	Food products	15
4	Total textile and wood activities	17–20
5	Total petroleum, chemical, rubber, plastic products	23–25
6	Total metal and mechanical products	27–28
7	Total machinery, computers, RTV, communication	29–33
8	Total vehicles and other transport equipment	34–35
9	Electricity, gas, and water	40–41
10	Construction	45
11	Trade and repairs	50–52
12	Hotels and restaurants	55
13	Transportation	60–62
14	Telecommunications	64
15	Financial intermediation	65–67
16	Real estate	70
17	Other business activities	71–74

Second, inflows into sectors 10 (construction) and 13 (transportation) are negatively correlated with left partisan orientation of the incumbent.

The evidence suggests that the sectoral allocation of inflows covaries with partisan orientation of the chief executive of the host government. This does not constitute a direct test of our theory, since it is not self-evident from the description of the sectors whether foreign investment complements or substitutes for domestic capital or for labor. For instance, we would expect that FDI is more likely to increase labor demand in manufacturing and possibly in the service sector, but less so in the primary sector.[27] To test for this, we conduct a pooled regression where we introduce an interaction between a measure of government partisanship with dummy variables that capture whether an industry is in the manufacturing or the service sector.[28] We expect workers in the manufacturing industry to benefit from investment inflows more than do workers in services. The omitted category is formed by industries in the primary sector, including agriculture and fishing (sector 1) and extractive industries (sector 2), where foreign investment is less likely to complement labor. The results from these tests, reproduced in table 4.3, are in line with our expectations: control of cabinet portfolios by left-leaning parties are associated with an increase in the proportion of foreign investment in industries in the manufacturing sector and less so in services, but not in the primary sector.

It is plausible that, even at this level of aggregation of the dependent variable, we could be missing the behavioral implications of investors' reaction to politics. Firms, for example, could have access to different production technologies, which they might selectively adopt in response to changes in the political environment. Hence, we would expect a large variance in the degree of complementarity or substitutability between foreign investment and domestic factors of production even within sectors. In equilibrium, we should, thus, expect that the endogenously determined FDI inflows (i.e., those that result from the strategic interaction between investors and host governments) should have different effects on the return to labor and capital depending on the political orientation of the incumbent. Inflows under the left should be of the type that has a positive effect on wages (and/or on the ability of governments to finance and supply government services to labor, or government transfers in our model), and inflows under the right-leaning government should be of the type that has a positive effect on the return to domestic capital owners.

FDI Inflows and Aggregate Wages

Our theory predicts that left-leaning governments would stimulate the entry of foreign capital flows into different sectors as long as aggregate wages unambiguously rise. In this section, we analyze whether the effect of endogenously determined capital inflows into different sectors on aggregate wages is systematically different when governments of different partisan orientation/ideology are in power. For this purpose, we estimate the model as follows:

TABLE 4.3. FDI Inflows and Government Political Orientation: Pooled Regressions

	DV: FDI Inflows into Sector I as a Proportion of Country's Investment			
	(1)	(2)	(3)	(4)
Lagged DV	0.290*	0.237	0.145	0.131
	(0.171)	(0.168)	(0.177)	(0.179)
Left share of Cabinet	−0.0020	−0.106	−0.139	−0.164
	(0.103)	(0.152)	(0.150)	(0.155)
Manufacturing	−0.0698	−0.138	−0.0160	0.0397
	(0.147)	(0.153)	(0.181)	(0.177)
Manufacturing × Left share of Cabinet	0.881**	0.843**	0.796**	0.763*
	(0.439)	(0.423)	(0.404)	(0.399)
Service	0.186**	0.175**	1.063***	1.176***
	(0.0923)	(0.0863)	(0.390)	(0.389)
Service × Left share of Cabinet	0.329**	0.317*	0.414**	0.401**
	(0.159)	(0.166)	(0.169)	(0.170)
Openness	0.0094***	0.0324	0.0398*	0.0600***
	(0.0028)	(0.0213)	(0.0211)	(0.0213)
Real GDP/capita (thousands)	0.0362***	−0.0195	−0.0267	0.0179
	(0.0115)	(0.0906)	(0.0886)	(0.131)
Population (millions)	−0.00031	−0.00387	−0.00156	0.0120
	(0.0011)	(0.0170)	(0.0167)	(0.0157)
Constant	−0.985***	1.144	0.539	−3.656
	(0.196)	(2.218)	(2.193)	(2.236)
Country dummies	No	Yes	Yes	Yes
Sector dummies	No	No	Yes	Yes
Year dummies	No	No	No	Yes
Countries	19	19	19	19
Sectors	17	17	17	17
Observations	2,434	2,434	2,434	2,434
R^2	0.061	0.086	0.116	0.125

Note: Heteroskedastic corrected standard errors in parentheses.
Two-tailed test: * significant at 10%; ** significant at 5%; *** significant at 1%.

$$\Delta \ln(W_{jt}) = \gamma_0 + \gamma_1 \text{ FDI}_{jt} + \gamma_2 \text{ Left}_{jt} + \gamma_3 \text{ FDI}_{jt} \times \text{Left}_{jt} + \delta' Z + \eta_{jt}, \qquad (2)$$

where $\Delta \ln(W_{jt})$ is the change in natural log of total wages (per employee) for country j at time t, which is equivalent to the rate of change in average wages.[29] The theoretical model introduced earlier assumes that the effect of capital inflows into different sectors have the same effect on the change in average wages economy wide. We argue that this should be true in equilibrium. If this was not the case, a left government would stimulate the entry of capital into those sectors where the effect on wages is greatest. Hence, our focus is on the coefficient γ_3: a positive estimate of γ_3 significantly different from zero would indicate that the increase in wages when foreign capital enters any sector in country j is higher when Left = 1.[30] Among the vector of control variables Z, we include the natural log of value added per employee (a proxy of the rate of change in labor productivity), the natural log of GDP per capita (a coarse proxy for the rate of change in capital endowment), the natural log of the ratio of trade to GDP (to control for changes in resource allocation), change in unemployment (since the effect of foreign investment inflows could be felt on wages or employment levels), and dummy variables for each country j and time period t.[31] The battery of dummy variables allows us to account for time-invariant characteristics of the host country (education, natural resource endowment, legal systems, labor market institutions, and other determinants of wages) and for common shocks across units, respectively. This specification follows Rodrik's (1999, 715–23) analysis of the effect of democracy on wages in manufacturing. Our main departure from Rodrik's analysis is that we estimate the model in differences, not levels. We perform a pooled regression, adjusting for heteroskedasticity and autocorrelation. Due to data constraints, the sample for these tests is limited to 18 countries for the period 1980–2003. Table 4.4 reproduces the results of these tests.[32]

These results suggest that after controlling for changes in productivity (change in the log of value added per employee), income, and other determinants of wages, the orientation of the government does not seem to be associated with changes in average wages, as indicated by the coefficient on the dummy variable Left.[33] Second, we also find that capital inflows do not systematically affect wages: the value of the coefficient on inflows is positive but not significantly different from zero. Finally, only when left governments are in power do foreign investment inflows increase total wages.[34] The latter results suggest that when dealing with foreign investors, left-leaning governments are selective: they would encourage inflows of FDI into those sectors that have the potential to improve aggregate labor welfare, consistent with our theory.

Summary of Results

We claim that different forms of FDI react differently to political incentives. Hence, we predict the existence of partisan cycles in the flow of FDI to different industries. We expect FDI to flow into sectors where it is a complement of labor when countries are governed by the left. Conversely,

TABLE 4.4. Effect of FDI Inflows on Average Wages and Labor Costs

	Dependent Variable	
	(1) ΔLn(Wages/ Employment)	(2) ΔLn(Labor Costs/ Employment)
Left (γ_1)	−0.00315	0.00020
	(0.00330)	(0.00216)
FDI Inflows, $ billion (γ_2)	0.00005	0.00006
	(0.00004)	(0.00004)
Left × FDI Inflows (γ_3)	0.00009**	0.00008**
	(0.00004)	(0.00004)
ΔLn(Value Added/Employee)	0.65675***	0.76565***
	(0.09199)	(0.04646)
ΔLn (Real GDP per capita)	−0.12538	−0.08530
	(0.11073)	(0.06385)
ΔOpenness	−0.00269***	−0.00184***
	(0.00089)	(0.00056)
ΔUnemployment	−0.00783***	−0.00657***
	(0.00228)	(0.00109)
ΔInflation	0.00094	0.00016
	(0.00148)	(0.00059)
Constant	0.00756	0.02813**
	(0.01188)	(0.01346)
Country dummies	Yes	Yes
Year dummies	Yes	Yes
Observations	232	409
Groups	18	24
R^2	0.8523	0.8834
Wald χ^2	1,027.2	3,015.0
Prob > χ^2	0.00	0.00

Source: Pinto and Pinto 2008, 245.
Note: Heteroskedastic panel corrected standard errors in parentheses.
Two-tailed test: *significant at 10%; **significant at 5%; ***significant at 1%.

foreign investment would be attracted to those sectors where it complements domestic capital when the pro-business party is in power. We find
that the pattern of FDI inflows covaries with government partisanship,
providing preliminary support to one of the implications of our theory. We
also find that under left-leaning governments, FDI inflows are more likely
to have a positive impact on aggregate wages, consistent with our assumptions on the distributive consequences of FDI flows.

Dynamics

Thus far, the model has neglected a crucial aspect of investment. Investment in general (and FDI in particular) is likely to generate returns
throughout several periods, possibly even beyond multiple elections and
incumbents' tenure. Hence, it would be reasonable to assume that when
making investment decisions, investors consider not only the current government partisanship but also the potential orientation of future governments. Modeling the interaction between foreign investors and host governments in a dynamic setting allows us to capture these calculations.

Adding this dynamic element leads to a well-known problem in the literature on capital taxation, which is that governments have an incentive to
tax capital more heavily once investment decisions have been made, since
the elasticity of capital to taxes becomes zero.[35] In other words, as bargains
become obsolete, it is ex-post optimal to choose the highest possible tax
rates on capital, even for governments that promise to maintain tax rates at
their ex-ante optimal levels (Kindleberger 1969; Vernon 1971). Investors
who face an exit cost will anticipate the government's behavior and will
likely decide not to enter, resulting in a suboptimal policy and missed investment opportunities (Pinto and Pinto 2011).

The extant literature argues that institutional constraints help solve the
commitment problem, since contracts are more likely to be honored when
the hands of the government are tied (North and Thomas 1973; North and
Weingast 1989; Henisz 2000). But tying a government's hands is equivalent
to adopting an inflexible policy, which may not be optimal—that is, the one
that would be adopted by a welfare-maximizing social planner (see Spiller
and Tommasi 2003). Moreover, the literature on capital taxation has shown
that, in practice, tax rates are not set at confiscatory levels; that is, even in
the absence of institutional constraints, outright expropriation is a rare
event (Chari and Kehoe 1990; Klein and Rios-Rull 2003).

To account for the absence of confiscatory tax rates, we develop a dynamic model where the host government only has access to partial commitment technologies.[36] From this model, we derive the conditions under which the host government's partisanship will result in qualitatively different tax schedules offered to foreign investors. The model also allows us to state conditions under which incumbents will have an incentive to opportunistically tax foreign investors. In our model, the incentives faced by the incumbent to tax foreign investors more or less heavily depend not only on the distributive consequences created by foreign investment but also on the costs of redeployment of that investment and the political uncertainty about the policy implemented by prospective partisan governments.

The implications of this dynamic model are in line with the predictions from the model discussed in the previous section, which predicted the existence of partisan cycles in the regulation of internationally mobile capital driven by the expected distributional consequences of inward investment. However, higher costs of redeployment, the costs to move investment and production to different sectors and different locations, are likely to mitigate those distributive motivations.

We adopt a modeling strategy that captures, under a unifying framework, the scope conditions for different predictions from the political economy of foreign investment literature (including those in the obsolescing bargain tradition) and those from the literature on capital taxation in macroeconomics. Implicit in our reasoning is the idea that the political process offers foreign investors a form of political insurance.[37] Since they anticipate that the capital flows will affect the return to owners of domestic factors of production, foreign investors will collude with local actors (labor or capital) when possible. This collusion forces the host government to internalize the costs of reverting the policy regime. Consequently, a partisan government will offer investment conditions preferred by its core constituent and will sustain those promises over time.

The Model with Capital Adjustment Costs

The predictions from the static analysis presented in the previous sections would still hold in a dynamic framework if, for instance, foreign investment perfectly adjusts to the new desired level when governments change capital tax rates. However, investors' reaction to changes in the host government's behavior may take some time.[38] Whether or not the reaction is immediate typically depends on the cost of adjusting capital to the new desired levels.

Consider a given set of tax rates that determine a specific initial allocation of foreign capital. An increase in tax rates would induce capital to leave the country; that is, there is an incentive to divest, and capital stocks are adjusted to the new tax levels.[39] With perfect capital mobility, the adjustment of foreign capital stock is immediate. When it is costly to change the stock of capital, only partial adjustment would take place, so the capital stock will not immediately jump to its new level when the tax rate on capital is changed.[40] The extreme case of immediate adjustment is consistent with the setup of the model in this chapter's appendix (see Pinto and Pinto 2008). Under these conditions, foreign capital adjusts perfectly to the new desired level; in every time period, then, partisan governments face the same exact problem as the one previously described.

Main Results

By extending the baseline model presented in the previous section and incorporating a dynamic approach, we are able to obtain additional results. First, we identify the conditions under which higher costs of redeployment will affect the incentives to tax foreign investment more heavily, rendering the predictions from the obsolescing bargain literature as a subcase in the broader framework that we defined as the politics of investment.

Second, governments have an incentive to impose heavier taxes on foreign capital that substitutes in production for the factor owned by the incumbents' core constituents. In this case, higher taxes are a consequence of both distributive effects (i.e., they would increase the return of the corresponding political group) and the fact that foreign capital is imperfectly mobile.

Third, the model shows that the orientation of the incumbent—namely, its allegiance to workers or capital owners—and the expected distributive pressure exerted by inflows and outflows of internationally mobile capital on labor and capital could either aggravate or mitigate the commitment problem that arises in the dynamic setting. For instance, the results of the model are consistent with lower taxes on capital in the second period. We claim that mitigation would be observed if the distributive effects more than compensate for the benefits of taxing a more inelastic tax base. Suppose that foreign capital complements in production the factor owned by the governments' constituents. In this case, the partisan government would maintain a relatively low capital tax rate (or at least taxes would not be raised). Otherwise, capital would have incentives to leave the country, negatively affecting the return of the domestic factors of production.

Finally, there are also two other determinants of the size of the tax breaks offered to foreign capitalists: (1) the opportunity costs faced by investors (i.e., the returns they could get abroad); and (2) the relative weight placed by domestic actors on government transfers financed with the revenue obtained from taxing capital (i.e., the trade-off between direct income effects and indirect income effects through government transfers), which was also central to the predictions in the earlier sections.

These predictions are consistent with our findings (presented in the previous section) on the differential sectoral allocation of FDI in OECD countries as the orientation of the incumbent changed and on the positive effect of FDI on wages under a left-leaning government.

Effect of FDI on Employment

In a previous section of this chapter, we introduced a political economy explanation of the variance in the regulatory regimes toward foreign investors, by focusing on the effect of FDI on the returns to domestic factors of production. Our findings are far from conclusive, since we could not identify the degree of complementarity or substitutability between labor and foreign capital in the different sectors. Still, the differential pattern of sectoral allocation of FDI under left- and right-leaning governments is indeed consistent with the predictions from our model: the positive correlation between left orientation of the government and inflows, on one side, and economy-wide wages, on the other, suggests that the argument is plausible.

Yet the emphasis on wages and factor returns should not be overstated. Journalistic accounts on the activity of multinational corporations and political debates around the politics of FDI usually stress the effects of foreign investment on employment.[41] Moreover, in the academic realm, there is clear empirical evidence that the quantity and quality of employment generated by domestic and foreign investment is systematically different.[42] Our own preliminary analysis suggests that the wage effects predicted in our earlier model might not attain in the absence of full employment at the economy and industry levels. Table 4.5 summarizes the results of the three regression models. Each model is specified as follows:

$$FDI_{ijt}/Investment_{jt} = \alpha_{0i} + \alpha_{1i} \, Left_{jt} + \varphi \, X + \varepsilon_{ijt}, \tag{3}$$

$$\Delta(Wage_{ijt}/Value\ Added_{ijt}) = \beta_{0i} + \beta_{1i}\,(FDI_{ijt}/Investment_{jt}) + \varphi\,X + \varepsilon_{ijt}, \tag{4}$$

$$\Delta(Employment_{ijt}/Population_{jt}) = \gamma_{0i} + \gamma_{1i}\,(FDI_{ijt}/Investment_{jt}) + \varphi\,X + \varepsilon_{ijt}, \tag{5}$$

where subscripts i, j, and t denote, respectively, sector i, country j, and time t, and X is a vector of sectoral and country-level controls.[43] The table reproduces the signs and significance levels of the estimated partial correlation coefficients α_{1i}, β_{1i}, and γ_{1i} for each sector i; note that for column 1, the sign and significance levels are those reported in the first column of table 4.5. Also note that the results for models 2 and 3 are fitted for a subsample of the data when the left-leaning party is in power only.[44] These results suggest that when the left is in power, sectoral FDI inflows are likely to have differential effects on sectoral wages and employment. For instance, consider sector 8 (vehicles and transportation): when the left is in power, FDI enters this sector not because it has an impact on wages but because it increases employment. A similar behavior is observed in sector 9 (electricity, gas, and water).

The Model

The empirical results shown in table 4.5 suggest that a model that focuses solely on the income effects of policies implemented by partisan government would only capture part of the story. Therefore, we add an employment motivation to the political economy model of FDI introduced in earlier in this chapter.[45]

Specifically, we assume that the utility of domestic labor depends on both the wages they receive and the employment level. Wages and employment are determined sequentially through a sector-specific process of wage bargaining. This implies that the host partisan government, when deciding the policy that maximizes the welfare of its constituents, is concerned about not only the return to domestic factors of production but also the level of employment. The weight placed on employment and/or factor returns depends on the incumbent's pro-labor or pro-business stance. We solve for the optimal policy bundle of taxes offered by the incumbent to foreign investors and the level of unemployment benefits offered to workers.

The model is built on a few assumptions. First, we assume that both domestic capital and labor are sector specific. Second, the utility of workers in each sector depends on sectoral wages, employment, and sector-specific unemployment benefits provided by the government. Third, wages and employment are determined through a process of sequential bargaining between labor and the firm. The bargaining process is specific to the sector. Finally, decisions are taken sequentially as follows: first, the govern-

TABLE 4.5.   FDI Inflows, Wages, and Employment

			Dependent Variable			
	(1) $FDI_{ijt}/$ Investment$_{jt}$		(2) $\Delta(Wage_{ijt}/$ Value Added$_{ijt})$		(3) $\Delta(Employment_{ijt}/$ Population$_{jt})$	
Sector (code and description)	Sign on Left	Signif.	Sign on FDI/Invest	Signif.	Sign on FDI/Invest	Signif.
1 Agriculture and fishing	+		+		+	
2 Mining and quarrying	+	**	−	***	+	
3 Food products	+	***	+		−	
4 Textile and wood	+		+		−	**
5 Petroleum, chemical, etc.	+		+	**	+	
6 Metal and mechanical	+	*	+	**	−	
7 Machinery, computers, etc.	+		+	**	−	
8 Vehicles and transport	+	***	+		+	*
9 Electricity, gas, and water	+	*	+		+	**
10 Construction	−	***	+		+	
11 Trade and repairs	+		+		−	
12 Hotels and restaurants	−		−		+	*
13 Transportation	−	*	+		−	
14 Telecommunications	+	*	+	***	+	*
15 Financial intermediation	+	***	+		+	
16 Real estate	−		+	***	+	
17 Other business activities	−		+	***	+	

Note: (1) Coefficient of Left$_{jt}$ (see table 4.1); (2) Coefficient of FDI$_{ijt}$/Investment$_{jt}$ (subsample Left$_{jt}$ = 1); (3) Coefficient of FDI$_{ijt}$/Investment$_{jt}$ (subsample Left$_{jt}$ = 1).

Two-tailed test: *significant at 10%; ** significant at 5%; *** significant at 1%.

ment chooses taxes on foreign capital and unemployment benefits for each sector; next, after observing the government's choice, workers make a wage demand; last, firms in each sector observe policy variables and wage demands and choose the amount of labor to employ.

Main Results

From the extended theoretical model, we establish two main conclusions. First, when foreign capital and domestic labor are complements, a pro-labor government will choose lower tax rates, encouraging the entry of foreign capital. The outcome of this policy is consistent with both lower and higher wages and/or lower or higher levels of employment. Second, also when foreign investment and labor are complements, domestic capitalists and domestic labor may agree on the tax policy; that is, the tax rates chosen by a pro-labor and a pro-capital government may be the same. These two results allow us to connect the theory with the correlations presented in table 4.5. The results presented there reveal that sectoral FDI inflows are likely to have differential effects on sectoral wages and employment. Moreover, they show that a left government may encourage the entry of foreign capital even if entry does not increase wages, as long as the level of employment rises, as observed in sectors 8 (auto industry) and 9 (utilities) among others.

Conclusion

This chapter argues that the partisan orientation of the incumbent government in a host country has the potential to affect the pattern of allocation of direct foreign investment. We discuss the predictions from a series of formal models aimed at capturing the interaction between investors, host governments, and owners of factors of production in the host country. Comparative static exercises from our models allow us to understand and explain the connection between partisanship and different types of foreign investment. The models emphasize the role of preferences of domestic actors derived from the expected distributive consequences of FDI and the link of those actors to different political parties.

We claim that the distributive consequences of FDI differ for different types of investment and are associated with the production technology available to investors. When foreign investment complements labor in production, its entry is likely to have a positive effect on labor demand; this differential demand is reflected in higher wages and employment opportunities to workers. When foreign investment substitutes for labor in production (e.g., by introducing labor-saving technologies), foreign capital's entry will result in reduced labor demand, lower wages, and lower levels of employment.

While distributive consequences of FDI affect domestic actors' incentives to demand different regulatory policies toward foreign investment, the political link between an incumbent government and its core constituents—whose well-being is affected by the inflow and outflow of mobile capital—determines the incumbent's incentives to supply policies that benefit those groups. Host governments will favor FDI when foreign investment enters into production as a complement to the factor owned by their core constituent, and they will try to keep investors out when their constituent owns a factor of production that is a substitute for foreign investment. Investors are likely to anticipate governments' behavior and decide to invest when the host government is of the "right" type or to withhold investment when it is not. More specifically, left-leaning governments are more likely to provide better investment conditions to lure foreign investment into those sectors where labor is a complement of FDI. Moreover, when in power, the party of the right will offer a more favorable investment environment to foreign investment that would flow into those sectors where FDI is a complement to domestic capital and will limit the inflow of foreign capital to those sectors where FDI substitutes for domestic capital, because direct investment inflows compete down the rents that would have otherwise accrued to domestic business owners. The predictions from these models are consistent with the differential pattern of sectoral allocation of FDI across countries and over time. Moreover, we show that under left-leaning governments, FDI inflow is likely to have a positive effect on wages, a finding that supports the underlying assumptions driving our models.

Depending on the cost of redeployment of their activities, some investors would also look for reassurances that the regulatory framework in the host country supports their activity and that the government will not act opportunistically against them as time goes by. Foreign investors react to the changes in the regulatory environment (and its consistency over time) by deciding to increase investment flow into a host country (and a specific sector in that country) if the owner of the factor of production that is their complement is politically influential, that is, if the preferences of these actors are likely to be internalized by those in position to change policy. In equilibrium, investors will stay out when the government is of the "wrong" type (i.e., when it represents their substitute in production). Partisan governments will internalize the preferences of their core constituents (the left, those of labor; the right, those of capital) and will abide by the conditions offered ex ante to lure investors in.

The implications of the model are in line with the predictions from earlier work on the existence of partisan cycles in the regulation of direct investment in the long run. While distributive motivations resulting from the technological relationship between foreign investment and domestic factors of productions are likely to drive the adoption of different regimes aimed at promoting or preventing the inflow of foreign investment, higher costs of redeployment mitigate these partisan effects. Our modeling strategy allows us to place the predictions from traditional arguments on the political economy of foreign investment under a common framework. We are able to identify the conditions under which rules and discretion matter in the regulation of foreign investment.

Appendix: Technical Presentation of the Model Developed

Consider a three-factor, two-sector, small-open economy, where world prices are fixed and normalized to unity. Production of output q^i in sector i = 1, 2 requires labor, domestic capital, and foreign capital: $q^i = f^i(K^i, k^i, L^i)$. We assume that $f^i(\cdot)$ is a constant-return-to-scale production function, where K^i is domestic capital, k^i foreign capital, and L^i labor in sector $i = 1$, 2. Total domestic capital and labor are assumed fixed in supply; that is, $\overline{K} = K^1 + K^2$, and $\overline{L} = L^1 + L^2$. Foreign capital is in (perfectly) elastic supply and can be rented at an exogenous rate, r (the opportunity cost of investing in the host). We assume that labor is mobile across sectors within the country but internationally immobile. Domestic capital, however, is sector specific; in other words, it is completely immobile.

We group domestic agents into two groups depending on their ownership of factors of production: workers (who only provide labor services), denoted with L; and capitalists (who only own capital), denoted with K. Then, $\overline{L}$ is the number of workers and $\overline{K}$ the number of capitalists in the economy. Consumers derive utility directly from income, denoted y_h, and from a government transfer, denoted g; the utility of individual h is given by $u_h = y_h + v(g_h)$, for $h = L, K$.[46]

Let t^i be the capital tax rate on foreign capital entering sector i. The allocation of foreign capital in sector i is determined by $f_k^i - t^i = r$, which states that the return to investing in the host country net of taxes should be at least as much as what the investor would have received abroad. Free mobility of labor assures that wages are equalized across sectors; that is, $w \equiv f_L^1 = f_L^2$, where w is the common wage to workers in all sectors.[47] Domestic capital owners in each sector are the residual claimants of the value of output net of payment to workers and foreign capital owners.[48] Due to constant returns to scale, the return to domestic capital in sector i is given by

$$\bar{r}^i = q^i - wL^i - (r + t^i)k^i, \text{ for } i = 1, 2,$$

and aggregate return to domestic capital is denoted as $\bar{r} = \bar{r}^1 + \bar{r}^2$.

The model assumes that decisions are taken sequentially. In the first stage, the government chooses the values of t^1 and t^2. In the second stage, labor and foreign investors decide in which sector to operate after observing the tax rates adopted by the government in the first stage. We find the subgame perfect Nash equilibrium of the game using backward induction; that is, we solve for the labor and capital allocation in the second stage and then derive the government's solution in the first stage.

Second Stage: Allocation of Foreign Capital and Domestic Labor

At the second stage, the sectoral allocation of domestic labor and foreign capital is simultaneously determined. Once foreign investors observe the regulatory framework affecting sectoral returns to investment, they decide to operate in any of those sectors. In equilibrium, the net returns across sectors must be equalized and must be equal to the return they would otherwise receive abroad. This decision affects the marginal product of labor in the sector, creating an incentive for workers to shift across sectors until wages in both sectors are equalized.

More formally, the Nash equilibrium at this stage (L^1, k^1, k^2) is implicitly defined by

$$f_k^1 - r - t^1 = 0, \qquad f_k^2 - r - t^2 = 0, \qquad \text{and } f_L^1 - f_L^2 = 0,$$

where $f_L^i \equiv w$, $i = 1, 2$. The equilibrium allocations of labor and foreign investment in different sectors of the economy are functions of the regulatory regime in both sectors. In other words, $L^1(t^1, t^2)$ and $k^i(t^1, t^2)$, $i = 1, 2$, where t^1 and t^2 are the tax rates selected by the host government in the first stage.

The conclusions of our model depend on the impact of tax rates t^i, $i = 1$, 2 on the returns to the domestic factors of production: wages, w, and the return to capital, $\bar{r}$. Since a change in t^i affects w and $\bar{r}$ indirectly through its effect on the allocation of factors of production, we first need to study how the equilibrium levels of L^1, k^1, and k^2 respond to changes in t^1 and t^2.

By implicit differentiation of the system of equations that determines the equilibrium allocation, we obtain the comparative static results $\partial k^i/\partial t^i$, $\partial k^j/\partial t^i$, and $\partial L^i/\partial t^i = -\partial L^j/\partial t^i$, $i, j = 1, 2, i \neq j$. Except for the signs of $\partial k^i/\partial t^i$, $i = 1, 2$, which is negative since higher taxes deter foreign investment, the results depend on the specific technological relationship between the factors of production k and L in each sector. This technological relationship is determined by the sign of the cross-partial derivative f_{Lk}, which accounts for the effect of an increase in foreign capital on the marginal productivity of domestic labor. For instance, suppose that k and L are complements in both sectors, that is, that $f_{Lk}^i > 0$, $i = 1, 2$. Then, $\partial k^2/\partial t^1 > 0$, and $\partial L^1/\partial t^1 < 0$. The intuition behind these results is straightforward. An increase in t^1 reduces the amount of foreign capital in sector 1. Given that k^1 and L^1 are complements, the marginal productivity of labor in sector 1 declines, so labor shifts to sector 2. As k^2 and L^2 are also complements, the marginal productivity of foreign capital increases in that sector, attracting foreign capital to sector 2. Similar conclusions apply for changes in t^2 and for different technological relationships between inputs.

The impact of taxes on the returns to the domestic factors of production is summarized in table 4A.1. The table considers all the different possibilities that may arise depending on whether labor and foreign capital are complements or substitutes, as specified in the first two columns of the table. We indicate with + or – the signs of the comparative static results of the effect of changing taxes in sectors $i = 1, 2$ on the returns to domestic capital owners ($\partial \bar{r}/\partial t^i$) and wages ($\partial w/\partial t^i$).

The effect of a change in t^i on wages only depends on the technological relationship between labor and foreign capital in that sector, given by f_{Lk}^i. Note that the partial derivatives of wages with respect to taxes in sector i

($\partial w/\partial t^i$) and the change in the marginal product of labor that results from foreign capital inflows ($f_{Lk}{}^i$) have opposite signs: if L and k are substitutes in sector i (i.e., $f_{Lk}{}^i < 0$), wages decline when t^i rises; if L and k are complements in sector i (i.e., $f_{Lk}{}^i > 0$), wages increase when t^i rises. These results can be explained as follows. A higher tax rate t^i lowers the amount of foreign capital in sector i. If labor and foreign capital are substitutes, then a lower level of capital increases labor productivity in that sector and, as a result, in the whole economy, so wages should increase. If labor and foreign capital are complements, then a lower level of capital in sector i reduces labor productivity, so wages go down with higher taxes. In sum, workers would support higher taxes on foreign capital when foreign capital substitutes labor in production, lower taxes when it acts as a complement.

Changes in tax rates may affect domestic capital owners in sectors 1 and 2 differently, and again these effects depend on the technological relationship between factors of production. An increase in t^i increases the total income received by foreign capitalists in k^i.[49] At the same time, it affects total labor income in ($\partial w/\partial t^i$)L^i. Since domestic capitalists are the residual claimants of profits, the change in total income of domestic capitalists in sector i is given by $\partial \bar{r}^i/\partial t^i = -[(\partial w/\partial t^i)L^i + k^i]$.[50] A rise in t^i also affects total income of domestic capitalists in sector j. The latter is given by $\partial \bar{r}^j/\partial t^i = -(\partial w/\partial t^i)L^j$. Since, in our model, the partisan government assigns the same weight to the well-being of domestic capitalists in all sectors, only the effect of t^i on the total income received by domestic capital owners, $\bar{r} = \bar{r}^i + \bar{r}^j$, matters. The total effect of an increase in t^i on $\bar{r}$ is given by $-[(\partial w/\partial t^i)\overline{L} + k^i]$.[51]

Suppose that labor and foreign capital are substitutes in sector i. Since, in this case, $\partial w/\partial t^i > 0$, when the tax rate on foreign capital in sector t^i increases, the return to domestic capital in both sectors decrease; that is, both

TABLE 4A.1. Effect of t^1 and t^2 on w and $\bar{r}$

Sector 1 Sector 2	Complements Complements	Complements Substitutes	Substitutes Complements	Substitutes Substitutes
$\partial \bar{r}/\partial t^1$	(+) or (−)[a]	(+) or (−)[a]	(−)	(−)
$\partial w/\partial t^1$	(−)	(−)	(+)	(+)
$\partial \bar{r}/\partial t^2$	(+) or (−)[a]	(−)	(+) or (−)[a]	(−)
$\partial w/\partial t^2$	(−)	(+)	(−)	(+)

[a]It is (+) when $|\partial w/\partial t^i|\overline{L} > k^i$; it is (−) when $|\partial w/\partial t^i|\overline{L} < k^i$.

$\bar{r}^i$ and $\bar{r}^j$ decrease with t^i. As a result, total income received by domestic capital owners, $\bar{r} = \bar{r}^i + \bar{r}^j$, unambiguously declines with an increase in t^i; that is, $\partial \bar{r}/\partial t^i < 0$. Now, if L^i and k^j are complements, then $\bar{r}^j$ increases with t^i, but the effect on $\bar{r}^i$ is ambiguous. Consequently, the impact of a change in t^i on total income received by domestic capital is ambiguous; that is, $\bar{r}$ may go either up or down with t^i. Since $\partial w/\partial t^i < 0$ when domestic labor and foreign capital are complements, the sign of $\partial \bar{r}/\partial t^i$ depends on the relative values of $|(\partial w/\partial t^i)| \bar{L}$ and k^j. If income received by owners of foreign capital (given by k^j) increases less than the decline of labor income when t^i is higher (given by $|(\partial w/\partial t^i)| \bar{L}$), then the total income of domestic capitalists tends to rise, that is, $\partial \bar{r}/\partial t^i > 0$. Everything else constant, this behavior would be observed in countries with relatively large labor endowments, $\bar{L}$. In these countries, $|(\partial w/\partial t^i)| \bar{L}$ would be larger than k^j. However, $\partial \bar{r}/\partial t^i$ can be negative if a higher t^i increases the income of foreign capitalists by more than what it decreases labor income. Thus, when foreign capital and labor are complements, a higher value of t^i can either increase or decrease total returns to domestic capital owners.

The results from the second stage partially explain the implementation of a specific policy by a partisan government. In general, they suggest that if workers and owners of domestic capital are only concerned about their income, they will tend to favor antagonistic policies toward FDI. For instance, when foreign capital substitutes for labor in production (e.g., the type that introduces labor-saving technologies), a higher tax rate on foreign investment would increase wages but would reduce total income received by domestic capitalists. If labor and foreign capital are complements, labor will support lower taxes on foreign investment to lure that type of FDI. Domestic capitalists, however, may support higher or lower taxes. Note, however, that owners of labor and owners of capital will never unanimously support restrictive policies on foreign investment, in the form of higher taxes on internationally mobile capital.

First Stage: Government Choice of Policy Variables

At this stage, governments, characterized by different political orientations (pro-labor or pro-capital), decide the optimal values of (t^1, t^2, g_L, g_K) anticipating the behavior of labor and foreign capital owners, that is, considering their responses represented by the functions $L^1(t^1, t^2)$ and $k^i(t^1, t^2)$, i = 1,

2. Specifically, a partisan government solves the following maximization problem: choose taxes and in-kind transfers (t^1, t^2, g_L, g_K) to maximize the function

$$\Omega = \beta (L^1 U_L^1 + L^2 U_L^2) + (1 - \beta) (U_K^1 + U_K^2),$$

subject to the budget constraint $\overline{L}g_L + \overline{K}g_K = T$, where $U_L^i = w + v(g_L)$ is the utility of workers in the economy, $U_K^i = \overline{r}^i + v(g_K)$ is the utility of domestic capital owners in sectors $i = 1, 2$, and $T = t^1 k^1 + t^2 k^2$. The budget constraint simply states that the amount of in-kind transfers to workers and domestic capital owners should be equal to the total revenue from taxing foreign investment.

This maximization problem is similar to the problem of optimal indirect taxation when the government has redistributive motivations. The objective function is a weighted sum of the aggregate welfare of workers and capitalists, where β is the weight attached to workers and $1 - \beta$ is the weight given to capitalists. The government's political orientation is defined by the value of β: governments with $\beta > 0.5$ have a pro-labor orientation, and those with $\beta < 0.5$ respond more heavily to the interests of capitalists.[52] The government's objective is to maximize the weighted utility of owners of labor and capital and not their income. If partisan governments wish to maximize the income of political group h, y_h, then their decisions would be exclusively driven by the results shown in the second stage. Additionally, as explained in the previous section, wages in all sectors are equalized in equilibrium $(w^1 = w^2 = w)$, because labor is mobile across sectors. Returns to capital $(\overline{r}^1$ and $\overline{r}^2)$ are not necessarily equalized, since we assumed that capital is sector specific. The budget constraint simply assures that the government's tax revenue is enough to finance the in-kind transfers.[53]

From the first-order conditions of the maximization problem, we derive the following results. First, the government follows the following rule to distribute tax revenue across individuals (i.e., the allocation of g_L and g_K): $v'(g_K)/v'(g_L) = b/(1 - b)$. Thus, if $b > 1/2$, then $v'(g_K) > v'(g_L)$, which implies that $g_K < g_L$ given that $v'' < 0$. As a result, governments with higher values of b will distribute g in favor of labor. Second, the first-order conditions with respect to the tax rates (t^i) can be rewritten as

$$b_k \left[\frac{(\partial w/\partial t^i)\overline{L} + k^i}{k^i} \right] - b_K \left[\frac{(\partial w/\partial t^i)\overline{L}}{k^i} \right] = \frac{\partial T/\partial t^i}{k^i}, \quad i = 1, 2, \quad \text{(A.1)}$$

where $\partial T/\partial t^i = k^i + t^i (\partial k^i/\partial t^i) + t^j (\partial k^j/\partial t^i)$ is the change in total tax revenue due to a change in t^i; $b_L = \beta/\lambda$ and $b_K = (1 - \beta)/\lambda$ are the government's valuation of a change in workers' and capitalists' income, respectively (measured in terms of government revenue); and λ is the Lagrange multiplier associated with the budget constraint. The variables b_L and b_K measure the government's marginal benefit of transferring one dollar to household h = L, K.

The expressions between square brackets on the left-hand side of equation A.1 represent the proportional change in income for group h when t^i is changed. The right-hand side is the increase in tax revenue due to an increase in t^i as a proportion of the tax base. Equation A.1 establishes the rule that a partisan government would follow when determining the tax rates.

Essentially, when choosing the level of t^i, the government considers two effects: a distributional effect, captured by the left-hand side of equation A.1; and an efficiency effect, captured by the right-hand side of that equation. An increase in tax rates would have different effects on the income received by domestic labor and domestic capitalists. A partisan government would value the changes in income using the weights b_K and b_L. At the same time, a higher level of t^i affects total tax revenue, which affects, in turn, the amount of transfers received by the political groups. In general, increasing the tax rates in different sectors may have different effects on total tax collection. For instance, suppose that $b_K = b_L$ (i.e., b = 1/2). Then, the left-hand side does not depend on i, so the distributional motive does not play any role. As a result, tax rates chosen by the government are such that the proportional change in tax revenue due to a change in t^i should be equalized across all sectors; that is, $(\partial T/\partial t^1)/k^1 = (\partial T/\partial t^2)/k^2$. In this way, the efficiency cost is minimized.

In general, when $b_K \neq b_L$, the expression $[(\partial w/\partial t^i)\bar{L}/k^i]$ will also affect the choice of the tax rates. Unfortunately, these rules only suggest general observations about the structure of the tax rates, and it is not possible to obtain precise implications. However, the following statements can be made when a smaller value of $(\partial T/\partial t^i)/k^i$ is consistent with a higher t^i while a larger $(\partial T/\partial t^i)/k^i$ is consistent with a lower t^i.

Suppose that $b_K = b_L$ initially, and consider a small increase in the value of β and b_L (or lower $(1 - \beta)$ and b_K), representing a shift toward a government that puts relatively more value on the well-being of labor. Then, the left-hand side of equation A.1 decreases for those sectors where labor and foreign capital are substitutes, given that $\partial w/\partial t^i > 0$, implying a smaller value of $(\partial T/\partial t^i)/k^i$ and, consequently, higher tax rates. In sectors where domestic labor and foreign capital are complements, the second term on the left-hand side of equation A.1 gets larger as b_L rises, because $\partial w/\partial t^i < 0$; but the first term can go either up or down as b_K gets smaller, since the sign of $[(\partial w/\partial t^i)\overline{L} + k^i]$ is ambiguous. The opposite effect takes place when we move from $b_K = b_L$ to a higher b_K.

CHAPTER 5

Political Institutions and the Effectiveness of Multinational Lobbying

THE EARLY CHAPTERS of this book were devoted to analyzing how particular constellations of political institutions and politics affect the flows of foreign direct investment. Certainly, investors are astute observers of political risk and take into account a diverse range of past, present, and expected future political factors before committing to a particular project. While analyzing foreign investment from this perspective is important to understanding FDI, doing so leaves part of the story untold. As we explained in chapter 1, political institutions and politics influence investment decisions, but they do not wholly determine them. There are times when the economic benefits and potential profitability of an investment project make it worthwhile to enter a politically risky environment. The obvious example of this is natural resource investment, where investors must go to the resources whatever the local politics might be. Large domestic markets and proximity to export locations provide similar attractions to investors.

The surge in FDI in Vietnam and Azerbaijan in recent years is testament to the fact that FDI is not entirely explained by the presence or absence of political institutions and politics favorable to investors. Even in politically risky environments, foreign investors are not simply passive actors subject to whims of the leaders of their host country. A host of new work in the business strategy literature has shown that investors have a number of tools at their disposal to ameliorate their political risk and even

115

alter the business environment of a host country after they have committed significant resources.

Multinational corporations believe that they can influence the economic policies, regulations, and even the political institutions of the countries in which they operate. They do not see their bargaining with host states as a one-shot game that is concluded after their agreement to invest, rendering them impotent to challenge future policies that materially affect their business. Foreign investors, in fact, often see themselves as agents of the reform process, providing information on regulation in other countries and helping shape the economic future of their host state (Prakash and Potoski 2007; Luo 2001). Such lobbying may take the form of individual interactions with decision makers, or investors may band together in business associations to collectively argue for general change.

In chapter 1, we outlined the four pathways by which MNCs can influence local policy decisions: (1) provide information and expertise to policy makers on regulations in other countries; (2) lobby officials, often allying with other local actors in the process; (3) use coercion, both positive (charitable giving or access to proprietary technology) and negative (threatening to leave); and (4) free policy makers from the grips of entrenched interests by offering alternative sources of revenue and employment generation.

The 2007 elections of the American Chamber of Commerce in Shanghai (AmCham Shanghai) provide a colorful example of these types of activities. As one would expect, given the importance of the Chinese economy, the list of office seekers was a veritable who's who of major U.S. MNCs, including, among others, Tyson Chicken, General Motors, CitiGroup, and a host of operations that were more regionally focused. The platforms were illustrative; two-thirds specifically mentioned expanding AmCham Shanghai's advocacy and lobbying capacity in regard to key national and local regulatory schemes. J. Norwell Coquillard of Cargill was the most forceful: "AmCham Shanghai must strengthen its Government Affairs team and utilize the expertise within the membership to make our voice heard in the halls of government." Coquillard went on to offer his own successful experience in planning and executing advocacy programs in Beijing to "strengthen the influence of AmCham and improve business conditions for members" (AmCham Shanghai 2007). Coquillard was not only elected to AmCham Shanghai's Board of Governors; in 2009, he was elected to chair the organization (AmCham Shanghai 2009).

Platforms of candidates discussed a number of tactics for improved influence on Chinese regulations, including (1) regularizing multilevel dialogues with key decision makers; (2) exploiting legislative commentary periods by mobilizing regulations experts from other countries to discuss reforms with Chinese leaders; (3) working collectively with other chambers, representing business from Europe, Australia, and Japan, to present a common front to Chinese authorities on key issues; and (4) building on healthy collaborations with like-minded domestic stakeholders.

The election materials are merely the tip of the iceberg; they reveal a glimpse into well-organized and systematic effort on the part of foreign investors to influence economic policies of their host state. China is not unique. Hundreds of AmCham offices exist throughout the world, reaching as far as tiny economies such as Nicaragua and Uzbekistan. Vietnam, despite formally opening its economy to FDI only two decades ago, has AmCham offices in Hanoi and Ho Chi Minh City. Indeed, the AmChams in Vietnam, along with other foreign chambers, were seen by Vietnamese officials as particularly helpful in shaping the new 2005 Investment Law as it wound its way through the drafting process (Linh 2005; Viet Lam and Linh 2005).

While there is now substantial anecdotal and empirical evidence that foreign investors are capable of mounting lobbying campaigns and pushing through policy change in their host countries, the research in this area has overwhelmingly focused on the relative success of tactics employed by foreign investors and much less so on the political conditions under which such tactics may or may not be successful. Drawing on the literature on the political economy of lobbying, we here explore how variance in political institutions affects the ability of MNCs to lobby for economic reforms in 26 transition states. We begin by analyzing the literature on the influence of foreign investors over economic policy. Next, we test how this influence is contingent on two critical dimensions of a country's polity discussed in earlier chapters of this book: (1) the number of constraints on executive decision making and (2) the degree of electoral competition and, consequently, the diversity of political views. We find little evidence that veto points mediate the political influence of investors, but we find relatively strong evidence that MNCs are less successful when their policy perspectives must compete against other interests in a robust political environment. Building on these findings, we next analyze the policy dimensions where foreign investors are most likely to be successful, discovering that investors have strong influence over economic liberalization and regulation but comparatively little influence over areas that are not of immediate concern to their businesses and that require greater institutional change.

Our analysis makes use of data on FDI and economic reform among the 26 transition states in Eastern Europe and the former Soviet Union to probe these two questions. We focus on these transition states for both theoretical and methodological reasons. Theoretically, the transition states provide a unique testing ground because their economic reform objectives of unwinding their states' central planning apparatuses were broadly similar and began at roughly the same time. Of course, there are plenty of historical and cultural confounders within the region, but they are far less problematic than in data sets pooling all developing countries. At the same time, the transition states demonstrate widespread variance on measures of political institutions, specifically the degree of political participation and the number of veto points over policy choices. Methodologically, the European Bank of Reconstruction and Development (EBRD) provides a unique annual data set extending back to the beginning of the reform era, in 1991 (EBRD 2006). This data set can be disaggregated to analyze eight critical dimensions of reform progress.

Literature on MNC Bargaining Power

When an earlier generation of political science scholars looked into the interaction of FDI and developing states in the 1960s and 1970s, they were explicitly interested in how FDI impacted local institutions and policymaking processes. Though their work was highly influenced by research on industries of natural resource extraction, they took seriously the notion that foreign investors could influence political institutions of a host country, primarily because the economic strength and access to external resources of MNCs gave them a bargaining advantage over very poor and isolated developing countries. For a while, these arguments provided fuel for the raging *dependencia* fires, because they confirmed the fears of developing countries and *dependentistas* that industrialized countries manipulated local institutions in order to exploit them for raw materials (Diebold 1974; Biersteker 1978; Moran 1974, 1978a; Evans 1979).

This view of investors as agents of change spent several decades in the wilderness outside of mainstream scholarship on the international political economy, due to the predominant theoretical paradigm suggesting that investors need credible commitments from host states (Weingast 1993a).

Without contracts backed by credible commitments, any investment deal with a developing nation would obsolesce over time, because local leaders would be free to incrementally rescind commitments made at the inception. The term *obsolescing bargain* was coined to describe this phenomenon of deteriorating investment arrangements with a host country (Vernon 1971, 1980). Because of the substantial costs of ex-ante contract infringement on large issues like expropriation and smaller regulatory and tax issues, foreign investors are much less likely to invest sizable amounts where the risk of obsolescence and policy uncertainty is at a maximum (Dixit and Pindyck 1994; Rajan and Marwah 1998). As a result, MNCs are thought to rely on overt signals of a country's ex-ante credibility, such as whether it is a democracy (Jensen 2003; Li and Resnick 2003) or has plausible checks on the powers of key decision makers (Henisz and Williamson 1999; Henisz 2000). Along these lines, chapter 2 in this volume explored, in new ways, the political risk signaling provided by democracy, while chapter 3 drilled down deeper into the variation across institutions within democracy, finding critical value in the role of political institutions that protect property rights and enforce contracts.

Seeing investors as agents of change in the realm of economic policy in host countries has recently begun to make a comeback, however. In the business strategy literature, this view has been quite prevalent for some time. Strategy analysts have long understood that no contract is ironclad and that the political risk faced by MNCs has to be actively managed (Henisz and Zelner 2004). Consequently, the strategy field has devoted great attention to how MNCs can mitigate bargaining advantages for host governments through strategic alliances with local partners (Boddewyn and Brewer 1994; Eden and Molot 2002), broad alliances with other investors (Stopford and Strange 1991), staged entry and incentive alignment with local actors (Henisz and Delios 2004; Pinto 2004, 2013), the use of home governments and international organizations to spearhead discussions (Ramamurti 2001), and the tactical allocation of proprietary technology and international finance (Luo, Shenkar, and Nyaw 2002). The general consensus in the business strategy literature is that MNCs have become quite adept at functioning politically within host countries and that the obsolescing bargain is of limited utility today as a theoretical framework (Hillman and Hitt 1999; Eden, Lenway, and Schuler 2005; Wint 2005). As one investor interviewed by Henisz and Zelner (2004, 167) put it, a lot of political risk is relationships, "not picking the right people, but rather articulating your views and cultivating ties with people who share your goals."

The consensus from the business strategy scholars has now begun to infiltrate the political economy literature in the wake of survey evidence indicating that foreign investors believe that they have influence over economic policy in host states (Desbordes and Vauday 2007), detailed case studies of the specific mechanisms used to achieve policy change (Hewko 2002–3; Lewis 2005), chronicles of the strategic lobbying alliances MNCs forge with state-owned enterprises and subnational governments (Kennedy 2007; Malesky 2008), and quantitative analysis isolating the impact of exogenous changes of FDI stocks and domestic economic reform choices (Li and Reuveny 2003; Rudra 2005; Mosley and Uno 2007; Malesky 2009).

The literature on FDI influence dovetails with an extensive American politics literature on business lobbying and policy choice in the United States (Grossman and Helpman 1994, 2002; Gawande and Bandyopadhyay 2002; Brasher and Lowery 2006). Of particular interest are the finding by Gordon and Hafer (2005) that business lobbying can affect the implementation of national policies and the Blonigen and Figlio (1998) analysis of FDI influence on individual legislator behavior.

Moreover, viewing foreign investors as political actors also helps provide one plausible pathway for the well-documented empirical pattern of regulatory policy diffusion across similarly situated countries: states develop very similar economic regulations despite vastly different endowments and starting points (Simmons and Elkins 2004; Kopstein and Reilly 2000). Simmons, Dobbins, and Garret (2006, 10) highlight coercion, competition, learning, and emulation as the four causal mechanisms undergirding policy diffusion. MNCs play critical roles as actors within all four mechanisms. States compete over the revenue and employment opportunities they provide and can be coerced when preexisting investments threaten to leave for policy regimes that are more welcoming. MNCs also drive learning and emulation, by providing immediate feedback to policy makers on issues under consideration and relating their experiences with policies in other countries (Hewko 2002–3; Henisz and Zelner 2003; Prakash and Potoski 2007).

Despite these achievements, the literature on investors as reform agents remains incomplete in two important ways. First, while attempts by foreign investors to influence economic policy are widespread, MNCs have found more success under certain political conditions than others. While there is a range of nuanced ways to depict differences in political institutions (as explored later in this chapter), it is helpful to begin with a simple illustrative example.

One of the easiest ways to group polities is by the executive-legislative relations depicted in their constitution. The largest categorization available is between presidential and parliamentary systems. Using this simple dichotomy, figure 5.1 analyzes how the relationship between the stock of FDI as a percentage of GDP and the average annual change in economic reform after that year, as measured by the EBRD (2006), is influenced by these simple differences in political institutions. The stock of FDI/GDP makes a reasonable proxy for aggregate bargaining strength because, as already demonstrated by the example from China, so much of the negotiations takes place between groups of businesses (organized as chambers or sectoral associations) and government officials. Two different lines are plotted. The solid line represents countries with parliamentary regimes according to the World Bank's Database of Political Institutions, while the dashed lines represent countries with presidential or semipresidential systems (Beck et al. 2001). While FDI is positively correlated with economic reform progress in both groups, the line for presidential systems is much steeper, with a slope roughly seven times the size of the parliamentary slope.

This relationship should be treated with some caution, as many of the parliamentary systems (e.g., Hungary, Slovenia, and the Czech Republic) are in Eastern Europe. These countries had already made significant reform efforts prior to 1994, thereby placing a ceiling on the subsequent progress they could make (Kitschelt 2003). Also, the high reformers are all in the middle of the distribution and therefore exert limited leverage on the estimated lines. Taking these issues into consideration, the graph is still quite illustrative. The influence of foreign investors on economic reform appears more muted in parliamentary systems. This finding provides tentative evidence that variance in political institutions might provide additional texture to previous findings that FDI can lobby for changes in economic regulations.

But what is it about parliamentary regimes in the transition states that limits the effectiveness of MNC lobbying? Two theoretical explanations are available. First, because parliamentary systems often necessitate large coalition governments comprising a number of parties and therefore disparate preferences, it is more difficult for foreign investors to exert influ-

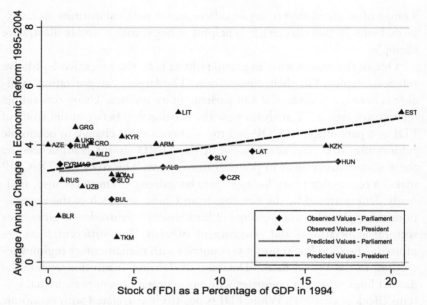

Fig. 5.1. Relationship between FDI stock in 1994 and average change in economic reform (1995–2006). This graph plots two different slopes through the scatter plot of transition states. The solid line plots the relationship in countries coded as parliamentary by the World Bank's Database of Political Institutions. The slope of this line is positive but substantively small (0.01) and statistically insignificant. The dashed line plots the relationship in countries with elected presidents or mixed systems with strong presidents. Among these states the slope is 0.07 and statistically significant at the .05 level.

ence or capture the entire range of decision makers. Alternatively, presidential systems may be the preferred governmental form of quasi dictators, such as in Turkmenistan or Azerbaijan. As a result, the elected legislatures are weak and do not play their constitutional role of constraining executive decisions. Moreover, in more authoritarian contexts, it may be more difficult for disparate groups to have their preferences heard and acknowledged by decision makers. In these cases of weak political competition, perhaps it is easier for MNCs to exert influence on the limited range of key decision makers. In the pages that follow, we use more nuanced measures of executive constraints and political competition to rigorously analyze the hypothesis that political institutions moderate the bargaining influence of FDI.

A second lacuna in the FDI bargaining literature is a lack of precision as to the key reform goals of foreign investors. MNCs have limited time and resources that they can devote to government affairs over the other elements of their business. Given these constraints, where do investors concentrate their persuasive activities? Anecdotal examples are plentiful as to investors arguing for changes in tax and trade policy, which directly impact their bottom line, or for privatization and enterprise reform, which affect the quality of their suppliers and business partners. There is little reason, however, to think that nonbank MNCs would be as interested in bank reform, as they are unlikely to use local banks and always have the option of accessing international capital markets. In this chapter, we disaggregate different types of reform in search of patterns of FDI behavior.

The Theoretical Relationship between Institutions and Lobbying by MNCs

The dense theoretical literature on the effectiveness of lobbying provides evidence of two general dimensions of political institutions that could potentially impede lobbying efforts of foreign investors who are pushing for economic reform. First, a number of scholars have demonstrated empirically that the number of actors in a polity with the ability to waylay legislation (veto players) is critical for understanding the influence of interest groups on policy making (McCubbins, Noll, and Weingast 1987; Immergut 1992; Huber, Ragin, and Stephens 1993; Tsebelis 2002). Henisz and Zelner (2006) apply the same logic to investors interested in lobbying for regulatory change. The more veto players there are (i.e., the more constraints there are on an individual executive deciding policy), the more effort and resources MNCs must expend to convince policy makers to change particular regulations or policy. When veto points are few, lobbyists must only convince a small group of key actors. To the extent that the preferences of the actors with veto power differ, institutional structures with more political constraints limit the range of feasible policy choices. According to this logic, veto points have the effect of moderating the response of political actors to a range of pressure from interest groups, including coalitions of foreign investors. More perniciously, capture of the policy regime has been shown to be easier in regimes characterized by limited executive constraints (Hellman 1998). As Max Weber (1922, 283–84) put it, "The monocratic chief is more open to personal influence and is more easily swayed, thus making it more readily possible to influence the administration of justice and other governmental activity in favor of such powerful interests." This logic generates the following hypothesis:

The number of veto players will decrease the effectiveness of foreign direct investors in lobbying for economic reforms.

Evidence shows that the influence of investors stems in great part from their aggregate bargaining power and ability to coordinate policy objectives through investor forums and international chambers (Pyle 2006; Gillespie 2006). The horse-trading in these sessions should lead to policies that are generally beneficial and less particularistic. While individual investors could potentially exercise inordinate influence on a specific reform, it is rare that a single investor is large and important enough to the economy to possess that power. Moreover, MNCs have an incentive to focus on long-term policy reforms and institutional changes rather than the capture of individual officials, because they cannot vote and therefore have limited direct influence over the selection of leaders from year to year. Focusing on general policies and institutional changes, while not a perfect guarantee, does grant foreign-invested enterprises more confidence that the reforms will outlast a particular administration.

Recent contributions by Sean Ehrlich (2007, 2008) place a fascinating twist on the theory of veto points. Rather than focusing on those who can kill policy initiatives, Ehrlich highlights "access points," actors who are relevant in a policy arena and have the ability to influence policy. Because access points have limited time and energy to devote to a specific policy, they cannot be receptive to all interest groups. But the more access points there are in a polity, the more opportunities interest groups will have to influence policy direction. Thus, Ehrlich finds that increasing access points both formally and empirically enhances the probability of legislation that benefits the business goals of the lobbying firms. If Ehrlich is correct, increasing veto (access) points should enhance the voice of foreign investors—just the opposite of what is predicted by our first hypothesis. If both predictions are simultaneously true to some extent, we might observe a nonresult as the two effects countervail one another.

In addition to the formal power to veto policy change, the more voices there are representing salient political positions, the more diffuse is the effectiveness of lobbying. Here again, political economy work with deep antecedents has established that robust electoral competition has important implications for the effectiveness of lobbying and the efficiency of policy making (Hillman 1989; Magee, Brock, and Young 1989; Grossman and Helpman 1994; Dixit and Londregan 1995; Faulhaber 1999). Most recently, Bueno de Mesquita et al. (2003) use a measure of competitiveness of participation as their proxy for the size of the coalition necessary to wrest control of policy making.[1] The greater the size of the winning coalition is, the less likely it is that policy will be oriented toward selective groups of insiders. The implications for MNC lobbying are obvious. Foreign investors must present their arguments against competing positions in a forum, where their views can be publically challenged and criticized. The more opportunities there are for such a competition of views, the less immediate effect FDI will have on policy change. The ability of foreign investors to provide unique information that influences policy makers will be curtailed, as will the provision of more selective benefits to policy makers, such as campaign contributions. Thus we arrive at our second hypothesis:

> *The level of competition in the political system will decrease the effectiveness of foreign direct investors in lobbying for economic reforms.*

Data, Measurement, and Specification

The dependent variable for this analysis is the EBRD ranking of countries from 1 to 4.3 on eight different economic reform policies between 1992 and 2004, the most commonly used indicator of reform in the transition literature.[2] A score of 1 means that the country has not yet begun to reform, while a score of 4.3 denotes the level of a typical advanced industrial economy. The scale originally had a maximum score of 4. The awkward score of 4.3 stems from an artifact of revised EBRD coding; EBRD wanted a value to denote a country surpassing the developed country threshold (4.0) but still making reform progress. We avoid the interpretative problems of this coding choice by standardizing reform measures to a scale of 0–100 points, where 100 represents maximum reform progress on the EBRD scale.

The eight reform policies include price liberalization, foreign exchange and trade liberalization, privatization of small state-owned enterprises, privatization of large state-owned enterprises, enterprise reform/corporate governance, competition policy, bank reform, and reform of nonbank financial institutions.[3]

For the first part of the empirical analysis, we rely on a measure of total economic reform that aggregates these individual policies. Focusing on aggregate reform has two intuitive features. First, legislative packages often group together several reforms as part of logrolling agreements or omnibus acts, leading to correlations between somewhat disparate measures. Second, as Hellman (1998) demonstrated in his discussion of the partial reform equilibrium, disproportionate progress on one policy creates new sets of winners that may use their newfound economic advantage to block advancement on other reform items. Focusing on aggregate reform also helps us identify which states avoided the trap of partial reform equilibrium by making consistent progress across many dimensions and whether FDI is associated with these escapes. At the end of this chapter, however, we return to the individual reform measures to see if investors have predilections for particular types of liberalization and changes in regulation. In the panel analysis, we standardize reform measures to a scale of 0–100 points and take the first difference in reform progress as our dependent variable in order to avoid spurious correlation caused by nonstationarity.[4]

We measure the cumulative stock of FDI as a percentage of GDP in the economy based on the United Nations Conference on Trade and Development (UNCTAD) database, after confirming that the data was highly correlated with other measures commonly used (UNCTAD 2005). Our key causal variable is annual change in the stock of FDI as a percentage of GDP.[5] Note that the annual change in the stock of FDI/GDP is not necessarily equivalent to measuring FDI flows.[6] The goal is to examine changes in the relative bargaining power of foreign investors over time. While a decline in FDI flows can lead to a decrease in the ratio, so can increases in domestic production and investment. In either case, FDI should have a weaker voice in relevant policy debates. Flows are often used as a measure of FDI attraction in many of the studies previously cited, but they are inappropriate for this analysis because they capture only single-year surges and not relative changes in existing bargaining power.

Assessing the causal effect of FDI is complicated by the fact that there are also strong theoretical foundations for concluding that investors consider economic reform progress prior to investment. Investors have reason to favor environments with low regulatory costs, adequate property rights protection, and reasonable tax laws. Consequently, to attract foreign investment, transition and developing countries need to make the institutional changes that foreign-invested enterprises desire and to offer a credible commitment that these institutions will remain in place in the long term (Weingast 1993a; Knack and Keefer 1995; Henisz and Williamson 1999; Elster, Offe, and Preuss 2000). This theory has been tested around the world, with scholars finding important correlations between policy and investment attraction, including the predictability of economic and foreign policies (Gastanaga, Nugent, and Pashamova 1998), structural reform progress (Schneider and Frey 1985; Jensen 2002), reductions in corporate taxation (Svenson 1994), limited bureaucratic corruption (Wei 2000), effective legal systems (Perry 2000), and property rights protection (Li and Resnick 2003). In the transition states specifically, scholars have focused on economic reform progress using the EBRD measures and also found correlations (Resmini 2000; Campos and Kinoshita 2003; Shiells 2003; Johnson 2004; Bevan, Estrin, and Meyer 2004; Jensen 2002; Diechman et al. 2003; Dunning 2005).

In testing the causal impact of FDI, we cannot simply ignore this rich and important literature. Consequently, we instrument for FDI using the predicted exchange rates from movements in baskets of OECD currencies in an IV-2SLS model, a technique successfully employed by Malesky (2009). Exogenously determined exchange rates offer a useful instrument because investors will often swoop in to take advantage of fire sales on assets when international price movements cause exogenous declines in the exchange rate. The theoretical conclusions of a conditional effect of FDI on economic reform, mediated by political institutions, survive this more rigorous analysis.[7]

To measure the number of actors with the ability to block legislation (veto points), we use the most recent version of Henisz's POLCON V data set, combining the number of political constraints on executive decision making, modified by the party composition of the different branches of government. These political constraints are analogous to the concept of veto points pioneered by Tsebelis (2002) and used by Frye and Mansfield (2003) in their analysis of trade reform in transition states. As we stated in chapter 3, countries characterized by high veto points are states with cross-checking political institutions (i.e., separate executives and bicameral legislatures that all have the power to impede new legislation) or parliamentary systems with electoral institutions that favor multiple parties, such as proportional voting. In these cases, multiple parties must be assembled into a coalition to win control over the parliament. Because each party can withdraw from the coalition and bring down the government, all parties, however small, have an effective veto over legislation.

To measure political competition, we take advantage of the same measure of competitiveness of participation used by Bueno de Mesquita et al. (2003), from the well-known Polity IV data set of political institutions. Measured on a five-point scale, with the score of 5 designating a fully open and competitive political system, *parcomp* measures the extent to which alternative preferences for policy and leadership can be pursued in the political arena (Marshall and Jaggers 2008). It measures, essentially, the ease of entry for new candidates and political parties and, thereby, the ability of voters to select alternative voices. This variable has been employed by Pinto and Zhu (2008) to measure the conditional effect of FDI on corruption, and they found that FDI has limited impact on corruption when political competition is high. However, Jensen (2008) did not find a correlation between *parcomp* and measures of political risk produced by rating agencies.

Parcomp takes on a value of between 1 and 5. Scores of 1 (repressed) and 2 (suppressed) are reserved for authoritarian political systems with limited competition (i.e., single-party systems or monarchy). Repressed systems, such as those of Turkmenistan and Uzbekistan in 1992, must possess the state authority to actively thwart activities, while suppressed systems either condone some limited competition but actively harass the limited opposition or do not have the state capacity to prevent competition. Azerbaijan, Belarus, and Kazakhstan are coded 2 throughout the period. Countries, such as Tajikistan, Armenia, and Estonia (in 2002), receive a score of 3 on *parcomp* if they have "factional" competition, defined in the *Polity IV Codebook* as "polities with parochial or ethnic-based political factions that regularly compete for political influence in order to promote particularist agendas and favor group members to the detriment of common, secular, or cross-cutting agendas" (Marshall and Jaggers 2008, 27). A *parcomp* score of 4 is a catchall score that implies a state in a "transition" away from suppressed or factional politics and toward a "competitive" political system, scored 5. At the beginning of reform, countries such as Macedonia and Slovakia received scores of 4, while Poland and Hungary were considered competitive systems.

In competitive systems, foreign investors must lobby for policy change against competing interest groups with alternative points of view, such as environmental and labor activists. The more rigorous the competition is, the more difficult it will be for investors to exert sole influence over policy makers. In less competitive systems, when foreign investment generates a large proportion of the economy, their arguments may face limited dissent. As a result, we expect the influence of foreign investors to be magnified in less competitive environments.

It is important to note that *parcomp* makes up one-third of the Polity IV democracy score. A second third of that score is accounted for by constraints on executive decision making, which essentially mirrors Henisz's *polcon* measure. As such, it would be duplicative to add an additional control variable for the entire Polity IV democracy score. Rather than using an ambiguous proxy for democracy, we are actually testing the precise impact of its component parts on policy making.[8]

While political constraints and *parcomp* may be seen as conceptually distinct, their measurement is highly correlated (0.73) in practice. Figure 5.2 provides a scatter plot of the relationship between the two variables, with political constraints on the *y*-axis and *parcomp* on the *x*-axis. Dashed lines depict the median values for each measure, so it is possible to identify countries like Estonia with high political constraints but below-average levels of competitiveness, resulting from the constitutional exclusion of the Russian minority. Alternatively, Russia, Albania, and Poland represent countries with above-average competition but more constraints on executives.

Both political constraints and political competition are plausibly endogenous to economic reform. Particular reform choices made by host governments may engender new political opposition, empower previously weak actors, or simply alter the dynamics of political competition. Dissatisfaction with rapid privatization or trade liberalization, for instance, led to the strengthening of reform communist and agricultural parties in much of Eastern Europe (Grzymala-Busse 2002). Indeed, there are changes in veto points across the countries in the data set. Over the time period covered by the data set, Poland, Croatia, and Russia all have constitutional changes that took place in the midst of economic reform choices and that are therefore hard to disentangle. Poland (1997) and Croatia (2000) specifically made changes that weakened the power of the president and favored stronger parliaments and more veto points. Russia, however, has systematically strengthened the power of the president in recent years and thereby reduced the constraints on executive decision making.

To address this problem, we hold the measures of each country's politi-

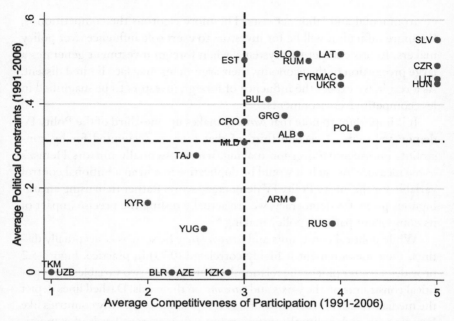

Fig. 5.2. Political institutions in transition states. This graph presents a scatter plot with the number of political constraints (Henisz 2000) on the *y*-axis and the competitiveness of participation (Polity IV) on the *x*-axis. Circles represent average scores over the reform era. Dashed lines represent the median values for each of the indicators. Note that there is a 0.73 bivariate correlation between the two variables; however, it is possible to identify countries that perform well on one and not the other.

cal institutions (veto points and competition) constant at their initial values at the beginning of the reform era in 1991 for Eastern Europe and 1993 for members of the former Soviet Union. As a robustness check, we rerun all specifications using the average value of political institutions from across the time period and also allowing political institutions to vary annually over time. These results are presented in the online appendix for this chapter.[9]

We also include a measure of the number of seats in the highest branch of the national parliament that are occupied by unreformed communist successor parties (postcommunist). If high numbers of communist leaders continue to be elected, it is an indication that significant portions of the population, including pensioners and former employees of state-owned enterprise, support a slower approach to economic reform (Norgaard

2000). High seat proportions held by communists can also exacerbate polarization, which has been shown to waylay reform efforts (Frye 2002). At the extremes, communists averaged over 30 percent of the seats in Moldova and Uzbekistan between 1992 and 2004 (Armingeon and Careja 2004).

Incentive for accession to the European Union provides another medium-term pathway for economic reform (Vachudova 2005), by providing a reward structure and "off-the-shelf" regulatory models for reformers (Mattli and Plumper 2002). A four-point categorical variable is used to track the level of association or membership a country has with the European Union and measures the impact of pull the EU has on economic reform motivations. In the scale used, 4 = member, 3 = candidate/application received, 2 = associate member/potential member, 1 = leadership has expressed formal desire to join, and 0 = neither the country nor the EU has formally expressed a desire for the country to join.[10] Robustness tests employ dummy variables for all levels of EU accession status in order to compare countries at similar levels of pull. *War* is a dichotomous variable measuring whether the country was at war during a particular year in the time series (Horowitz 2003).

Specification

We analyze 12 years of economic reform progress in 27 transition states using panel-corrected standard errors (Beck and Katz 1995). The key terms in the analysis are the change in the stock of FDI, the initial political constraints and competition, and a multiplicative term capturing the interaction of the variables.

One dilemma of analyzing changes in economic reform is that major leaps in economic reform were made very early in the transition period and decline over time. This issue is exacerbated by the EBRD's ceiling score of 4.3, marking a country's rise to the level of a "western, capitalist system." Obviously, the closer a country is to that ceiling in a particular reform area, the more difficult subsequent reforms become. We capture this ceiling effect by using a series of annual dummy variables, known as year fixed effects, for the number of years that a country has been engaging in reform, under the assumption that latter years should be significant and negative. A robustness test achieved similar results by using a lagged measure of reform to capture previous reform progress as a proxy for ceiling effects.

In addition, many of the variables in the model demonstrate trending over time. There is a good reason for this; economic reform was only one of the multiple transitions taking place in these countries. Many countries were becoming more democratic, hardening institutions, and shedding the strength of communist successor parties over the same period. Because these changes were taking place simultaneously with economic reform, there is a strong possibility of confusing such trending with a causal relationship—a spurious correlation, in other words. The standard econometric approach is to detrend nonstationary variables by using the first difference.[11] In cases of significant nonstationarity, we use the first difference of the variable, as noted in the regression tables.[12]

Results

The six models in table 5.1 provide the results of the regression analysis. Model 1 shows the unconditional effect of changes in the share of FDI and constraints on executive decision making, after controlling for structural determinants. The model reveals that both FDI and constraints have strongly significant and positive effects on annual changes in economic reform. A 1 percent change in a country's share of FDI is associated with about a 1 percent change in annual economic reform, roughly the same substantive effect that Malesky (2009) uncovered. A one-unit change in political constraints is also associated with a large, substantive change in economic reform, as has been demonstrated by Malesky (2009) in the case of FDI and by Hellman (1998), Frye and Mansfield (2003), and Gehlbach and Malesky (2010) in the case of veto points.

Care should be taken in interpreting the substantive size of effect of veto points, however, as the measure of executive constraints is standardized to a 0–1 scale. Thus a one-unit change represents a movement across the entire spectrum, from complete authoritarianism to complete gridlock. It is perhaps more helpful to think of a change of one standard deviation in initial political constraints, about 0.28, which is roughly the difference between Romania at the beginning of the reform process (0.31) and Slovenia in 1992 (0.59). If we could somehow perform an experiment where we kept economic conditions, culture, and history at the start of the reform process exactly the same for Romania but could superimpose on it Slovenia's vigorous parliamentary system and coalition government, Romania would then average annual economic reform that was 0.4 percent higher annually.

Model 2 performs the exact same analysis but replaces constraints on executive decision making with the competitiveness of political participation from the Polity IV data set. Chapter 2 of this book also explores the impact of this variable, finding that it is not as important for the attraction of FDI as other political institutions. Here, we find that FDI once again has the same, 1 percent effect. Competitiveness of participation has a strongly significant and positive effect on economic reform. A one-unit change on the five-point competitiveness scale is associated with a 0.2 percent change in annual economic reform progress. Thus, if Uzbekistan, with very poor initial competitiveness (1), could improve to the level of Slovakia (4) without any changes in the structural conditions of its economy, we would expect about a 0.6 percent improvement in annual economic reform progress.

Models 3 and 4 provide more sophisticated analyses, however, where we allow the impact of FDI to vary depending on the level of political institutions in the country; that is, rather than observing the independent effect of FDI and veto points on reform choices, we test whether FDI has a differential effect under different institutional settings. The results of these tests are reported in three coefficients shown in Models 3 and 4. The coefficient on FDI reveals the marginal impact of a one-unit change in FDI share when political institutions are 0. The coefficients on political constraints and competitiveness, respectively, reveal marginal impact of a one-unit change when the change in the share of FDI is 0. Finally, the table displays the coefficient on the conditional effect after multiplying the two variables. The most important thing to notice about these models is that while the coefficients on the component variables are significant in both models, the interactive effect is only statistically significant in Model 4 for the competitiveness of participation.

This is tentative evidence that the political influence of FDI is conditional on competitiveness but not on political constraints; however, more analysis is necessary. First and most important, both FDI and the political institution variables are continuous, including many different values. The coefficient on the interaction is hard to interpret, because it conflates several different levels into a single number. The only way to truly understand the conditional effect of FDI is to analyze the impact of FDI at specific values of the institutional measures.

Second, to address multicollinearity, when covariance between two variables is so high that it is hard to disentangle the individual impact of both factors, the political institutions were considered separately in Mod-

TABLE 5.1. Conditional Effect of FDI and Political Institutions on Economic Reform

Dependent Variable: Annual Change in Total Economic Reform (measured by EBRD scores) Independent Variables	Competitiveness (unconditional) (1)	Political Constraints (unconditional) (2)	Competitiveness (conditional) (3)	Political Constraints (conditional) (4)	Competitiveness and Political Constraints (conditional) (5)	Robust to Dropping Azerbaijan (6)	Fully Specified (7)
Change in stock of FDI/GDP (ln, lag)	1,047** (0.443)	1.098** (0.440)	1.478*** (0.448)	4.258*** (1.031)	4.485*** (1.083)	5.134*** (1.387)	4.556*** (1.084)
Initial Polcon	2.068*** (0.571)		2.784*** (0.788)		2.061** (0.939)	2.348** (0.967)	2.626*** (1.015)
FDI × Initial Polcon			-3.520 (2.788)		0.936 (3.073)	0.919 (3.204)	0.337 (3.072)
Initial PARCOMP		0.203** (0.079)		0.417*** (0.133)	0.197 (0.152)	0.280* (0.154)	0.183 (0.151)
FDI × Initial PARCOMP				-1.147*** (0.366)	-1.277*** (0.415)	-1.390*** (0.451)	-1.252*** (0.417)
GNP per Capita in 1989	0.134 (0.269)	0.126 (0.274)	0.153 (0.267)	0.149 (0.263)	0.158 (0.267)	-0.084 (0.218)	-0.188 (0.104)
Natural Resources 1989	-0.158 (0.099)	-0.048 (0.076)	-0.173* (0.102)	-0.054 (0.077)	-0.164 (0.102)	-0.191* (0.105)	0.090 (0.291)
GDP per Capita (ln, d)	6.532 (5.207)	7.910 (5.284)	7.048 (5.231)	8.900* (5.263)	7.840 (5.241)	10.320*** (5.657)	7.040 (5.219)
Postcommunists in Legislature (d)							-0.710 (1.872)
Accession to European Union (d)							-0.323 (0.241)
War (dummy)							0.758* (0.458)
Constant	7.956*** (0.235)	8.312*** (0.484)	7.111*** (0.527)	7.025*** (0.544)	7.766*** (0.645)	7.489*** (0.935)	7.649*** (0.575)
Time Fixed Effects	Yes	Yes	Yes	Yes	Yes	Yes	Yes
Observations	272	272	272	272	272	263	272
Panels	26	26	26	26	26	25	26
R^2	0.435	0.427	0.439	0.439	0.448	0.458	0.451
Root Mean Squared Error	3.177	3.221	3.179	3.204	3.197	3.188	3.211

Note: OLS with panel corrected standard errors in parentheses.

Two-tailed test: *significant at 10%; **significant at 5%; ***significant at 1%.

els 3 and 4. There are strong reasons to prefer such an approach, but it can lead to omitted-variable bias; that is, we may think the substantive effect of competitiveness of participation is larger than it really is, because we have not taken into account that impact of veto points in the same model. Model 5 corrects for this problem by running both interactions within the same specification. The size of the coefficients for the key variables does not change very much as compared to the results in Models 3 and 4, so we can rest assured that this model is not plagued by multicollinearity. Once again, we find that the effect of FDI is conditional on competitiveness but not on executive constraints.

Model 6 replicates Model 5 but drops Azerbaijan, which, due to its large oil resources, is an outlier in terms of investment attraction. The omission makes little difference in the substantive results. Finally, Model 7 provides the fully specified model, which includes the full set of control variables (postcommunists in the legislature, EU accession, and civil wars). Coefficients hardly change after the inclusion.

Political Constraints

Figure 5.3 delves deeper into these results by showing the predicted economic reform for different combinations of FDI and executive constraints based on the results of Model 7. This figure displays the change in the share of FDI/GDP along the horizontal axis and the percentage change in economic reform on the vertical axis. Three lines are drawn, dividing states into whether the executive constraints were at the 25th percentile (0 constraints, or the level of Uzbekistan), 50th percentile (0.3 constraints, about the level of Croatia in 1992), or 75th percentile (0.51 constraints, about the level of the Czech Republic after separation from Slovakia). The three lines have the distinctive curved shape of the natural log function used to constrain the distribution of the dependent variable to a more normal distribution, thereby facilitating hypothesis testing.

Figure 5.3 reveals that both FDI and political constraints have positive influences on reform progress. A positive increase along the *x*-axis for any of the three lines would lead to higher economic reform. Similarly, the measure of political constraints has a positive impact; shifting upward from the lowest level of political constraints at the same level of FDI would yield an increase in reform. For instance, when the change in FDI is 5 percent, expected economic reform is about 7.5 percent at the 25th percentile of

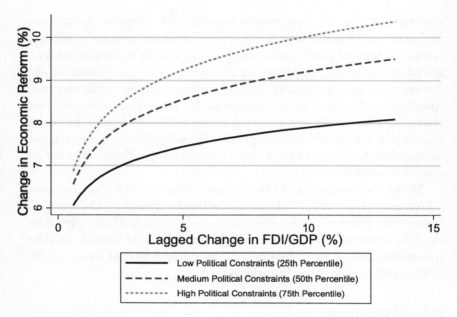

Fig. 5.3. Predicted effect of FDI on economic reform. This figure charts the predicted effects from a panel regression, interacting changes in FDI/GDP with initial levels of political constraints at the beginning of the reform era. Essentially, each line represents the predicted effect of FDI given a particular level of political constraints. We can see that while FDI and political constraints have individually positive effects on FDI their interactive effect is not significantly different from 0. The slopes of the predicted lines are almost exactly the same. In sum, the analysis reveals that political constraints do not mediate the impact of FDI on economic reform choices.

political constraints and 9.5 percent at the 75th percentile. Nevertheless, this increase results from independent increases in political constraints and not from the interaction between FDI and veto points. We can observe this directly, because the slopes of the three lines are almost identical; they vary only in their intercepts. One line is not significantly steeper or more pronounced than the other, and we certainly do not see evidence of a shift to a negatively sloped line as FDI increases. At each level of political constraints, a one-unit change in FDI returns roughly the same level of economic reform. Imposing confidence intervals on these lines would reinforce this conclusion but would mar our ability to make out the differences in the lines, because the confidence intervals would overlap so greatly.

The implication of figure 5.3 for the analysis of FDI lobbying is critical. Stocks of FDI and political constraints exert strong but independent effects on the pace of economic reform in transition countries. Their joint effect is not significantly different from zero. Foreign investors do not have significantly different probabilities of successful lobbying in regimes characterized by high veto points as opposed to regimes with less constrained executives.

Competitiveness of Participation

Figure 5.4 repeats the same analysis for the competitiveness of participation. Here, we observe a very different story. The slope of the FDI line changes dramatically across different levels of competition, which affects economic reform greatly. When competitiveness is restricted to the 25th percentile (a score of 2, about the level of the Krygyz Republic in 1992), there is a strongly significant upward slope. In these cases, investors play an important role as the primary providers of expert information on regulation and economic policy. FDI would appear to dramatically influence the progress of reform through lobbying and information provision. At the median level (a score of 3, or the level of Bulgaria in 1992), this influence is much less pronounced. The slope is only slightly greater than 0 and not statistically significant. Finally, at the 75th percentile (a score of 4, or the level of Latvia after independence), the slope is actually negative but not statistically significant. When FDI must compete for influence with other actors in a world of multiple policy ideas, its effect is drowned out; it does not have near the impact on reform choices and regulatory decisions that it does in other policy environments.

On graphs displaying the economic reform, like figures 5.3 and 5.4, it is difficult to simultaneously plot the level of statistical significance of the regression analysis. This can have important implications for our confidence in the conclusions, because we do not know if our findings would be robust to a similar analysis on a different set of countries. Statistical significance allows us to calculate confidence intervals, which provide us with a theoretical range for our predicted values that we know are replicable in repeated analysis. Figure 5.5 supplements figure 5.4 using a slightly different method of displaying interaction effects.

Whereas figure 5.4 plots just the predicted values at different levels of competitiveness and participation, figure 5.5 plots just the estimated slopes

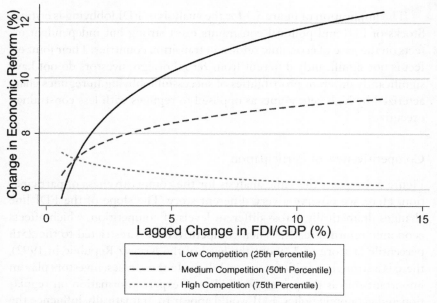

Fig. 5.4. Predicted effect of FDI on economic reform. This figure charts the predicted effects from a panel regression, interacting changes in FDI/GDP with initial levels of competitiveness at the beginning of the reform era. Essentially, each line represents the predicted effect of FDI given a particular level of competition. We can see that the slope of the FDI line is strongly contingent on the level of competitiveness. At the 25th percentile of competitiveness, FDI has a positive slope. At median level of competitiveness, the slope is nearly flat. And at the 75th percentile, the slope actually turns slightly negative, though this result is statistically insignificant. In sum, competitiveness mediates the policy influence of FDI. Investors have less influence on reform choices when they must compete in a robust policy environment.

of the lines and the confidence intervals around those slope predictions. On the x-axis is the level of competitiveness, which ranges in value from 1 to 5. The diamonds display the theoretical impact of a 1 percent change in FDI at each level of political competition. It is immediately obvious that FDI is highly influential when there are few alternative voices in the polity. When initial competitiveness is equal to 1, a 1 percent change in the stock of FDI/GDP yields nearly a 3 percent increase in total economic reform— a substantively enormous result that is significant at the .01 level. The marginal impact of FDI is only salient in uncompetitive regimes. When competitiveness is 3.55, about the average level of Georgia and Armenia over

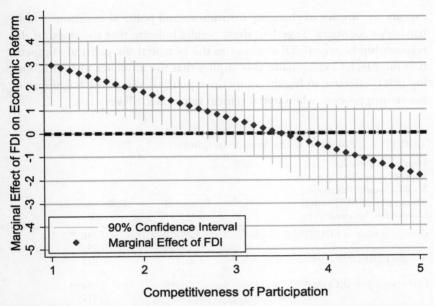

Fig. 5.5. Marginal effect of FDI on economic reform. This figure charts the marginal effect from a panel regression interacting changes in FDI/GDP with initial levels of competitiveness at the beginning of the reform era. The marginal effect is not uniformly positive, dipping below 0 at about 3.5. The 90% confidence intervals cross the zero line at 2.7, demonstrating that marginal effects are statistically significant only at low levels of political competition but not at high levels where the confidence intervals cross the 0 threshold.

the course of the 1990s, the impact of FDI dips below 0. At high levels of competitiveness, the level of full-fledged Western-style democracies, the confidence intervals cross over 0, illustrating that the marginal effect of FDI on reform is insignificant in highly competitive regimes; that is, the coefficient could be negative or positive, and we cannot differentiate with certainty about results at high levels of competitiveness. In practical terms, this means that while we know that FDI is less effective in competitive regimes, we cannot say that FDI actually damages reform efforts, as we could if the coefficient was significantly negative.

These results are robust to dropping measures of initial political constraints at the beginning of the time period and replacing them with average levels of political constraints between 1990 and 2004 (see table 5.2) to capture the impact of changing institutions and political coalitions within particular countries. Together, these results indicate that the slope of the relationship between FDI declines as the potential for political competition increases. Conceptually, this implies that the influence of FDI lobbying is less effective in highly competitive polities even at the beginning of the reform process, when initial reform values are still very low.

TABLE 5.2. Robust to Using Average Institutions

Dependent Variable: Annual Change in Total Economic Reform (measured by EBRD scores) Independent Variables	Restricted (1)	Fully Specified (2)
Change in stock of FDI/GDP (ln, lag)	5.205***	5.348***
	(1.297)	(1.293)
Average PARCOMP (1992–2004)	–0.021	–0.025
	(0.227)	(0.222)
FDI × Average PARCOMP	–1.360***	–1.374***
	(0.519)	(0.518)
Average Polcon	3.045*	3.403*
	(1.654)	(1.751)
FDI × Average Polcon	–1.400	–1.729
	(3.066)	(3.106)
GNP per Capita in 1989	0.451	–0.040
	(0.320)	(0.075)
Natural Resources 1989	–0.043	0.426
	(0.076)	(0.330)
GDP per Capita (ln, d)	7.776	7.260
	(5.439)	(5.429)
Postcommunists in Legislature (d)		–0.987
		(1.799)
Accession to European Union (d)		–0.335
		(0.217)
War (dummy)		0.512
		(0.388)
Constant	7.242***	7.036***
	(0.563)	(0.500)
Time Fixed Effects	Yes	Yes
Observations	272	272
Panels	26	26
R^2	0.451	0.452
Root Mean Squared Error	3.189	3.205

Note: OLS with panel corrected standard errors in parentheses. Replicating table 5.1 (Models 5 and 7) with average instead of initial effects.

Two-tailed test: *significant at 10%; **significant at 5%; ***significant at 1%.

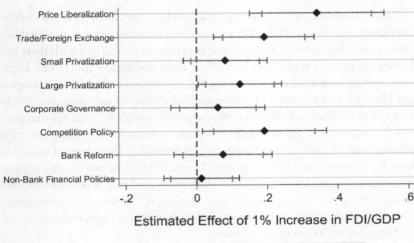

Estimated Effect of 1% Increase in FDI/GDP

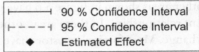

Fig. 5.6. Impact of FDI on individual economic reforms. This graph charts the substantive effect of a 1% change in the stock of FDI/GDP on the individual reforms that comprise the EBRD transition index. Confidence intervals around the slope predictions demonstrate the statistical significance of the estimated effects. Each line represents the results of panel regression of economic reform on the stock of FDI/GDP. The model uses time-fixed effects and controls for time variant confounders, such as EU entry status, postcommunist seats in the legislature, participation in a civil war, and GDP per capita.

Individual Economic Reforms

From a policy perspective, the focus on aggregate reform is opaque. It is more interesting to know on which types of reform foreign investors have the most pronounced impact. Figure 5.6 takes the analysis a step further by disaggregating the impact of FDI on individual reforms. Basically, figure 5.6 is the result of rerunning the Model 2 results from table 5.1 and calculating the impact of FDI on different dependent variables. It shows that FDI has a significant and substantively large effect on four reform categories: price liberalization, trade liberalization, and large privatization, and competition policy.

Trade liberalization is certainly an area where investors choose to lobby extensively. Hewko's (2002–3) discussion of the impact of multinational investors on policy reform, for instance, is primarily concerned with their influence on tax and trade laws that affect their ability to export. The large privatization results shown in figure 5.6 confirm the finding of Campos and Horvath (2006) that FDI prevents backsliding of privatization. Similarly, the privatization analysis confirms Lewis's anecdotal findings that foreign investors are at the forefront of efforts to improve efficiency through privatization of small and medium-size businesses as they depend on small firms for sourcing and other services (Lewis 2005). The results on changes in competition policy confirm the qualitative evidence from Henisz and Zelner (2006) that foreign investors in the electricity and telecommunications sectors are active in lobbying for better antitrust regulations to allow for fair competition in those sectors.

Four other areas shown in figure 5.6 have positive effects but statistically insignificant relationships. In these areas, other factors were the key drivers of policy change. Most foreign investors have little need for domestic banking services and therefore are unlikely to be involved in discussions on bank reform. It is probably still premature to assess the impact of FDI on nonbank institutions in the financial sector. Large financial investors were slow to move into all but a few Central Eastern European economies. The impact of foreign investment in these areas may be just a few years off, as Hewko's (2002–3) story of the Czech derivative market illustrates. Small privatization and corporate governance are more mysterious. Even if they did not influence national policy regarding corporate governance directly, foreign-invested enterprises should have been expected to at least influence individual firms' decisions through their own examples. We return to this issue shortly, when we discuss contingent effects.

This section is just a brief glimpse into the impact of FDI on different policy arenas. Nevertheless, the results at this stage are illustrative. MNCs are clearly more effective lobbyists in some arenas than in others. This may be because investors find certain reforms critical and therefore utilize more energy in achieving these changes. Alternatively, the differential effect across policy arenas may reflect the level of international expertise vis-à-vis local knowledge. Perhaps investors are more effective when they have regulatory ideas that local politicians cannot learn about in other contexts. The effectiveness of MNC lobbying may also be contingent on the saliency of reform efforts for local politicians and the national sensitivity of allowing foreign influence on particular economic sectors. Foreign investors may have a greater impact on trade liberalization because this is a policy arena within which local politicians want their expertise. Bank reform may be less malleable because local politicians have political and strategic reasons for keeping the banking sector in domestic hands.

Of course, the impact of FDI on each of these arenas may also depend on political institutions. The next step is to parse out the conditional effect for each policy arena as we did for the aggregate measure of reform earlier in this chapter. We analyze conditional effects of this in table 5.3. We find that small privatization, large privatization, and competition policy conform to the general pattern discovered in the case of aggregate reform; that is, FDI is influential on reform choices, but the impact of FDI is mediated by the strength of competition in these environments—stronger political competition means smaller effectiveness of FDI lobbying efforts. On trade reform, corporate governance, bank reform, and nonbank financial reform, we find that the interaction terms are insignificant, indicating that the impact of FDI is not conditional on institutional settings, in terms of either competition or veto points.

There are a few surprises, however, that are contrary to the findings for aggregate reform. On three individual reforms (price liberalization, small privatization, and competition policy), the interaction term for political constraints is positive, indicating that veto points positively modify the impact of FDI. In other words, the more players there are who have influence over policy, the stronger the effect of FDI is. Two theories explain these surprising findings. First, as previously discussed, Ehrlich's (2007) theory of "access points" predicts this counterintuitive finding. The large number of individuals with policy influence increases their individual receptiveness. Second, Gehlbach and Malesky (2010) show that a high number of veto points can, in special cases, encourage positive reform progress by weakening the power of special interests that prefer inefficient outcomes. Future research will need to sort out which of these hypotheses best explains these findings on individual reform outcomes.

Conclusion

This chapter has striven to stitch together a disparate number of robust literatures—ranging from strategic business theory, international economics, international political economy, and the comparative analysis of interest

TABLE 5.3. Conditional Effect of FDI and Political Institutions on Individual Reform Types

Dependent Variable; Annual Change in Total Economic Reform Independent Variables	Price (1)	Trade (2)	Small Privatization (3)	Large Privatization (4)	Corporate Governance (5)	Competition Policy (6)	Bank Reform (7)	Financial Reform (8)
Change in stock of FDI/GDP (ln, lag)	2.013	0.977	10.907***	12.255***	2.504	4.913**	−1.025	0.809
	(2.496)	(2.756)	(2.405)	(3.439)	(3.278)	(2.487)	(3.228)	(2.436)
Initial Polcon	0.444	1.679	−4.800**	4.674	8.006***	−0.695	10.532***	7.864***
	(2.796)	(2.242)	(1.884)	(3.499)	(2.597)	(2.144)	(3.499)	(2.606)
FDI × Initial Polcon	26.797***	0.299	9.537**	13.565	−11.234	13.261*	−5.926	−9.211
	(7.202)	(6.618)	(3.994)	(9.430)	(7.787)	(7.359)	(9.018)	(7.982)
Initial PARCOMP	1.425***	2.108***	2.406***	1.840***	1.003**	1.462***	0.601	1.305***
	(0.316)	(0.554)	(0.354)	(0.919)	(0.444)	(0.308)	(0.475)	(0.363)
FDI × Initial PARCOMP	−1.390	0.267	−3.508***	−4.013***	−0.083	−2.012**	0.245	−0.676
	(1.122)	(0.954)	(0.805)	(1.243)	(1.095)	(0.797)	(0.987)	(1.195)
Constant	14.062***	19.861***	14.947***	6.556***	6.136***	1.512	6.959***	2.251**
	(1.625)	(2.335)	(1.027)	(1.270)	(1.807)	(2.458)	(1.920)	(1.103)
Fully Specified Controls	Yes	Yes	Yes	Yes	Yes	Yes	Yes	Yes
Time Fixed Effects	Yes	Yes	Yes	Yes	Yes	Yes	Yes	Yes
Observations	272	272	272	272	272	272	272	272
Panels	26	26	26	26	26	26	26	26
R^2	0.169	0.330	0.457	0.257	0.344	0.201	0.175	0.231
Root Mean Squared Error	10.21	9.120	5.867	8.382	6.321	5.605	7.597	7.150

Note: OLS with panel corrected standard errors in parentheses, controlling for natural resources, GNP89, GDP growth, postcommunists in the legislature, EU accession, and war, as well as year fixed effects.

Two-tailed test: *significant at 10%; **significant at 5%; ***significant at 1%.

group lobbying—into a cohesive framework for understanding the success of multinational lobbying within transition countries.

While the aggregate stock of foreign investment in transition economies is strongly associated with economic reform, indicating that investors do have some influence over economic policy, this analysis has shown that success is highly contingent on political institutions. Surprisingly, it is not veto points that drive the divergence. The story of MNC lobbying is not one of capture of elite decision makers. The key political institutional marker is the competitiveness of participation. The more an electoral system allows open entry of new political parties and unfettered competition of political groups, the less influence investors have on the reform process. In states with limited competitiveness, investors are among the limited number of purveyors of information regarding market choices. This allows them to provide guidance on key regulatory challenges facing policy makers without needing to rigorously compete with dissenting expertise.

In addition, this chapter has shown that investors have been most effective in arguing for price liberalization, trade openness, large privatization, and competition policy. They have less influence over small-scale development in the private sector and the proliferation of good corporate governance, and they have virtually no relationship with reform in banking and other financing institutions.

CHAPTER 6

Conclusion

WE HAVE ATTEMPTED in this book to solve a puzzle that has vexed academics and policy makers for what sometimes seems forever: what is it that allows some countries to attract foreign investment at high levels and yet prevents others from doing so? Many argue that politics matters, and we demonstrate in this work that this is surely the case. We do more than that, however—we also demonstrate *how* politics matters. In this concluding chapter, we sketch our contribution to understanding the complex relationship between politics and multinational enterprises.

One overarching theme of our book is that political institutions and politics affect the risk environment within which foreign investors have to operate, both before and after committing resources to a host country. This can range from major events, such as the expropriation of foreign investment, to more day-to-day activities, such as the perceptions on how courts help in the enforcement of contracts. We maintain that this risk environment is central to understanding foreign direct investment and helps to explain the tremendous variation among countries in attracting multinational firms. There is another avenue through which politics affects the attractiveness of host countries to foreign investors: the policies, laws, and regulations that govern investment activity and impact their bottom line are the outcome of complex political interactions among political actors who may disagree on the desirability of foreign investment flows. While politics permeates every stage of the investment process and has a continuous impact on the operations of multinational firms, forward-looking firms factor in the political environment before committing resources to an investment project.

Related to this point, one of the biggest disagreements in the FDI literature over recent years is whether democracy or authoritarian rule is superior for attracting foreign investment. We believe we have helped answer this question rather definitively throughout this book, and our answer comes down on the side of democracy, although with caveats. Our central finding is that democracies have the ability to lessen not only the perception of political risk in the minds of foreign investors but the actual risk as well. Development scholars have made these arguments before, but the theoretical underpinnings of such notions and the empirical proofs always seemed sufficiently short of the mark as to leave the issue in doubt.

Our specific contribution on this debate begins, in chapter 2, with a discussion of the importance of political risk. Many scholars in international business, economics, and political science have employed composite indicators of political instability or risk to assess the impact of political risk on international business.[1] At the same time, many other scholars attempting to understand the determinants of FDI have found that political institutions influence investment and entry-mode decisions of international businesses by shaping investors' perception of the political risk in the host environment.[2] Very rarely, though, do those investigating FDI offer a direct evaluation of the link between political institutions and political risk. We begin to fill this important gap by demonstrating in chapter 2 how political regime type, a central feature of political institutions, influences not only the perception of risk in the minds of investors but also the actual risk, the most extreme form of which is manifested when the host government expropriates investor assets. We then go on in later chapters to show the nuances of how political institutions and the politics that operate within them affect the risk environment for FDI.

As we show in this book, political institutions and politics matter at all stages of FDI in the host country—not just at the beginning of the bargain, when foreign investors are deciding whether or not to enter a particular venue. What happens after the bargain is struck matters as well. Moreover, while much of the extant literature portrays MNC investors as passive or politically reactive (certainly not proactive) both before and after the decision to enter has been made, we show that such investors are able to and do actively engage the host country's political process at all stages, by supplying vital information to policy makers, lobbying government, and encouraging prospective and existing local affiliates to do likewise. Similarly, much of the development literature treats all FDI as essentially the same, for both the investor and the recipient country, whereas we show that the industrial sector targeted by foreign investment matters a great deal, as does whether the investment can be withdrawn relatively easily and at low cost. It also matters whether the investment will have beneficial or detrimental effects on labor or domestic capital or both in the host country. The expected distributional consequences of foreign investment could make the politics of regulating FDI a contested political issue in the host country. To the extent that foreign investment activity has the potential to affect—positively or negatively—the demand for their services in the marketplace, workers, domestic business owners, and other economic agents would support or oppose pro-investment policies.

Chapter 2 begins the discussion on the effects of political institutions on FDI by studying, theoretically and empirically, the links between regime type and political risk. While political risk encompasses a number of political outcomes affecting firms, we focus on expropriation risk. In chapter 2, we identify various theoretical mechanisms by which democracy could be thought to either raise or lower the risk of expropriation against multinationals. Using a data set containing actual expropriations in 63 countries from 1960 to 1990 and data from ONDD, the Belgian Export Credit Agency, we examine simultaneously the net impact of democracy on both actual expropriations and the perceived risk of expropriation. This is a novel approach, since studies prior to this have looked at either expropriation (e.g., Jensen 2008) or perceived risk (e.g., Li 2009), but not both together.

While the existing literature is divided on the question of whether democracy enhances or diminishes risk, our evidence, using large-N empirical analyses, demonstrates that both democracies and autocracies expropriate foreign investment but that democracies do so less frequently. Based on our analysis of actual expropriations, democracies better protect property rights of foreign investors than do authoritarian regimes, presumably because democracies contain an array of institutional veto players, such as competitive legislatures and independent courts, which constrain the impulse toward predation by other key players in the political system. Our findings offer direct empirical support for arguments advanced by Feng (2001), Li and Resnick (2003), Li (2009), and Jensen (2003, 2006) that democracies attract investment because they expropriate less often. As we also demonstrate, insurance premiums to protect against government misdeeds are higher in authoritarian regimes than in democracies. This further confirms that democracies are safer, but it also shows that investors face higher costs when approaching authoritarian regimes, something that surely lessens inward flows of FDI.

While the analysis provided in chapter 2 focuses on the relationship between political regimes and political risk, the use of aggregate data makes it difficult to identify the exact causal mechanism by which democracies lower risk. Chapter 3 takes on that task, using both firm-level and aggregate data to show that institutional constraints are important to understanding the ebb and flow of FDI. The existing development literature has paid scant attention to the effect that democratic political institutions have on the investment decisions of individual firms. Most previous studies use large data sets from the World Bank, the International Monetary Fund, and other sources to arrive at conclusions about the forces that drive FDI, but these studies can only indirectly hint at what investors take into account when deciding to invest or not; they cannot prove such things. For that, we need to get information from the foreign investors themselves— those that make the decisions to invest or not and in what amounts. We do that in chapter 3 with the use of data obtained from a survey questionnaire administered by Biglaiser and Staats (2010) to CEOs of U.S. corporations with investments in Latin America. The survey results we report in chapter 3 indicate that uppermost in the minds of investors when deciding where to invest is whether the prospective host country adheres to the rule of law, recognizes and upholds private property rights (i.e., enforces contracts and eschews government expropriation), has a relatively high level of political stability, and has a relatively efficient and effective court system.

As we indicate in chapter 3, the factors that the corporate survey respondents identify as important are connected in theory to the presence or absence of institutional features that constrain political actors. Thus, adherence to the rule of law, of prime importance according to the survey, requires the presence of independent and strong courts, which the survey participants also told us they want. According to the insurance policy theory discussed in chapter 3, independent and strong courts are most likely to flourish in a system with robust political competition, the very kind of political competition able to prevail in institutionalized democratic systems. Democratic competition is also a key to understanding political stability, something high on the list of the survey responders. Under competitive circumstances, those in power are persuaded to support strong and independent courts that limit their own prerogatives while in office but protect their rights when they are likely out of power. This, in turn, convinces those in the opposition to support the democratic bargain and not try to overturn the existing regime through extralegal means. Strong courts that come about through competitive circumstances also allow those in power to make credible commitments to investors that their assets will be safe, not only under the current administration, but under future administrations as well.

To connect theory with results, chapter 3 turns to analysis of aggregate data to empirically explore the relationship between political constraints and risk. Through use of the POLCON V data set (Henisz 2010), we show that political competition and the presence of veto points in the political system is associated with higher levels of FDI. We also show the same thing for the presence of well-performing courts; that is, strong and independent courts attract FDI.

Chapter 4 continues the discussion of the relationship between political institutions and politics, on the one hand, and FDI, on the other, by focusing on FDI's distributive consequences and highlighting the importance of adding coalitional motivations to the foreign investment equation. Chapter 4 shows that not all FDI is the same, at least not in terms of the willingness of the host government to encourage foreign capital inflows or in terms of the willingness of investors to devote assets to any particular country.

Given that the definition of FDI implies that management responsibility flows with capital, the exit option of FDI is more limited and costly than would be the case for portfolio investment. There is usually an efficient market for realization of returns on portfolio assets but no relatively frictionless way that allows an MNC to leave a country once invested there, although the impediment to exit varies from industry to industry. It is precisely this frictional component that makes inflows of FDI preferable to other forms of investment for the host country, by which we mean that the income effect associated with an inflow of capital is not negated by the volatility effect associated with mobile capital (see Pinto 2004, 2005, 2013). As we argue in chapter 4, these high redeployment costs force investors to look for reassurance that they will not be taken advantage of once they have deployed their assets in a foreign venue. Given that FDI is vulnerable to opportunistic behavior by host governments and that investors are forward looking, adoption of investor-friendly policies alone might not be enough to lure in investors, who face a classic problem of time consistency

(Kydland and Prescott 1977; Calvo 1978). The likelihood that governments will exploit them over time reduces foreign investors' propensity to invest. This is the very type of issue discussed in chapter 3 in reference to how institutional constraints on policy makers can allow for a credible commitment that policies will remain relatively friendly in the outer years.

Certain kinds of capital, even in the form of FDI, are relatively mobile and show high elasticity to host countries' policies, including tax policy, because investors are able to withdraw without major effort or cost; governments in such circumstances face the problem of a "race to the bottom." By contrast, immobile types of foreign investment, which are often sector specific, become inelastic to unfavorable policies and differential tax rates immediately after investment takes place, rendering them virtual hostages of host governments. Investors holding sector-specific assets with high costs of redeployment are exposed to opportunistic behavior by host governments. Foreign investors have two options to reduce the risk that governments will take advantage of them: they can pay a redeployment cost and leave the country after government intentions become apparent, or they can withhold investment ex ante in the shadow of opportunistic government behavior. Both conditions are economically inefficient and politically sensitive. The higher the level of location-specific assets involved in an investment project is, the more salient the dilemma of the obsolescing bargain is. Consequently, the determinants of FDI and MNC activity are tied to local conditions, and their consequences are likely to vary with type of firm and investment strategies (see Pinto and Pinto 2008, 2011).

Foreign investors have to contend with a number of factors, pertaining to probable investment return and investment risk, that convince them whether and in what amounts to invest in any given country. These are the pull factors that attract outside investment into a country. The host country has control over these factors to the extent that it can reduce investment risk through fortifying political and legal institutions and adhering to the rule of law, all things that give investors some assurance that their investments will be protected and given the opportunity to flourish. In addition or alternatively, they can increase the probable rate of return on investments through various policy incentives that (among other things) lessen tax and regulatory burdens. Each country has to decide for itself how to go about enhancing the pull factors, but strategies directed at reducing risk are most difficult to accomplish and take time to effectuate, so we would expect many or most developing countries to devote considerable attention to policies directed at increasing the rate of return on investments as a means of pulling in FDI.

Much of the existing literature looks on the willingness of the host government to encourage FDI as based on what the government can do to improve the risk climate and/or what it can afford or is willing to do to mitigate risk through tax breaks and other inducements. The conventional view is to ask whether the host government has calculated that the costs of improving conditions or offering inducements is offset by the benefits to economic growth and development that FDI is expected to bring. Yet, as chapter 4 shows, it would be a mistake to assume that economic growth and development are the only ends in the minds of policy makers in a host country when they are deciding how much and what FDI they wish to draw into the country and what measures they want to utilize in doing so. Domestic politics enters into the equation. These policy makers have to consider the needs and demands of their core constituents before deciding on policies conducive to attracting FDI. In chapter 4, we show that the focus of these policies will depend to a great degree on the partisan nature of the government in power, principally whether the government receives its greatest support from labor or capital interests.

The economic conditions in a host country are important in this regard, as is the particular economic sector within which FDI operates and whether the FDI is capital or labor intensive. Depending on local conditions and sector, some forms of FDI will complement the local labor pool and either not diminish employment or actually increase it. In other cases, however, FDI will supplant the labor pool and lead to diminished employment, at least in the short run. Economists may argue that the long-run benefits of industrial upgrading outweigh the short-run labor dislocations, but politicians in a host country who depend on labor's political support will be hard pressed to make this argument to their core constituents. Along the same lines, some forms of FDI in certain sectors will compete with and overwhelm local firms. This may benefit consumers in the form of lower prices and pave the way for future growth spurred on by technology spillovers, but it will not sit well with local investors, and a government that depends on their support will be severely constrained in the policies that it can or is willing to implement. Thus, chapter 4 identifies how the partisan orientation of the ruling coalition conditions the type of investment politicians try to attract and how this affects the risk environment for investors.

The first four chapters of this book begin with a focus on firm entry, examining how political institutions affect the risk environment. Yet entry is only one part of the calculus for firms. As shown in chapter 3, firms consider the court systems and investment stability as critical, and chapter 4 examines how the sector of investment conditions the treatment of firms by partisan politicians. Firms that provide the right types of spillovers, such as employment under left-wing governments, find more profitable entry deals and an overall better operating environment than other firms. Yet our focus in the first four chapters of this book is on investors as passively accepting the investment environment or avoiding environments that are not conducive to their operations.

In chapter 5, we add our final level of complexity to the examination of firm-government interactions, by exploring how MNCs can actively lobby for policy change to influence the policy environment, reduce political risks, and increase profitability for their firms. Building on the work of Malesky (2008, 2009), we use FDI data and data from the European Bank of Reconstruction and Development on economic reform among the 26 transition states in Eastern Europe and the former Soviet Union, to show how and under what conditions MNC lobbying and other forms of communications to policy makers in host countries can affect the risk environment under which MNCs operate—both before and after commitment of investment capital. To aid in this effort, chapter 5 stitches together a disparate number of literatures—ranging from strategic business theory, international economics, international political economy, and the comparative analysis of interest group lobbying—into a cohesive framework for understanding the success of multinational lobbying within transition countries.

While the aggregate stock of foreign investment in transition economies is strongly associated with economic reform, indicating that investors have influence over economic policy, our analysis shows that success is highly contingent on political institutions. Surprisingly, it is not veto points per se that drive the divergence. The story of MNC lobbying is not one of capture of elite decision makers. Rather, the key political institutional marker is the competitiveness of participation. We show empirically, using data from 26 countries in economic transition, that investors have a more difficult time influencing key decision makers when their views on regulatory reforms must do battle with other perspectives in free and fair electoral competition. The more an electoral system allows open entry of new political parties and unfettered competition of political groups, the less influence investors have on the reform process. In states with limited competitiveness, investors are among the limited number of purveyors of information regarding market choices. This allows them to provide guidance on key regulatory challenges facing policy makers without needing to compete rigorously with dissenting expertise.

The constraints on executive decision making talked about in earlier chapters, especially chapter 3, prove more important for investment attraction than postinvestment influence of MNCs. The influence of FDI on the policy process does not appear to be mediated by checks and balances or coalition politics. Furthermore, we show that some policy arenas are more subject to investor persuasion than others. Both of these insights are important for our ability to predict the directions of economic reform in developing and transition countries. It is important as well to understanding the overall puzzle this book sought to solve: the conditions under which FDI is attracted to countries and allowed to thrive after arriving.

Beyond the insights and conclusions reached in chapter 5, there remains a great deal of work to be done relating to the political influence of MNCs. One particularly rich target arena is to apply these policy lessons to firm-level data sets that are now available in many countries. The firm-level data sets will help us better understand the effectiveness of particular political tactics for MNCs, which cannot be disaggregated when the country is the unit of analysis.

Taken together, the chapters of this book provide insights into the relationship between politics and FDI and introduce avenues for future research. While we highlight the positive influence of democracy for reducing risks for investors, our chapter on lobbying highlights that political competition, often associated with democracies, does limit the influence of firms over economic reforms. Thus, while democracies often are business friendly and limit the ability of politicians to nationalize firms or engage in sweeping policy changes that harm firms, democratic institutions also check the power of investors and could even empower domestic actors who are in direct competition with them.

Notes

1. See Caves (1996), Dunning (1993), and Navaretti and Venables (2004) for broad discussions of multinationals.

2. Calculated based on the figures in the UNCTAD *World Investment Report* (2007, 253). The share of developing and emerging markets in inflows has increased in recent years, accounting for roughly half of world inflows in 2009. Moreover, a handful of emerging markets, particularly the BRICs (Brazil, Russia, India, and China), have become important sources of direct investment, commanding one-fourth of world outflows; see UNCTAD (2010) and Pinto (2013, chapter 1).

3. See, e.g., Graham (1996), Moran (1999), and Lipsey (2002).

4. Gartzke, Li, and Boehmer (2001); Gartzke and Li (2003); Li and Reuveny (2003); Rosecrance and Thompson (2003).

5. Jensen and Rosas (2007) find that FDI decreases income inequality in Mexico.

6. See, e.g., Gilpin (1987), Moran (1978a, 1978b), and Choucri and North (1995). The *dependentista* thesis that domestic and foreign capital coalesce to exploit the popular sectors in Latin America receives limited empirical support: to the extent that the alliance between foreign and domestic capital existed, it proved unstable and short lived. See Dominguez (1982) and Pinto (2004, 2013).

7. For literature on the economic determinants, see, e.g., the classic works by Caves (1996), Dunning (1977), and Markusen (1995).

8. There is a growing consensus that FDI can be an important contributor to economic growth. See Moran, Graham, and Blomstrom (2005) for a recent contribution.

9. See Pinto (2004, 2013).

CHAPTER 2

1. See, e.g., Schneider and Frey (1985), Fatehi-Sedeh and Safizadeh (1989), Li (2006b, 2008), Loree and Guisinger (1995), Olibe and Crumbley (1997), Wood-

ward and Rolfe (1993), Sethi, Guisinger, Phelan and Berg (2003), and Globerman and Shapiro (2003).

2. See, e.g., Oneal (1994), Resnick (2001), Li and Resnick (2003), Jensen (2003, 2006), Harms and Ursprung (2002), Busse (2004), and Busse and Hefeker (2005), and Henisz (2000, 2002a, 2002b).

3. See Elkins, Guzman, and Simmons (2006) for work on the diffusion of BITs. See Yackee (2007), Allee and Peinhardt (2010), and Crisp et al. (2010) on the variation in content of BITs.

4. For a select set of papers on FDI and BITs, see UNCTAD (1998), Neumayer and Spess (2005), Salacuse and Sullivan (2005), Tobin and Rose-Ackerman (2005), Yackee (2007, 2008), and Kerner (2009).

5. See Jensen (2006, 2008), Li and Resnick (2003), and Li (2009) for a more detailed discussion of these factors, including evidence of actual expropriation behaviors and evidence from investors, location consultants, and political risk insurers.

6. See Rosendorff and Vreeland (2006).

7. There is considerable evidence that financial markets respond and react to the probability of individual leaders being elected in democratic systems (Herron et al. 1999; Leblang and Mukherjee 2004; Jensen and Schmith 2005; Vaaler, Schrage, and Block 2005, 2006).

8. Also see Herschman (2005). Some voters or groups may prefer keeping foreign investors out, as discussed in chapter 4. In this case, we could expect that the coalitions representing these groups may be less constrained by the reputation costs of opportunistic behaviors (see Pinto and Pinto 2011).

9. See Franzese (2002a) for a review.

10. One might wonder about the role of some independent bureaucratic agency in expropriations. In some issue areas, such as monetary policy, politicians often delegate authority to independent agencies like the central bank to remove the incentives to manipulate economic policy for short-term gains due to the traditional problem of time inconsistency (e.g., Kydland and Prescott 1977; Calvo 1978; Cukierman 1992). But with respect to the initiation of expropriation against multinationals, as far as we know, no independent government agency has been delegated with such authority in any country. Hence, the notion of central bank independence or other independent agency is not relevant to our study of expropriation initiations. Still, the legal system in a country is relevant to the adjudication of investment disputes over imposed expropriations, which we investigate in chapter 3.

11. An extensive literature in political science has stressed that authoritarian governments, unconstrained by popular pressures and domestic firms' interests, can be favorable to foreign investors (Huntington 1968; Bornschier and Chase-Dunn 1985; Oneal 1994; Li and Resnick 2003; Li 2006a).

12. Sebastian Saiegh (2005) demonstrates that the median voter under democracy may hamper debt repayment.

13. The left government has its core constituency in labor and often tends toward an interventionist policy against capital owners, such as imposing capital controls. In contrast, the right government is more oriented toward laissez-faire poli-

cies and appeals to multinational corporations, capital owners, and the financial community. See, e.g., Alesina, Grilli, and Milesi-Ferretti (1994), Grilli and Milesi-Ferretti (1995), Quinn and Inclan (1997), Li and Smith (2002), Pinto and Pinto (2008), and Pinto (2013). In chapter 4, we will investigate in detail the impact of this partisan bias on FDI.

14. See, e.g., Truitt (1970), Knudsen (1974), Jodice (1980), Kobrin (1980, 1984), and Minor (1994).

15. This definition does not cover "creeping expropriation" cases, where governments change taxes, regulation, access, or laws to reduce the profitability of foreign investment.

16. Kobrin (1980, 1984) and Minor (1994) suggest that compared to using the individual plant level, aggregating expropriation acts to the industry level allows greater comparability across heterogeneous industries. This avoids the absurd possibility of treating, say, a plantation and an oil field as implicitly equivalent in worth. For regional, sectoral, and temporal distributions of these expropriation acts, see Minor (1994).

17. This count excludes four expropriation acts whose years are missing values. The number of countries is identified by comprehensive data collection through a variety of sources. For details, see Kobrin (1980, 1984) and Minor (1994). Countries that did not commit any expropriation that fits the definition during the period are excluded from the sample because the causal process of expropriation in such countries is likely to be qualitatively different from those experiencing at least one expropriation act. We elaborate on the sample selection issue in the statistical modeling section in chapter 3.

18. The ACLP data ends at 1990, though there were no expropriations in 1991–92 (Minor 1994).

19. See Hansen (2004) for a brief overview and history of MIGA and OPIC. See also MIGA (2004).

20. http://www.opic.gov.

21. See Hamdani, Liebers, and Zanjani (2005).

22. Information on OPIC pricing can be found on the OPIC website and in various annual reports. OPIC pricing on individual projects is not available, and OPIC pricing is exempt from the U.S. Freedom of Information Act.

23. See Jensen (2008).

24. See Jensen (2006, 2008).

25. http://www.ducroire.be.

26. Jensen (2008) reports interviews with risk insurers and underwriters that point to similar ratings and price convergence across providers. Also, plant location consultants use the ONDD data for the evaluation of political risks.

27. See Jensen (2006) and Li (2009) for a review.

28. The sample includes Algeria, Angola, Argentina, Bangladesh, Benin, Bolivia, Brazil, Cameroon, the Central African Republic, Chad, Chile, Colombia, Congo, Costa Rica, the Dominican Republic, Ecuador, Egypt, El Salvador, Ethiopia, Gabon, Gambia, Ghana, Guatemala, Guinea, Guyana, Haiti, Honduras, India, Indonesia, Iran, Iraq, Jamaica, Kenya, Liberia, Malagasy, Malawi, Malaysia, Mauritania, Mexico, Morocco, Mozambique, Myanmar, Nepal, Nicaragua, Niger,

Pakistan, Panama, Peru, the Philippines, Senegal, Sierra Leone, Somalia, Sri Lanka, Sudan, Swaziland, Syria, Tanzania, Thailand, Trinidad and Tobago, Uganda, Venezuela, Zaire, and Zambia.

29. However, based on our statistical inferences, one might easily conjecture the impact of including these irrelevant OECD countries into our analysis: that is, the effect of democracy will undoubtedly become even more significant and larger. This is so because almost all the OECD countries have been democratic in the sample period and because none of them committed any expropriation act. The increase in the sample size and the nature of data for the OECD countries will necessarily strengthen the negative effect of democracy on the count of expropriation acts.

30. Note that the measure controls for preferences by counting the number of political parties that control veto points, rather than employing actual information on preferences of veto players with regard to foreign investment.

31. In an additional model not reported here due to space, we also estimate Model 1 by adding an additional control variable for the number of bilateral investment treaties signed by a country in a year. It turns out that democracy remains negative and significant, whereas the effect of the BIT variable is statistically not different from zero. Also see Li (2009) for related additional analysis.

32. The countries dropped from the analysis due to lack of data are Afghanistan, American Samoa, Andorra, Antigua, Aruba, the Bahamas, Barbados, Belize, Bermuda, Bosnia, Brunei, Cape Verde, the Cayman Islands, the Channel Islands, Cote d'Ivoire, Cuba, Dominica, the Faeroe Islands, French Polynesia, Greenland, Grenada, Guam, Hong Kong, Iceland, Iraq, the Isle of Man, Kiribati, the Democratic Republic of Korea, Lebanon, Libya, Liechtenstein, Luxembourg, Macao, the Maldives, Malta, the Marshall Islands, Mayotte, Micronesia, Monaco, Myanmar, the Netherlands Antilles, New Caledonia, the Northern Mariana Islands, Palau, Puerto Rico, Qatar, Samoa, San Marino, Sao Tome, Serbia, Seychelles, the Solomon Islands, Somalia, St. Kitts, St. Lucia, St. Vincent, Suriname, Timor-Leste, Tonga, Vanuatu, the Virgin Islands, and the West Bank and Gaza.

33. The regional dummy variables are Western Europe, Latin America, sub-Saharan Africa, North Africa and the Middle East, Eastern Europe and the former Soviet Union, Asia, and Oceania.

34. We also tested for nonrandom selection, as outlined by Jensen (2008). Even after accounting for nonrandom selection, democratic institutions are still associated with lower political risk scores.

35. We utilize CLARIFY for all predicted values. See King, Tomz, and Wittenberg (2000) and Tomz, Wittenberg, and King (2003).

CHAPTER 3

1. Busse (2004); Feng (2001); Henisz (2000); Jensen (2003, 2006, 2008); Li (2006a, 2006b, 2009); Li and Resnick (2003).

2. Brunetti, Kisunko, and Weder (1997); Brunetti and Weder (1999); Levine (1998); North (1990); Sherwood, Shepherd, and De Souza (1994); Shihata (1995).

3. Huntington (1968); O'Donnell (1978); Oneal (1994); Tuman and Emmert (2004).

4. Biglaiser and DeRouen (2006); Crenshaw (1991).

5. Rummel and Heenan (1978); Baer and Miles (2001).

6. Jones and Kane (2005); Biglaiser and DeRouen (2007).

7. Martínez, Esperança, and de la Torre (2005) surveyed executives in the United States and Europe but without consideration of political criteria. MIGA (2002) surveyed firms on FDI determinants but did not include possible political factors.

8. See Kobrin (1984) on the history of asset expropriation in the 1960s and 1970s.

9. See Akinsanya (1980), Kobrin (1984), and Vernon (1998) for details on expropriation.

10. See chapter 5, wherein we study the effects of political institutions in mediating the lobbying effectiveness of MNCs.

11. Harms and Ursprung (2002) argue that FDI is not boosted by civil and political repression identified with authoritarian regimes.

12. Lehmann (1999) claims that political risk adversely affects FDI.

13. See, e.g., Pinto and Pinto (2008), for discussion about disparate treatment of investors by ideologically driven governments.

14. On the importance of regional trade agreements, see Büthe and Milner (2008). There has also been increased interest in bilateral investment treaties (Neumayer and Spess 2005). The effects of trade agreements and investment treaties are important but beyond the scope of our survey.

15. Good relations between the United States and the host country do not suggest that investors favor increased politicization that could jeopardize their investments depending on the political parties in power. However, cordial relations imply that allies will attempt to work together and reach settlements when disputes arise, unlike countries that have histories of hostile relations.

16. The countries in the study are Argentina, Bolivia, Brazil, Chile, Colombia, Costa Rica, Ecuador, El Salvador, Guatemala, Honduras, Mexico, Nicaragua, Panama, Paraguay, Peru, Uruguay, and Venezuela.

17. Pearce and Zahra (1991) report a return rate of 20 percent, but this is only after they exclude responses from companies that refused to participate.

18. Because of the small number of service corporations in our survey, we were unable to conduct meaningful statistical comparisons as we did between manufacturing corporations and all other types of corporations.

19. We included a label for regional trade because of the growth in outsourcing and the recent expansion in regional trade agreements in Latin America (e.g., NAFTA, Mercosur, CAFTA, and the Andean Pact) that increase the potential importance of trade blocs for U.S. investors.

20. Factor analysis involves a variety of statistical techniques "whose common objective is to represent a set of variables in terms of a smaller number of hypothetical variables" (Kim and Mueller 1978, 9). We employed principal-component analysis as our extraction method and Varimax with Kaiser normalization for rota-

tion of the data. For our first factor (protection of property rights), which is of particular interest to us, we obtain an Eigenvalue of 2.957 and 73.9 percent explanation of variation. For the remaining factors, we see the highest level of explanation of variation at 76.1 percent and the lowest at 58.2 percent. The question "had relatively high levels of literacy and education" did not seem to fit into any broad category and loaded only weakly with the other questions. Because of this, we dropped it from further consideration.

21. The survey results suggest the importance of investment risk but do not tap into the possible role that investment return also might play. Perhaps investors have different time horizons and preferences, with some investors more willing than others to bear higher risks if the returns are substantial. Such inquiries are beyond the scope of our research but are explored in the next chapter.

22. For an excellent exposition of separable and nonseparable preferences in survey responses, see Lacy (2001).

23. One might argue that policy stability is not always attractive to investors if the policies in place fail to respond to emergency situations such as currency crises or economic recessions. However, such crises are relatively uncommon, and it is unclear, in any event, that governments with institutional restraints on policy change are any less able to respond to urgent circumstances than are authoritarian regimes (see Molinas, Liñan, and Saiegh 2004).

24. At this point, we are looking at all developing countries to show how representative our survey is to the developing world, but we will examine panel data of Latin America exclusively later in the chapter. We also will consider the effects of judicial institutions separately. The survey results suggest that the strength of judicial institutions gives investors confidence, which conforms to the courts literature. The literature suggests that the courts are usually unwilling to act as agents of change without support from the political branches and society in general (Epp 1998; Rosenberg 2008). Although not specifically addressing court systems, Sabatier and Jenkins-Smith (1993) argue that we too often treat political institutions as separate entities, when we could learn more about how they operate by studying them simultaneously as collaborative enterprises—what they call "the advocacy coalition approach."

25. Because our dependent variable is calculated as a percentage of GDP and because some of our independent variables have GDP as numerators, there is concern about biased estimates. However, the results hold up even when GDP variables are removed from the model.

26. We do not include a separate measure of democracy, because POLCON V is partly constructed from the Polity IV democracy measure.

27. That Chávez offered Nicaragua power plants, tractors, and factories financed by soft loans from Venezuelan state banks supports Ortega's closeness to him (*Economist* 2007b).

28. While in certain instances or types of transactions, investors may actually prefer arbitration to litigation, this is not universally true. If it were, we would see business interests using arbitration at much higher levels in countries where effective and efficient court systems are in place, such as the United States.

29. Block and Vaaler (2004) argue that democratic election cycles may cause policy makers to adopt short-term policies that are harmful for growth and development. Similarly, Bhagwati (1966) suggested that democracies face a cruel dilemma between the need to satisfy short-term demands of the electorate that may be inimical to long-term growth and development. However, more than a quarter century later, Bhagwati (2002) has had a change of heart and now argues that democracy may, when accompanied by markets and openness, actually be good for development.

30. For a discussion of constitutionalization of rights, see Schneiderman (2001, 521), Gill (2002, 48), and Hirschl (2004, 146–47).

31. We recognize the possibility that, under certain conditions, a government can make a credible commitment to investors through means other than formal institutions. For example, Haber, Mauer, and Razo (2003) show the importance of informal institutions in the Mexican petroleum industry during the period 1911–29, and Fisman (2001) shows how political connections benefited investors in Indonesia during and after the Suharto regime. However, our argument is that formal commitments are more consistent and reliable in most instances.

32. For discussion of insurance policy theory in the Latin American context, see Finkel (2003, 2004) and Chavez (2004).

33. Realization of the importance of strong courts was a major factor in Chile's decision to reform its criminal justice system. The changes included converting from an outmoded written inquisitorial system that was closed to the public to an accusatorial system employing public proceedings and proofs presented through oral testimony subject to cross-examination (see Riego 2008).

34. For access to the data, see http://www.bea.gov/international/di1usdbal .htm.

35. We used the average scores of three of the individual measures that comprise the EFW judicial measure: judicial independence, impartial courts, and protection of property rights. We opted not to use two measures in the EFW data. One related to "military interference in rule of law and the political process," which we deemed too specific for our purposes and more conceptually related to authoritarianism. The other is labeled as "integrity of the legal system," but this conflates "law" with maintenance of "order," leading to the anomaly that North Korea and Cuba are ranked high in this category.

36. We test the logged version of GDP to account for data outliers.

37. We did not include corruption in table 3.6, because our corruption data begin in the mid-1980s. If we included it, we would lose 10 years of data.

CHAPTER 4

1. We have no systematic evidence to support these claims, but we plan on exploring the empirical content of these predictions more systematically in future research. Anecdotal evidence, however, suggests that this calculation was present in South Korea's regulation of foreign investment from the 1960s through the financial crisis of 1997. The restrictive investment regime legislated under the Foreign

Capital Inducement Act of 1960 and revised in 1961 and 1973 limited the sectors where foreign investors were allowed to be active and mandated the formation of joint ventures aimed at allowing local firms to master technologies developed by foreign MNCs. There are two interpretations for the restrictiveness of South Korea's foreign investment regime. One account argues that the regime was functional to the government's developmental program—the Economic Planning Agency would allow foreign investment, but only in those sectors that needed technological assistance from abroad (Mardon 1990; Sachwald 2003). Alternatively, it is plausible that restrictions on foreign ownership were aimed at protecting the interests of the *chaebols*, the politically influential industrial conglomerates. The *chaebols* would have direct access to the government and demand the preservation of their prominent status in the Korean economy (Haggard and Mo 2000; Pinto 2004; Pinto 2013).

2. The financial statements of the affiliates of U.S. MNCs are likely to reflect their response to political changes in host countries. The U.S. Bureau of Economic Analysis collects such data (see Mataloni 1995 for a description of the BEA's surveys of U.S. direct investment abroad). Nathan Jensen, Pablo Pinto, and Santiago Pinto are in the process of testing these additional implications of our models using microlevel data on the activity of affiliates of U.S. MNCs.

3. The role of inflexible policy is underscored in the recent literature on transaction costs (Williamson 1985; Henisz and Williamson 1999; Spiller and Tommasi 2003).

4. Right-leaning governments (and parties) are associated with open trade policies in developed (capital-abundant) countries, while left-leaning governments are more protectionist (Dutt and Mitra 2005; Milner and Judkins 2004). The outcomes are reversed for capital-scarce countries, which is consistent with the predictions derived from the Hecksher-Ohlin model of trade (see Stolper and Samuelson 1941).

5. Exceptions are Evans (1979), Evans and Gereffi (1982), Gereffi (1983), Pinto (2004, 2005, 2013), Vaaler (2008), and Jensen (2008).

6. In the appendix to this chapter, we present a more technical discussion of the baseline model, which was originally published in Pinto and Pinto (2008).

7. Both domestic factors of production are assumed to be internationally immobile.

8. These assumptions follow those prevalent in the literature on the politics of trade and FDI (Grossman and Helpman 1996) and in standard economic theories of MNCs (Caves 1996). Note that the predictions from our model would be substantively similar if domestic capital is assumed to be mobile while labor is sector specific. If both labor and domestic capital are mobile across sectors, governments will not be able to implement sector-specific policies. Essentially, for the conclusions of our model to hold, we require one of the domestic factors to be relatively more specific than the other. Under the assumption of fixed world prices, this setting allows capital flows to affect factor returns, rather than output mixes.

9. To simplify the bargaining protocol for factor returns, we assume perfect

competition in the input market, so factors are paid their respective marginal productivity.

10. Recall that we define foreign investment as a combination of capital and technology, which we assume is available in (relatively) infinite supply. Implicitly, it is assumed that foreign investors have access to different technologies that allow them to enter the country as either a complement to or substitute of labor or domestic capital.

11. This tax could be interpreted as the net effect of the numerous policy instruments that governments use to regulate foreign investment. Among those instruments, we find, for example, screening and approval procedures, limits on the share that nonresidents are allowed to hold, differential tax schedules, regulatory regimes on sectoral activity and market structure, trade policy, local procurement rules, differential exchange rate regimes, training programs, and active labor policies. All these instruments and regulations affect either the cost of doing business or the price that firms can charge for their goods and services, and they are hence likely to affect the firm's bottom line (see Pinto 2004, 2005, 2013; Pinto and Pinto 2008).

12. The framework can be extended to account for the effect of FDI on competition in product and factor markets, wage bargaining structures, and any other conditions that have the potential to affect the relative return to workers and capital owners in the host country. Depending on their effect on market structure, the establishment of foreign firms could also affect the relative bargain between labor and capital owners in the host country and, indirectly, the return to domestic factors.

13. Those links could result from the constraints and incentives created by political institutions and from structural conditions in the host economy, such as the degree of organization and centralization of labor and business interests.

14. Political parties build and nurture ties to groups of voters, whether organized or not, and tend, when in government, to deliver policies valued by those groups for material (or ideological) reasons. The assumption that governments have partisan (and electoral) incentives in regulating economic activity is pervasive in the literature that explores the links between politics and macroeconomic management. Hibbs (1977, 1992) and Tufte (1978) are the precursors in this tradition. For more recent models of partisan and electoral business cycles, see, e.g., Alesina (1987, 1988); Alvarez, Garrett, and Lange (1991); Alesina and Rosenthal (1995); Boix (1997, 1998); Garrett (1998); Iversen (1999); and Franzese (2002b). The existence of a partisan business cycle has received more support than its electoral counterpart. See Franzese (2002a) for an excellent review of this literature.

15. Parties of the left and right alike may be at odds with the interests of foreign investors for ideological reasons, usually associated with nationalism. Chavez's nationalization of Cargill's rice plants on March 2009, Kirchner's call to boycott Shell gas stations in 2005, and the reaction in the United States against Japanese investment in the 1980s and Chinese investment in recent years are clear examples of the rally-around-the-flag rhetoric against foreign interest (see Pinto and LeFoulon

2007; Milhaupt 2008; Frye and Pinto 2009). However, we bracket such ideological concerns from our analysis, since we have no reason to believe that they predominate on one side of the political spectrum compared to the other.

16. Our theoretical model focuses on one feature of foreign investment: capital inflows. However, FDI may also lead to technology transfers or generate "spillover" effects to domestically owned firms. If this other aspect of FDI benefits domestic capitalists, right-leaning governments would adopt policies that give special treatment to foreign investment.

17. The motivation to raise or lower taxes is, in fact, twofold: on one hand, taxes can be used to restrict or promote FDI inflows and affect factors' returns; on the other hand, they can finance a transfer that governments could use to benefit their constituents. Note, however, that the tax that maximizes revenue does not necessarily coincide with the tax that maximizes factor return. In this regard, regulating foreign investment creates a similar problem to the one identified in the literature on the political economy of trade: workers and capital owners are forced to trade off the utility they derive from this government transfer for the income received from their participation in the market. In our theoretical model, we derive precise conditions that determine the pattern of sectoral tax rates under different assumptions about the technological relationship between factors of production and government partisanship.

18. FDI inflows is the yearly amount of net direct investment inflows to a host country broken down by individual sectors, in current U.S. dollars. The source for this variable is the OECD's *International Direct Investment Statistics Yearbook* (OECD 2005a). Data is available for OECD countries for the period 1980–2003.

19. Investment is calculated using CI (investment share of GDP), CGDP (real GDP per capita, in current prices), and POP (population). The source for this data is the Penn World Table, version 6.1 (Heston, Summers, and Aten 2002).

20. Alternative normalizations of the dependent variable yield similar results to those reported in this chapter.

21. *Left* is a dummy variable coded 1 when the party of the chief executive is listed as "Left" in the World Bank's Database of Political Institutions (Beck et al. 2001). The ideological position assigned to each country corresponds to the orientation of the chief executive for political systems classified in the database as presidential and to that of the majority or largest government party for systems classified as parliamentary.

22. Openness is the sum of exports and imports as a percentage of GDP; population is in thousands; real GDP per capita is the GDP (in thousands of U.S. dollars) divided by total population. The source for these variables is the Penn World Table, version 6.1 (Heston, Summers, and Aten 2002). In alternative specifications, we control for GDP growth, exports of natural resources as a percentage of GDP, educational attainment of the workforce, government consumption, fiscal deficits, and political and institutional constraints. The inclusion of these control variables does not affect the substantive conclusions of the results obtained from the baseline models presented in table 4.1. The results from the alternative specifications, not reproduced here, are available from the authors on request.

23. We conduct similar tests with FDI inflows into sector i expressed in levels, and using the logarithmic of FDI as a proportion of GDP and as a proportion of sectoral employment, yielding identical results.

24. Data on FDI inflows is only available for 17 sectors (OECD 2005a).

25. Results also hold when we use an alternative measure of ideological orientation of government from Duane Swank's (2001) Comparative Parties Data Set: left party cabinet portfolios as a percent of all cabinet portfolios. Swank's data set is available online at http://www.marquette.edu/polisci/documents/part19502006 .xls. It covers the period 1950–99 for 21 countries: Australia, Austria, Belgium, Canada, Denmark, Finland, France, Germany, Greece, Ireland, Italy, Japan, the Netherlands, Portugal, New Zealand, Norway, Spain, Sweden, Switzerland, the United Kingdom, and the United States.

26. Sectoral information is not readily available for most countries throughout the period under analysis, so we instead use country aggregates, in addition to country and year dummies.

27. The positive correlation between the left and investment flows in mining and quarrying is puzzling in this regard, particularly given our findings in chapter 2 on the propensity of left-leaning governments to expropriate more than their right-leaning counterparts. To the extent that investors in extractive industries are more sensitive to this risk, the positive correlation may be capturing fiscal motivations on the side of left-leaning governments in light of this sensitivity that dominates the factor market effects identified in our theoretical model.

28. In these tests, we use Swank's measure of left party control of cabinet portfolios discussed in note 26. The dummy variable for manufacturing takes a value of 1 for sectors 3–8 in table 4.2; the variable for service includes sectors 9–17. In some industries in the service sector, we would also expect foreign investment to affect the demand for business services, hence attenuating the differences between pro-labor and pro-business incumbents.

29. The data source for the dependent variable is the OECD STAN (STructural ANalysis) Database for industrial analysis (OECD 2005b). It is constructed as the ratio of wages and salaries to employees.

30. FDI is the yearly amount of net direct investment inflows to a host country in current U.S. dollars. FDI enters the model in levels, since this variable is measured as net flows in the data source. It can take negative values in case of amortization, divestment, and/or profit, interest, and royalty repatriation. The source for this variable is the OECD's *International Direct Investment Statistics Yearbook* (online resource, OECD 2005a). Data is available for OECD countries for the period 1980–2003. Value added comprises labor costs (compensation of employees), consumption of fixed capital, taxes less subsidies, and net operating surplus and mixed income. The source for this data is the OECD STAN database (OECD 2005b).

31. Data on unemployment rates was obtained from the UN Common Statistical Database (http://unstats.un.org/unsd/databases.htm). For definition and sources of the other explanatory and control variables, see notes 22 and 23.

32. Alternatively, we use the rate of change of labor costs per employee, with identical results. Labor costs include wages and salaries, supplements, taxes, and

other contributions paid by employers. This variable has broader country and year coverage than wages. The source for this data is the OECD STAN Database (online resource, OECD 2005b).The countries included in the analysis are Australia, Austria, Belgium, Canada, the Czech Republic, Denmark, Finland, France, Germany, Greece, Hungary, Italy, Japan, Korea, the Netherlands, New Zealand, Norway, Poland, Portugal, the Slovak Republic, Spain, Sweden, the United Kingdom, and the United States.

33. This coefficient is negative but not significantly different from zero at conventional levels.

34. Significance tests show that g_1, g_2, and g_3 are jointly significantly different from zero: Wald χ^2 (3) = 20.34; $p > \chi^2 = 0.0001$.

35. This is a form of the classical problem of time inconsistency (Kydland and Prescott 1977; Calvo 1978; Drazen 2000). There is no external enforcement mechanism that can reassure that conditions offered will be honored, resulting in policy sequencing. As inflow and outflow of capital has a different effect on different domestic actors given their location in the economy, the distributive effect of factor movements on the return to domestic actors determines the existence of ex-post heterogeneity.

36. See Pinto and Pinto (2011) for a complete explanation of the dynamic model.

37. Following Williamson (1983a, 1983b), Pinto (2004, 2013) argues that this mechanism is analogous to a mutual exchange of hostages between governments and investors: "Investment will be secure when government's attempts to target investors hurt domestic actors that the government cannot afford to ignore; i.e.: when investors can take a pivotal domestic actor hostage" (Pinto 2004, 66). On the analogy of the mutual exchange of hostages, see also Williamson (1983a). Janeba (2001) offers an alternative explanation that is driven by distributive concerns and voter backlash. Governments initially compete by offering investors subsidy packages but later reverse these policies. Voters disagree over the net benefits of attracting corporations, because of distributive concerns. Economic shocks change the identity of the policy maker over time by affecting the number of people who support the corporation.

38. Several papers (e.g., Wildasin 2003) analyze the determination of capital tax rates in dynamic settings under different degrees of capital mobility. These models assume that capital stocks do not completely adjust to changes in capital taxation.

39. The model in Pinto and Pinto (2011) assumes that, at each time period, decisions are taken sequentially as follows: (1) at the beginning of period τ, a partisan government chooses the tax rates in sectors 1 and 2; (2) after observing tax rates, domestic labor and foreign capitalists decide in which sectors to operate; (3) in period $(\tau + 1)$, nature chooses a pro-labor government with probability β and a pro-capital government with probability $(1 - \beta)$; (4) once the state of nature is realized, each government chooses tax rates according to its partisan orientation, and later domestic labor and foreign capitalists adjust to the new environment as in stages 1 and 2. We find the subgame perfect Nash equilibrium of the game; that is, we solve the game using backward induction.

40. For example, suppose that foreign capital owners face the following capital adjustment cost function in sector i: $C^i(k^{i\prime}, k^i) = (\varphi^i/2) [(k^{i\prime} - k^i)/ k^i]^2 k^i$, where $\varphi^i \geq 0$, k^i is capital in period τ, and $k^{i\prime}$ is capital in period $(\tau + 1)$. Note that $C^i(k^i, k^i) = 0$, $\partial C^i/\partial k^{i\prime} > 0$ if $k^{i\prime} > k^i$, $\partial C^i/\partial k^{i\prime} > 0$ if $k^{i\prime} < k^i$, and $\partial^2 C^i/(\partial k^{i\prime})^2 > 0$. The dynamic model developed in Pinto and Pinto (2011) includes a capital adjustment cost function of this type.

41. Mosley and Uno (2007) are an exception in that they find that economic integration (including trade and foreign investment) has the potential to affect labor rights in developing countries; while trade has the potential to depress labor collective rights, FDI leads to better working conditions.

42. See Lipsey (2004) and Hanson (2001) for reviews of this literature.

43. The results reported for model (3) correspond to those shown earlier in table 4.1.

44. The signs and significance levels are obtained by fitting OLS models with robust standard errors corrected for panel effects on the subsample of country and years when the incumbent government is coded as "Left" in the Database of Political Institutions. All regressions include year dummies.

45. Pinto and Pinto (2007) develop the model in detail. Here, we discuss the intuition behind the model and some of the results.

46. The results will not change if g is interpreted as an in-cash transfer. v(g) is increasing at a diminishing rate; that is, $v' > 0$, $v'' < 0$, and $v'(0) \rightarrow \infty$.

47. To simplify the factor return bargaining protocol, we assume perfect competition in the input market, so factors are paid their respective marginal productivity. This assumption could also be interpreted as the effect of FDI on the returns to labor and capital in the long term.

48. We normalize the amount of domestic capital in each sector to one; that is, $K^1 = K^2 = 1$, and $\overline{K} = 2$. Equivalently, we can also think that $f^i(K^i, L^i, 1)$ represents production in sector i in its intensive form.

49. Since foreign capital is perfectly mobile, the marginal productivity of k^i must increase when t^i rises in order to attract capital to that sector. In other words, the net return to foreign capital must remain unchanged and equal to the opportunity cost represented by r. Otherwise, foreign capital would not enter.

50. This is a consequence of the constant-returns-to-scale assumption: if $q^i = f^i(K^i, k^i, L^i)$ exhibits CRS, then, by the Euler theorem, $q^i = \bar{r}^i + (r + t^i) k^i + wL^i$.

51. The constraint that the government weighs equally the return to owners of capital in both sectors can be relaxed, leading to a different pattern of political coalitions.

52. We assume that the welfare weights attached to L and K are the same across sectors. We could assume that governments are identified with workers or domestic capitalists operating in specific sectors, which would require using different welfare weights for each group in each sector. As labor is mobile and wages are equalized across sectors, the latter is irrelevant for L. It would still seem reasonable, though, to consider different weights for the fixed factors K^1 and K^2. For simplicity, we assume that domestic capitalists are treated identically regardless of the sector where they operate.

53. We do not restrict tax rates to be nonnegative. However, given the budget constraint, it is clear that they cannot be negative or zero in both sectors at the same time.

CHAPTER 5

1. The variable for competitiveness of participation (*parcomp*) is from the Polity IV data set (Marshall and Jaggers 2008).

2. See Falcetti, Lysenko, and Sanfey (2005) for a review of the literature using EBRD scores. Transition indicators were first presented in 1994, but backdating to 1992 did not occur until the year 2000. This means that early years of transition must be treated with caution.

3. For a complete discussion of these, see the annual EBRD *Transition Report* (1994–2006).

4. Tests were implemented using the STATA *hadrilm* command.

5. The natural log of FDI/GDP is taken to minimize the skewness caused by outliers, such as Estonia, Hungary, Azerbaijan, and Kazakstan. Without the natural log, the relationship would appear to be much stronger.

6. While controlling for the sector of FDI would be ideal, the UNCTAD data does not differentiate by sector. Other data sets provide sectoral FDI data but are limited in the countries and time periods they cover (see Malesky 2009 for a discussion). To maintain the full sample, we do not control for sector but do provide a dummy variable to capture whether the particular economy is highly dependent on natural resources.

7. To ease interpretation of results for a wider audience, we here report the naive single-stage regressions, but two-stage models are available on request.

8. At the request of an anonymous reviewer, all specifications were rerun with an additional control for Freedom House's measure of civil liberties, to capture the noninstitutional components of democracy. While the substantive size of the coefficients is robust to this specification, the high correlation between the three separate measures of democracy and their interaction terms renders all of the demo-cratic variables statistically insignificant. An F-Test reveals the joint significance of the variables, while a high variance inflation factor (10.37) on the civil liberties variable provides additional evidence of multicollinearity. In short, while the notion of capturing noninstitutional aspects of democracy would be extremely interesting and useful, it is unfortunately impossible given the blunt nature of our current metrics. To reduce confusion, we report only the variables without the civil liberties measure.

9. The online appendix for chapter 5 can be found on the SSRN page for Edmund J. Malesky, at http://papers.ssrn.com/sol3/cf_dev/AbsByAuth.cfm?per_id= 915350.

10. Milestone dates were obtained from the European Commission website on enlargement, http://ec.europa.eu/enlargement/index_en.htm (accessed on June 7, 2007).

11. We ran the Hadri Lagrange multiplier test for panel models on all variables (Hadri 2000), implemented in STATA using *hadrilm*.

12. Engle-Granger two-step tests demonstrated that cointegration of the de-trended variables did not pose significant problems for this analysis. When tests revealed autocorrelation of residuals in the models, violating standard OLS assumptions, a panel-specific AR1 process was applied.

CHAPTER 6

1. See, e.g., Schneider and Frey (1985), Fatehi-Sedeh and Safizadeh (1989), Li (2006b, 2008), Loree and Guisinger (1995), Olibe and Crumbley (1997), Woodward and Rolfe (1993), Sethi et al. (2003), and Globerman and Shapiro (2003).

2. See, e.g., Oneal (1994), Resnick (2001), Li and Resnick (2003), Jensen (2003, 2006), Harms and Ursprung (2002), Busse (2004), and Busse and Hefeker (2005), and Henisz (2000, 2002a, 2002b).

References

Agarwal, Jamuna P., Andrea Gubitz, and Peter Nunnenkamp. 1992. *Foreign Direct Investment in Developing Countries: The Case of Germany.* Ann Arbor: University of Michigan Press.

Aitken, Brian, and Ann E. Harrison. 1999. "Do Domestic Firms Benefit from Direct Foreign Investment? Evidence from Venezuela." *American Economic Review* 89, no. 3:605–18.

Akinsanya, Adeoye A. 1980. *The Expropriation of Multinational Property in the Third World.* New York: Praeger.

Alesina, Alberto. 1987. "Macroeconomic Policy in a Two-Party System as a Repeated Game." *Quarterly Journal of Economics* 102, no. 3:651–78.

Alesina, Alberto. 1988. "Macroeconomics and Politics." *National Bureau of Economic Research Macroeconomics Annual* 3:13–36.

Alesina, Alberto, Vittorio Grilli, and Gian Maria Milesi-Ferretti. 1994. "The Political Economy of Capital Controls." In *Capital Mobility: The Impact on Consumption, Investment, and Growth,* ed. Leonardo Leiderman and Assaf Razin, 289–321. Cambridge: Cambridge University Press.

Alesina, Alberto, and Dani Rodrik. 1994. "Distributive Politics and Economic Growth." *Quarterly Journal of Economics* 109, no. 2:465–90.

Alesina, Alberto, and Howard Rosenthal. 1995. *Partisan Politics, Divided Government, and the Economy.* New York: Cambridge University Press.

Alesina, Alberto, and Guido Tabellini. 1990. "A Positive Theory of Fiscal Deficits and Government Debt." *Review of Economic Studies* 57, no. 3:403–14.

Allee, Todd, and Clint Peinhardt. 2010. "Delegating Differences: Bilateral Investment Treaties and Bargaining over Dispute Resolution Provisions." *International Studies Quarterly* 54, no. 1:1–26.

Allison, P. D., and R. P. Waterman. 2002. "Fixed-Effects Negative Binomial Regression Models." *Sociological Methodology* 32:247–65.

Alvarez, M., J. A. Cheibub, F. Limongi, and A. Przeworski. 1996. "Classifying Political Regimes." *Studies in Comparative International Development* 31, no. 2:3–36.

Alvarez, R. Michael, Geoffrey Garrett, and Peter Lange. 1991. "Government Partisanship, Labor Organization, and Macroeconomic Performance." *American Political Science Review* 85, no. 2:539–56.

AmCham Shanghai (American Chamber of Commerce in Shanghai). 2007. *AmCham Shanghai 2007 Board of Governors Election: Candidate Information.* Shanghai, China: AmCham Shanghai. http://www.amcham-shanghai.org/NR/rdon lyres/7DFFD379-CE0C-434C-B62F-6303819129E1/2364/CandidateInfor mation.pdf.

AmCham Shanghai. 2009. *Announcement of the 2009 Shanghai Board of Governors.* Shanghai, China: AmCham Shanghai. http://www.amchamshanghai.org/Am ChamPortal/MCMS/Presentation/Template/Content.aspx?Type=41&Guid={ 27 E46FE4-E5CA-4DC5-91A4-7F824885E2FB.

Arana, Mario. 2007. Interview with the former Nicaraguan president of the Central Bank and finance minister, Managua, Nicaragua, July 9.

Armingeon, Klaus, and Romana Careja. 2004. Comparative Data Set for 28 Post-communist Countries, 1989–2004. Institute of Political Science, University of Berne.

Baer, Werner, and William R. Miles, eds. 2001. *Foreign Direct Investment in Latin America: Its Changing Nature at the Turn of the Century.* Binghamton, NY: International Business Press.

Bajpai, Nirupam, and Jeffrey D. Sachs. 2000. "Foreign Direct Investment in India: Issues and Problems." Development Discussion Paper 759, Harvard Institute for International Development.

Barro, Robert J., and Xavier Sala-i-Martin. 2003. *Economic Growth.* 2nd ed. Cambridge, MA: MIT Press.

Beck, Nathaniel, and Jonathan N. Katz. 1995. "What to Do (and Not to Do) with Time-Series Cross-Section Data." *American Political Science Review* 89, no. 3: 634–47.

Beck, Nathaniel, Jonathan N. Katz, R. Michael Alvarez, Geoffrey Garrett, and Peter Lange. 1993. "Government Partisanship, Labor Organization, and Macroeconomic Performance—a Corrigendum." *American Political Science Review* 87, no. 4:943–48.

Beck, Nathaniel, Jonathan N. Katz, and R. Tucker. 1998. "Taking Time Seriously: Time-Series Cross-Section Analysis with a Binary Dependent Variable." *American Journal of Political Science* 42, no. 4:1260–88.

Beck, Thorsten, George Clarke, Alberto Groff, Philip Keefer, and Patrick Walsh. 2001. "New Tools in Comparative Political Economy: The Database of Political Institutions." *World Bank Economic Review* 15, no. 1:165–76.

Becker, David G. 1999. "Latin America: Beyond 'Democratic Consolidation.'" *Journal of Democracy* 10, no. 2:138–51.

Bergsten, C. Fred, Thomas Horst, and Theodore H. Moran. 1978. *American Multinationals and American Interests.* Washington, DC: Brookings Institution.

Bevan, Allan A., Saul Estrin, and Klaus Meyer. 2004. "Foreign Investment Location and Institutional Development on Transition Economies." *International Business Review* 13:43–64.

Bhagwati, Jagdish N. 1966. *The Economics of Undeveloped Countries.* London: Weidenfeld and Nicolson.

Bhagwati, Jagdish N. 2002. "Democracy and Development: Cruel Dilemma or Symbiotic Relationship?" *Review of Development Economics* 6, no. 2:151–62.

Bhagwati, Jagdish N., Elias Dinopoulos, and Kar-yiu Wang. 1992. "Quid Pro Quo Foreign Investment." *American Economic Review: Papers and Proceedings* 82, no. 2:186–90.

Biersteker, Thomas J. 1978, *Distortion or Development? Contending Perspectives on the Multinational Corporation.* Cambridge, MA: MIT Press.

Biglaiser, Glen, and Karl DeRouen, Jr. 2006. "Economic Reforms and Inflows of Foreign Direct Investment in Latin America." *Latin American Research Review* 41, no. 1:51–75.

Biglaiser, Glen, and Karl DeRouen. 2007. "Following the Flag: Troop Deployment and U.S. Foreign Direct Investment." *International Studies Quarterly* 51, no. 4:835–54.

Biglaiser, Glen, and Joseph L. Staats. 2010. "Do Political Institutions Affect Foreign Direct Investment? A Survey of U.S. Corporations in Latin America." *Political Research Quarterly* 63, no. 3:508–22.

Block, Steven A., and Paul M. Vaaler. 2004. "The Price of Democracy: Sovereign Risk Ratings, Bond Spreads, and Political Business Cycles in Developing Countries." *Journal of International Money and Finance* 23:917–46.

Blonigen, Bruce A., and David N. Figlio. 1998. "Voting for Protection: Does Foreign Direct Investment Influence Legislator Behavior?" *American Economic Review* 88, no. 4:1002–14.

Blonigen, Bruce, and Miao Wang. 2004. "Inappropriate Pooling of Wealthy and Poor Countries in Empirical FDI Studies." NBER Working Paper 10378, National Bureau of Economic Research.

Boddewyn, Jean, and Thomas Brewer. 1994. "International-Business Political Behavior: New Theoretical Directions." *Academy of Management Review* 19, no. 1:119–43.

Boix, Carles. 1997. "Political Parties and the Supply Side of the Economy: The Provision of Physical and Human Capital in Advanced Economies." *American Journal of Political Science* 41, no. 3:814–45.

Boix, Carles. 1998. *Political Parties, Growth, and Equality: Conservative and Social Democratic Economic Strategies in the World Economy.* New York: Cambridge University Press.

Boix, Carles. 2003. *Democracy and Redistribution.* Cambridge Studies in Comparative Politics. Cambridge: Cambridge University Press.

Bollen, Kenneth A., and Scott T. Jones. 1982. "Political Instability and Foreign Direct Investment: The Motor Vehicle Industry, 1948–65." *Social Forces* 60:1070–88.

Borner, Silvio, Aymo Brunetti, and Beatrice Weder. 1995. "Policy Reform and Institutional Uncertainty: The Case of Nicaragua." *Kyklos* 48, no. 1:43–64.

Bornschier, Volker, and Christopher Chase-Dunn. 1985. *Transnational Corporations and Underdevelopment.* New York: Praeger.

Brasher, Holly, and David Lowery. 2006. "The Corporate Context of Lobbying Activity." *Business and Politics* 8, no. 1:1–25.

Brewer, Thomas. 1993. "Foreign Direct Investment in Emerging Market Countries." In *The Global Race for Foreign Direct Investment*, ed. L. Oxelheim, 177–204. New York: Springer.

Broad, Robin, ed. 2002. *Global Backlash: Citizen Initiatives for a Just World Economy.* Lanham, MD: Rowman and Littlefield.

Brunetti, Aymo, Gregory Kisunko, and Beatrice Weder. 1997. "Credibility of Rules and Economic Growth: Evidence from a Worldwide Survey of the Private Sector." Background report carried out for *World Development Report 1997.* Unpublished report. Washington, DC: World Bank.

Brunetti, Aymo, and Beatrice Weder. 1999. *Investment and Institutional Uncertainty: A Comparative Study of Different Uncertainty Measures.* Washington, DC: World Bank.

Bueno de Mesquita, Bruce, George W. Downs, and Alastair Smith. 2005. "Thinking Inside the Box: A Closer Look at Democracy and Human Rights." *International Studies Quarterly* 49, no. 3:439–58.

Bueno de Mesquita, Bruce, Alastair Smith, Randolph M. Siverson, and James D. Morrow. 2003. "The Logic of Political Survival." Cambridge, MA: MIT Press.

Bunn, D. W., and M. M. Mustafaoglu. 1978. "Forecasting Political Risk." *Management Science* 24, no. 15:1557–67.

Bureau of Economic Analysis. 2007. U.S. Direct Investment Abroad: Balance of Payments and Direct Investment Position Data. http://www.bea.gov/international/di1usdbal.htm.

Busse, Matthias. 2004. "Transnational Corporations and Repression of Political Rights and Civil Liberties: An Empirical Analysis." *Kyklos* 57, no. 1:45–66.

Busse, Matthias, and Carsten Hefeker. 2005. "Political Risk, Institutions, and Foreign Direct Investment." Multinational Enterprise Working Paper 3-2005, Washington University.

Büthe, Tim, and Helen V. Milner. 2008. "The Politics of Foreign Direct Investment into Developing Countries: Increasing FDI through Trade Agreements?" *American Journal of Political Science* 52, no. 4:741–62.

Calvo, Guillermo. 1978. "On the Time Consistency of Optimal Policy in a Monetary Economy." *Econometrica* 46, no. 6:1411–28.

Calvo, Guillermo, Leonardo Leiderman, and Carmen Reinhart. 1993. "Capital Inflows and the Real Exchange Rate Appreciation in Latin America: The Role of External Factors." *IMF Staff Papers* 40, no. 1:108–51.

Calvo, Guillermo, Leonardo Leiderman, and Carmen Reinhart.1996. "Inflows of Capital to Developing Countries in the 1990s." *Journal of Economic Perspectives* 10, no. 2:123–39.

Cameron, A. C., and P. K. Trivedi. 1998. *Regression Analysis of Count Data.* Cambridge: Cambridge University Press.

Campos, Nauro F., and Ramon Horvath. 2006. "Reform Redux: Measurement, Determinants, and Reversals." Discussion Paper 2093, Institute for the Study of Labor.

Campos, Nauro F., and Yuko Kinoshita. 2003. "Why Does FDI Go Where It Goes? New Evidence from the Transition Economies." IMF Working Paper 03/228, International Monetary Fund.

Caves, Richard E. 1996. *Multinational Enterprise and Economic Analysis*. 2nd ed. New York: Cambridge University Press.

Chari, Varadarajan V., and Patrick J. Kehoe. 1990. "Sustainable Plans." *Journal of Political Economy* 98:784–802.

Chavez, Rebecca Bill. 2004. *The Rule of Law in Nascent Democracies*. Palo Alto, CA: Stanford University Press.

Chinn, Menzie D., and Hiro Ito. 2008. "A New Measure of Financial Openness." *Journal of Comparative Policy Analysis* 10:307–20. Data accessed at http://www.ssc.wisc.edu/~mchinn/research.html.

Choucri, Nazli, and Robert North. 1995. *Nations in Conflict: National Growth and International Violence*. New York: W. H. Freeman.

Clarke, Donald C. 2003. "Economic Development and the Rights Hypothesis: The China Problem." *American Journal of Comparative Law* 51:89–111.

Collier, Paul, and Catherine Pattillo. 2000. "Investment and Risk in Africa." In *Investment and Risk in Africa*, 3–30. London: MacMillan.

Correa, Carlos M., and Nagesh Kumar. 2003. *Protecting Foreign Direct Investment: Implications for a WTO Policy Regime and Policy Options*. New York: Zed Books.

Cox, Gary W., and Mathew D. McCubbins. 1993. *Legislative Leviathan: Party Government in the House*. California Series on Social Choice and Political Economy 23. Berkeley: University of California Press.

Crenshaw, Edward. 1991. "Foreign Direct Investment as a Dependent Variable." *Social Forces* 69:1169–82.

Crisp, Brian F., Nathan M. Jensen, Guillermo Rosas, and Thomas Zeitzoff. 2010. "Vote-Seeking Incentives and Investment Environments: The Need for Credit Claiming and the Provision of Protectionism." *Electoral Studies* 29, no. 2:221–26.

Cukierman, Alex. 1992. *Central Bank Strategy, Credibility, and Independence: Theory and Evidence*. Cambridge, MA: MIT Press.

Curtin, Richard, Stanley Presser, and Eleanor Singer. 2000. "The Effects of Response Rate Changes on the Index of Consumer Sentiment." *Public Opinion Quarterly* 64:413–28.

Dahl, Robert A. 1971. *Polyarchy: Participation and Opposition*. New Haven: Yale University Press.

Dahl, Robert A. 1998. *On Democracy*. New Haven: Yale University Press.

Degregori, Carlos Ivan. 1998. "Ethnicity and Democratic Governability in Latin America: Reflections from Two Central Andean Countries." In *Fault Lines of Democracy in Post-Transition Latin America*, ed. Felipe Agüero and Jeffrey Stark, 203–34. Coral Gables, FL: North-South Center Press, University of Miami.

De Melo, Martha, Cevdet Denizer, Alan Gelb, and Stoyan Tenev. 1997. "Circumstance and Choice: The Role of Initial Conditions and Policies in Transition Economies." World Bank Working Paper 1866, Washington, DC.

Desbordes, Rodolphe, and Julien Vauday. 2007. "The Political Influence of Foreign Firms in Developing Countries." *Economics and Politics* 19, no. 3:422–50.

De Soto, Hernando. 2000. *The Mystery of Capitalism: Why Capitalism Triumphs in the West and Fails Everywhere Else*. New York: Basic Books.

Diamond, Larry Jay. 1999. *Developing Democracy toward Consolidation*. Baltimore: Johns Hopkins University Press.

Diebold, J. 1974. "Why Be Scared of Them?" *Foreign Policy* 3:79–95.

Diechman, Joel I., Abdolreza Eshghi, Dominque M. Haughton, Selin Ayek, and Nicholas C. Teebagy. 2003. "Foreign Direct Investment in the Eurasian Transition States." *East European Economics* 41, no. 1:5–34.

Dixit, Avanish, and John Londregan. 1995. "Redistributive Politics and Economic Efficiency." *American Political Science Review* 89, no. 4:856–66.

Dixit, Avanish, and Robert Pindyck. 1994. *Investment under Uncertainty*. Princeton: Princeton University Press.

Dominguez, Jorge I. 1982. "Business Nationalism: Latin American National Business Attitudes and Behavior toward Multinational Enterprises." In *Economic Issues and Political Conflict: US–Latin American Relations*, ed. Jorge I. Dominguez, 16–68. Boston: Butterworth Scientific.

Drazen, Allan. 2000. *Political Economy in Macroeconomics*. Princeton: Princeton University Press.

Dunning, John H. 1977. "Trade, Location of Economic Activity, and the MNE: A Search for an Eclectic Approach." In *The International Allocation of Economic Activity*, ed. B. G. Ohlin, P.-O. Hesselborn, and P. M. Wijkman, 395–418. London: Macmillan.

Dunning, John H. 1981. *International Production and Multinational Enterprise*. London: George Allen and Unwin.

Dunning, John H. 1993. *Multinational Enterprises and the Global Economy*. Wokingham, England: Addison-Wesley.

Dunning, John H. 2005. "Institutional Reform, Foreign Direct Investment, and European Transition Economies." In *International Business and Government Relations*, ed. Robert Grosse, 49–78. Cambridge: Cambridge University Press.

Durham, J. Benson. 1999. "Economic Growth and Political Regimes." *Journal of Economic Growth* 4:81–111.

Dutt, Pushan, and Devashish Mitra. 2005. "Political Ideology and Endogenous Trade Policy: An Empirical Investigation." *Review of Economics and Statistics* 87, no. 1:59–72.

Easton, J., and M. Gersovitz. 1983. "Country Risk: Economic Aspects." In *Managing International Risk*, ed. R. Herring, 75–108. Cambridge: Cambridge University Press.

EBRD (European Bank of Reconstruction and Development). 2006. *Transition Report 2006: Finance in Transition*. London: EBRD.

Economist. 2005. "A Bulgarian Software House Looks to Vietnam." December 1. http://www.economist.com/displayStory.cfm?Story_ID=E1_VNQGNSD.

Economist. 2007a. "Bolivia: Tin Soldiers." February 15. http://www.economist.com/world/la/displaystory.cfm?story_id=8706221.

Economist. 2007b. "Nicaragua: Ortega's Crab Dance." October 11. http://www.economist.com/world/la/PrinterFriendly.cfm?story_id=9947023.

Economist. 2007c. "Venezuela: It's Our Oil." June 28. http://www.economist.com/world/la/displaystory.cfm?story_id=9410681.

Eden, Lorraine, Stefanie Lenway, and Douglas A. Schular. 2005. "From the Obsolescing Bargain to the Political Bargaining Model." In *International Business and Government Relations*, ed. Robert Grosse, 251–73. Cambridge: Cambridge University Press.

Eden, Lorraine, and Maureen Appel Molot. 2002. "Insiders, Outsiders, and Host-Country Bargains." *Journal of International Management* 8, no. 4:359–88.

Ehrlich, Sean D. 2007. "Access to Protection: Domestic Institutions and Trade Policy in Democracies." *International Organization* 61, no. 3:571–605.

Ehrlich, Sean D. 2008. "The Tariff and the Lobbyist: Political Institutions, Interest Group Politics, and U.S. Trade Policy." *International Studies Quarterly* 52, no. 2:427–45.

Elkins, Zachary, Andrew T. Guzman, and Beth A. Simmons. 2006. "Competing for Capital: The Diffusion of Bilateral Investment Treaties, 1960–2000." *International Organization* 60, no. 4:811–46.

Elster, Jon, Claus Offe, and Ulrich K. Preuss. 2000. *Institutional Design in Post-communist Societies: Rebuilding the Ship at Sea*. Cambridge: Cambridge University Press.

Epp, Charles R. 1998. *The Rights Revolution: Lawyers, Activists, and Supreme Courts in Comparative Perspective*. Chicago: University of Chicago Press.

Epstein, David L., Robert Bates, Jack Goldstone, Ida Kristensen, and Sharyn O'Halloran. 2006. "Democratic Transitions." *American Journal of Political Science* 50, no. 3:551–69.

España, Mario. 2007. Interview with the investment advisor for ProNicaragua, an investment promotion agency, Managua, Nicaragua, July 10.

Evans, Peter. 1979. *Dependent Development: The Alliance of Multinational, State, and Local Capital in Brazil*. Princeton: Princeton University Press.

Evans, Peter B., and Gary Gereffi. 1982. "Foreign Investment and Dependent Development: Comparing Brazil and Mexico." In *Brazil and Mexico: Patterns in Late Development*, ed. Sylvia A. Hewlett and Richard S. Weinert, 111–68. Philadelphia: Institute for the Study of Human Issues.

Falcetti, Elizabeth, Tatania Lysenko, and Peter Sanfey. 2005. "Reforms and Growth in Transition: Re-Examining the Evidence." EBRD Working Paper 90, European Bank of Reconstruction and Development.

Fatehi-Sedeh, Kamal, and Hossein M. Safizadeh. 1989. "The Association between Political Instability and Flow of Foreign Direct Investment." *Management International Review* 29:4–13.

Faulhaber, Gerald. 1999. "Lobbying, Voting, and the Political Economy of Price Regulation." INSEAD Working Paper 97/85.

Feldstein, Martin S., James R. Hines, and R. Glenn Hubbard. 1995. *Taxing Multinational Corporations*. Chicago: University of Chicago Press.

Feliciano, Zadia, and Robert E. Lipsey. 1999. "Foreign Ownership and Wages in the United States, 1987–1992." NBER Working Paper 6923, National Bureau of Economic Research.

Feng, Yi. 2001. "Political Freedom, Political Instability, and Policy Uncertainty: A Study of Political Institutions and Private Investment in Developing Countries." *International Studies Quarterly* 45, no. 2:271–94.

Fernandez-Arias, Eduardo. 1996. "The New Wave of Private Capital Inflows: Push or Pull?" *Journal of Development Economics* 48:389–418.

Finkel, Jodi. 2003. "Supreme Court Decisions on Electoral Rules after Mexico's 1994 Judicial Reform: An Empowered Court." *Journal of Latin American Studies* 35:777–99.

Finkel, Jodi. 2004. "Judicial Reform in Argentina in the 1990s: How Electoral Incentives Shape Institutional Change." *Latin American Research Review* 39, no. 3:56–80.

Finkel, Jodi. 2005. "Judicial Reform as Insurance Policy: Mexico in the 1990s." *Latin American Politics and Society* 46, no. 4:87–113.

Fisman, Raymond. 2001. "Estimating the Value of Political Connections." *American Economic Review* 91, no. 4:1095–1102.

Franzese, Robert J., Jr. 2002a. "Electoral and Partisan Cycles in Economic Policies and Outcomes." *Annual Review of Political Science* 5:369–421.

Franzese, Robert J., Jr. 2002b. *Macroeconomic Policies of Developed Democracies.* Cambridge Studies in Comparative Politics. Cambridge: Cambridge University Press.

Freeman, Chris. 1982. *The Economics of Industrial Innovation.* London: Francis Pinter.

Frieden, Jeffry A. 1994. "International Investment and Colonial Control: A New Interpretation." *International Organization* 48, no. 4:559–93.

Frühling, Hugo. 1998. "Judicial Reform and Democratization in Latin America." In *Fault Lines of Democracy in Post-Transition Latin America,* ed. Felipe Aguero and Jeffrey Stark, 237–62. Coral Gables, FL: North-South Center Press, University of Miami.

Frye, Timothy. 2002. "The Perils of Polarization: Economic Performance in the Post-communist World." *World Politics* 54, no. 4:558–60.

Frye, Timothy, and Edward Mansfield. 2003. "Fragmenting Protection: The Political Economy of Trade Policy in the Post-communist World." *British Journal of Political Science* 33:635–57.

Frye, Timothy, and Pablo M. Pinto. 2009. "The Politics of Chinese Investment in the U.S." In *Investing in the United States: Is the U.S. Ready for FDI from China? Studies in International Investment,* ed. Karl P. Sauvant, 85–121. Cheltenham, UK: Edward Elgar.

Fung, K. C., Hitoma Iizaka, Chelsea Lin, and Alan Siu. 2002. "An Econometric Estimation of Locational Choices of Foreign Direct Investment: The Case of Hong Kong and U.S. Firms in China." Working paper, Center for International Economics, University of California, Santa Cruz.

Garland, Marshall W., and Glen Biglaiser. 2009. "Do Electoral Rules Matter? Political Institutions and Foreign Direct Investment in Latin America." *Comparative Political Studies* 42, no. 2:224–51.

Garrett, Geoffrey. 1998. *Partisan Politics in the Global Economy.* New York: Cambridge University Press.

Gartzke, Erik, and Quan Li. 2003. "The Shadow of the Invisible Hand: War, Peace, and Economic Globalization." *International Studies Quarterly* 47, no. 4:561–86.

Gartzke, Erik, Quan Li, and Charles Boehmer. 2001. "Investing in the Peace: Economic Interdependence and International Conflict." *International Organization* 55, no. 2:391–438.

Gastanaga, Victor M., Jeffrey B. Nugent, and Bistra Pashamova. 1998. "Host Country Reforms and FDI Inflows: How Much Difference Do They Make?" *World Development* 26, no. 7:1299–1314.

Gatignon, Hubert, and Erin Anderson. 1998. "The Multinational Corporation's Degree of Control over Foreign Subsidiaries: An Empirical Test of a Transaction Costs Explanation." *Journal of Law, Economics, and Organization* 4, no. 2:305–36.

Gawande, Kishore, and Usree Bandyopadhyay. 2000. "Is Protection for Sale? Evidence on the Grossman-Helpman Theory of Endogenous Protection." *Review of Economics and Statistics* 82, no. 1:139–52.

Geddes, Barbara. 1999. "What Do We Know about Democratization after Twenty Years?" *Annual Review of Political Science* 2:115–44.

Gehlbach, Scott, and Edmund Malesky. 2010. "The Contribution of Veto Players to Economic Reform." *Journal of Politics* 72 (4): 957–75.

Gereffi, Gary A. 1983. *The Pharmaceutical Industry and Dependency in the Third World*. Princeton: Princeton University Press.

Gill, Steven. 2002. "Constitutionalizing Inequality and the Clash of Globalizations." *International Studies Review* 4:47–65.

Gillespie, John Stanley. 2006. *Transplanting Commercial Law Reform in Vietnam*. Melbourne: Ashgate.

Gilpin, Robert. 1987. *The Political Economy of International Relations*. Princeton: Princeton University Press.

Ginsburg, Tom. 2003. *Judicial Review in New Democracies: Constitutional Courts in Asian Cases*. New York: Cambridge University Press.

Gleditsch, Kristian, and Michael D. Ward. 1997. "Double Take: A Reexamination of Democracy and Autocracy in Modern Politics." *Journal of Conflict Resolution* 41, no. 3:361–83.

Globerman, Steven, and Daniel Shapiro. 2002. "Global Foreign Direct Investment Flows: The Role of Governance Infrastructure." *World Development* 30, no. 11:1899–1919.

Globerman, Steven, and Daniel Shapiro. 2003. "Governance Infrastructure and US Foreign Direct Investment." *Journal of International Business Studies* 34, no. 1:19–39.

Gordon, Sanford, and Catherine Hafer. 2005. "Flexing Muscle: Corporate Political Expenditures as Signals to the Bureaucracy." *American Political Science Review* 99, no. 2:245–61.

Görg, Holger, and Eric Strobl. 2003. "Multinational Companies, Technology Spillovers, and Plant Survival." *Scandinavian Journal of Economics* 105, no. 4: 581–95.

Graham, Edward M. 1996. *Global Corporations and National Governments*. Washington, DC: Institute for International Economics.

Green, Robert, and Christopher Korth. 1974. "Political Instability and the Foreign Investor." *California Management Review* 17, no. 1:23–31.

Grilli, Vittorio, and Gian Maria Milesi-Ferretti. 1995. "Economic Effects and Structural Determinants of Capital Controls." *IMF Staff Papers* 42, no. 3:517–51.

Grosse, Robert. 1997. "Foreign Direct Investment in Latin America." In *Generating Savings for Latin American Development*, ed. Robert Grosse, 135–53. Coral Gables, FL: North-South Center Press, University of Miami.

Grossman, Gene, and Elhanen Helpman. 1994. "Protection for Sale." *American Economic Review* 84, no. 4:833–50.

Grossman, Gene, and Elhanan Helpman. 1996. "Foreign Investment with Endogenous Protection." In *The Political Economy of Trade Policy: Papers in Honor of Jagdish Bhagwati*, ed. Robert C. Feenstra, Gene M. Grossman, and Douglas A. Irwin, 199–223. Cambridge, MA: MIT Press.

Grossman, Gene, and Elhanen Helpman. 2002. *Interest Groups and Trade Policy*. Princeton: Princeton University Press.

Groves, Robert, Stanley Presser, and Sarah Dipko. 2004. "The Role of Topic Interest in Survey Participation Decisions." *Public Opinion Quarterly* 68:2–31.

Grzymala-Busse, Anna. 2002. *Redeeming the Communist Past: The Regeneration of Communist Successor Parties in East Central Europe*. Cambridge: Cambridge University Press.

Guillen, Mauro F. 2000. "Organized Labor's Images of Multinational Enterprise: Divergent Foreign Investment Ideologies in Argentina, South Korea, and Spain." *Industrial and Labor Relations Review* 53, no. 3:419–42.

Haber, Stephen, Noel Mauer, and Armando Razo. 2003. "When the Law Does Not Matter: The Rise and Decline of the Mexican Oil Industry." *Journal of Economic History* 63, no. 1:1–32.

Hadri, Kaddour. 2000. "Testing for Stationarity in Heterogeneous Panel Data." *Econometrics Journal* 3:148–61.

Haggard, Stephan, and Jongryn Mo. 2000. "The Political Economy of the Korean Financial Crisis." *Review of International Political Economy* 7, no. 2:197–218.

Hamdani, Kausar, Elise Libers, and George Zanjani. 2005. "An Overview of Political Risk Insurance." Working paper, Federal Reserve Bank of New York.

Hamilton, K., and M. Clemens. 1999. "Genuine Savings Rates in Developing Countries." *World Bank Economic Review* 13, no. 2:333–56.

Hansen, Kenneth W. 2004. "PRI and the Rise (and Fall?) of Private Investment in Public Infrastructure." In *International Political Risk Management: The Brave New World*, ed. Theodore H. Moran, 75–99. Washington, DC: World Bank.

Hanson, Gordon H. 2001. "Should Countries Promote Foreign Direct Investment?" G-24 Discussion Paper 9, United Nations Conference on Trade and Development.

Hanson, Gordon H., Raymond J. Mataloni, Jr., and Matthew J. Slaughter. 2001. "Expansion Strategies of U.S. Multinational Firms." *Brookings Trade Forum*, 245–82.

Harms, Philipp, and Heinrich W. Ursprung. 2002. "Do Civil and Political Repression Really Boost Foreign Direct Investment." *Economic Inquiry* 40:651–63.

Hausman, J., B. H. Hall, and Z. Griliches. 1984. "Econometric Models for Count

Data with an Application to the Patents-R&D Relationship." *Econometrica* 52, no. 4:909–38.

Hawkins, Robert G., Norman Mintz, and Michael Provissiero. 1976. "Government Takeovers of U.S. Foreign Affiliates." *Journal of International Business Studies* 7, no. 1:3–16.

Hegerty, W. Harvey, and Richard C. Hoffman. 1987. "Who Influences Strategic Decisions?" *Long Range Planning* 20:76–85.

Hellman, Joel, 1998. "Winners Take All:. The Politics of Partial Reform in Post-communist Transitions." *World Politics* 50, no. 2:203–34.

Hellman, Joel, Gerant Jones, and Daniel Kaufmann. 2002. "Far from Home: Do Foreign Investors Import Higher Standards of Governance in Transition Economies?" Discussion paper, World Bank Institute.

Helmke, Gretchen. 2002. "The Logic of Strategic Defection: Court-Executive Relations in Argentina under Dictatorship and Democracy." *American Political Science Review* 96, no. 2:291–303.

Helmke, Gretchen. 2004. *Courts under Constraints: Judges, Generals, and Presidents in Argentina.* New York: Cambridge University Press.

Henisz, Witold J. 2000. "The Institutional Environment for Multinational Investment." *Journal of Law, Economics, and Organization* 16, no. 2:334–64.

Henisz, Witold J. 2002a. "The Institutional Environment for Infrastructure Investment." *Industrial and Corporate Change* 11, no. 2:355–89.

Henisz, Witold J. 2002b. *Politics and International Investment.* Cheltenham, UK: Edward Elgar.

Henisz, Witold J. 2004. "Political Institutions and Policy Volatility." *Economics and Politics* 16, no. 1:1–27.

Henisz, Witold J. 2006. Political Constraints Database. http://www-manage ment.wharton.upenn.edu/henisz/.

Henisz, Witold J. 2010. The Political Constraint Index. http://www-manage ment.wharton.upenn.edu/henisz/.

Henisz, Witold J., and Andrew Delios. 2004. "Information or Influence? The Benefits of Experience for Managing Political Uncertainty." *Strategic Organization* 2, no. 4:389–421.

Henisz, Witold J., and Edward Mansfield. 2006. "Votes and Vetoes: The Political Determinants of Commercial Openness." *International Studies Quarterly* 50, no. 1:189–212.

Henisz, Witold J., and Oliver J. Williamson. 1999. "Comparative Economic Organization—within and between Countries." *Business and Politics* 1, no. 3:261–77.

Henisz, Witold J., and Bennet A. Zelner. 2001. "The Institutional Environment for Telecommunications Investment." *Journal of Economic and Management Strategy* 10, no. 1:123–47.

Henisz, Witold J., and Bennet A. Zelner. 2003. "The Strategic Organization of Political Risks and Opportunities." *Strategic Organization* 1, no. 4:451–60.

Henisz, Witold J., and Bennet A. Zelner. 2004. "Political Risk Management: A Strategic Perspective." In *International Political Risk Management: The Brave New World*, ed. Theodor Moran, 154–70. Washington, DC: World Bank.

Henisz, Witold J., and Bennet A. Zelner. 2006. "Interest Groups, Veto Points, and Electricity Infrastructure Deployment." *International Organization* 60, no. 1:263–86.

Herron, Michael, James Lavin, Donald Cram, and Jay Silver. 1999. "Measurement of Political Effects in the United States Economy: A Study of the 1992 Presidential Election." *Economics and Politics* 11, no. 1:51–81.

Herschman, Andrea. 2005. "Audience Costs and Veto Players: How Democracies Attract FDI." Unpublished manuscript, University of California, Los Angeles.

Heston, Alan, Robert Summers, and Bettina Aten. 2002. Penn World Table. Version 6.1. Center for International Comparisons of Production, Income, and Prices at the University of Pennsylvania.

Hewko, John. 2002. "Foreign Direct Investment: Does the Rule of Law Matter?" Working paper, Carnegie Endowment for International Peace, Washington, DC: 1–28.

Hewko, John. 2002–3. "Foreign Direct Investment in Transitional Economies: Does the Rule of Law Matter?" *East European Constitutional Review*, Fall/Winter, 71–79.

Hibbs, Douglas A., Jr. 1977. "Political Parties and Macroeconomic Policy." *American Political Science Review* 71, no. 4:1467–87.

Hibbs, Douglas A., Jr. 1992. "Partisan Theory after Fifteen Years." *European Journal of Political Economy* 8:361–73.

Hillman, Amy J., and Michael A. Hitt. 1999. "Corporate Political Strategy Formulation: A Model of Approach, Participation, and Strategy Decision." *Academy of Management Review* 24, no. 4:825–42.

Hillman, Arye. 1989. *The Political Economy of Protectionism.* Chur, Switzerland: Harwood Academic Publishers.

Hines, James R., Jr. 2001. *International Taxation and Multinational Activity.* Chicago: University of Chicago Press.

Hirschl, Ran. 2004. *Towards Juristocracy: The Origins and Consequences of the New Constitutionalism.* Cambridge, MA: Harvard University Press.

Hoffman, Richard C., and C. Gopinath. 1994. "The Importance of International Business to the Strategic Agenda of U.S. CEOs." *Journal of International Business Studies* 25, no. 3:625–37.

Holston, James, and Teresa P. R. Caldeira. 1998. "Democracy, Law, and Violence: Disjunction of Brazilian Citizenship." In *Fault Lines of Democracy in Post-Transition Latin America*, ed. Felipe Agüero and Jeffrey Stark, 263–96. Coral Gables, FL: North-South Center Press, University of Miami.

Horowitz, Shale. 2003. "War after Communism: Effects on Political and Economic Reform in the Former Soviet Union and Yugoslavia." *Journal of Peace Research* 40, no. 1:25–48.

Horstmann, Ignatius J., and James R. Markusen. 1992. "Endogenous Market Structures in International Trade (*Natura Facit Saltum*)." *Journal of International Economics* 32, nos. 1–2:109–29.

Hoti, Suhejla, and Michael McAleer. 2004. "An Empirical Assessment of Country Risk Ratings and Associated Models." *Journal of Economic Surveys* 18, no. 4:539–88.

Huber, Evelyne, Charles Ragin, and John Stephens. 1993. "Social Democracy, Christian Democracy, Constitutional Structure, and the Welfare State." *American Journal of Sociology* 99, no. 2:711–49.

Huntington, Samuel P. 1968. *Political Order in Changing Societies.* New Haven: Yale University Press.

Hymer, Stephen. 1976. *The International Operations of National Firms: A Study of Foreign Direct Investment.* Cambridge, MA: MIT Press.

Iaryczower, Matias, Pablo T. Spiller, and Mariano Tommasi. 2002. "Judicial Independence in Unstable Environments, Argentina 1935–1998." *American Journal of Political Science* 46, no. 4:699–716.

ICRG (International Country Risk Guide). 2007. http://www.prsgroup.com/.

Ikawa, Motomichi. 2004. Introduction to *International Political Risk Management: Exploring New Frontiers,* ed. Theodore H. Moran. Washington, DC: World Bank.

Immergut, Ellen. 1992. *Health Politics and Institutions in Western Europe.* Cambridge: Cambridge University Press.

Iversen, Torben. 1999. *Contested Economic Institutions: The Politics of Macroeconomics and Wage Bargaining in Advanced Democracies.* New York: Cambridge University Press.

Janeba, Eckhard. 2001. "Global Corporations and Local Politics: A Theory of Voter Backlash." NBER Working Paper 8254, National Bureau of Economic Research.

Jenkins, Barbara. 1986. "Reexamining the 'Obsolescing Bargain': A Study of Canada's National Energy Program." *International Organization* 40, no. 1:139–65.

Jensen, Nathan M. 2002. "Economic Reform, State Capture, and International Investment in Transition Economies." *Journal of International Development* 14:973–77.

Jensen, Nathan M. 2003. "Democratic Governance and Multinational Corporations: Political Regimes and Inflows of Foreign Direct Investment." *International Organization* 57, no. 3:587–616.

Jensen, Nathan M. 2004. "Crisis, Conditions, and Capital: The Effects of International Monetary Fund Agreements on Foreign Direct Investment Inflows." *Journal of Conflict Resolution* 48, no. 2:194–210.

Jensen, Nathan M. 2006. *Nation-States and the Multinational Corporation: Political Economy of Foreign Direct Investment.* Princeton: Princeton University Press.

Jensen, Nathan M. 2008. "Political Risk, Democratic Institutions, and Foreign Direct Investment." *Journal of Politics* 70, no. 4:1040–52.

Jensen, Nathan M., and Fiona McGillivray. 2005. "Federalism and Foreign Direct Investment." *International Interactions* 31, no. 4:303–26.

Jensen, Nathan M., and Guillermo Rosas. 2007. "Foreign Direct Investment and Income Inequality in Mexico, 1990–2000." *International Organization* 61, no. 3:467–87.

Jensen, Nathan M., and Scott Schmith. 2005. "Market Responses to Politics: The Rise of Lula and the Decline of the Brazilian Stock Market." *Comparative Political Studies* 38, no. 10:1245–70.

Jensen, Nathan M., and Leonard Wantchekon. 2004. "Resource Wealth and Political Regimes in Africa." *Comparative Political Studies* 37, no. 7:816–41.

Jensen, Nathan M., and Daniel J. Young. 2008. "Investment Risk: What Makes Developing World Countries Seem Prone to Violence?" *Journal of Conflict Resolution* 52, no. 4:527–47.

Jodice, David A. 1980. "Sources of Change in Third World Regimes for Foreign Direct Investment." *International Organization* 34, no. 2:177–206.

Johnson, Andreas. 2004. "FDI Inflows to the Transition Economies in Eastern Europe: Magnitude and Determinants." Working Paper Series in Economics and Institutions of Innovation 59, Centre of Excellence for Studies in Science and Innovation, Royal Institute of Technology, Sweden.

Jones, Garett, and Tim Kane. 2005. "U.S. Troops and Economic Growth: Regression Analysis with Robustness Tests." Working paper.

Jorquera, Carlos. 2003. Interview with the business attorney and board member of the National Chamber of Commerce of Chile, Santiago, Chile, May 23.

Kapstein, Ethan B. 1996. "Workers and the World Economy." *Foreign Affairs* 111(May/June): 16–37.

Karl, Terry Lynn. 1990. "Dilemmas of Democratization." *Comparative Politics* 23:1–21.

Katz, Lawrence F., and Kevin M. Murphy. 1992. "Changes in Relative Wages, 1963–1987: Supply and Demand Factors." *Quarterly Journal of Economics* 107, no. 1:35–78.

Keeter, Scott, Carolyn Miller, Andrew Kohut, Robert Groves, and Stanley Presser. 2000. "Consequences of Reducing Nonresponse in a Large National Telephone Survey." *Public Opinion Quarterly* 64:125–48.

Kennedy, Scott. 2007. "Transnational Political Alliances: An Exploration with Evidence from China." *Business and Society* 46, no. 2:174–200.

Keren, Michael, and Gur Ofer. 2002. "The Role of FDI in Trade and Financial Services in Transition: What Distinguishes Transition Economies from Developing Economies?" *Comparative Economic Studies* 44:15–45.

Kerner, Andrew. 2009. "Why Should I Believe You? The Costs and Consequences of Bilateral Investment Treaties." *International Studies Quarterly* 53, no. 1:73–102.

Kim, Hae-On, and Charles W. Mueller. 1978. *Introduction to Factor Analysis*. Newbury Park, CA: Sage.

Kindleberger, Charles P. 1969. *American Business Abroad: Six Lectures on Direct Investment*. New Haven: Yale University Press.

King, Gary, Michael Tomz, and Jason Wittenberg. 2000. "Making the Most of Statistical Analyses: Improving Interpretation and Presentation." *American Journal of Political Science* 44, no. 2:347–61.

Kitschelt, Herbert. 2003. "Accounting for Post-communist Regime Diversity. What Counts as a Good Cause?" In *Capitalism and Democracy in Central and Eastern Europe: Assessing the Legacy of Communist Rule*, ed. Grezgorz Ekiert and Stephen Hanson, 49–86. Cambridge: Cambridge University Press.

Klein, Naomi. 2000. *No Logo: Taking Aim at Brand Bullies*. New York: Picador.

Klein, Paul, and Jose-Victor Rios-Rull. 2003. "Time-Consistent Optimal Fiscal Policy." *International Economic Review* 44:1217–45.

Klein, Walter. 2003. Interview with the business attorney and board member of the National Chamber of Commerce of Argentina, Buenos Aires, Argentina, October 23.

Knack, Stephen, and Phillip Keefer. 1995. "Institutions and Economic Performance: Cross-Country Tests Using Alternative Institutional Measures." *Economics and Politics* 7, no. 3:207–27.

Knudsen, Harold. 1974. "Explaining the National Propensity to Expropriate: An Ecological Approach." *Journal of International Business Studies* 5, no. 1: 1–71, 86–89.

Kobrin, Stephen J. 1979. "Political Risk: A Review and Reconsideration." *Journal of International Business Studies* 10, no. 1:67–80.

Kobrin, Stephen J. 1980. "Foreign Enterprise and Forced Divestment in LDCs." *International Organization* 34, no. 1:65–88.

Kobrin, Stephen J. 1984. "Expropriation as an Attempt to Control Foreign Firms in LDCs: Trends from 1960 to 1979." *International Studies Quarterly* 28, no. 3:329–48.

Kobrin, Stephen J. 1987. "Testing the Bargaining Hypothesis in the Manufacturing Sector in Developing Countries." *International Organization* 41, no. 1:609–38.

Kopstein, Jeffrey, and David Reilly. 2000. "Geographic Diffusion and the Transformation of the Post-communist World." *World Politics* 53, no. 1:1–30.

Korten, David C. 2001. *When Corporations Rule the World.* San Francisco: Berrett-Koehler.

Krusell, P., L. Ohanian, V. Rios-Rull, and G. Violante. 2000. "Capital-Skill Complementarity and Inequality: A Macroeconomic Analysis." *Econometrica* 68, no. 5:1029–53.

Kydland, Finn E., and Edward C. Prescott. 1977. "Rules rather than Discretion: The Inconsistency of Optimal Plans." *Journal of Political Economy* 85:473–92.

Lacy, Dean. 2001. "A Theory of Nonseparable Preferences in Survey Responses." *American Journal of Political Science* 45, no. 2:239–58.

Lagos, Marta. 2001. "How People View Democracy: Between Stability and Crisis in Latin America." *Journal of Democracy* 12, no. 1:137–45.

Landes, William M., and Richard A. Posner. 1975. "The Independent Judiciary in an Interest-Group Perspective." *Journal of Law and Economics* 18, no. 3:875–901.

Lankes, Hans-Peter, and A. J. Venables. 1996. "Foreign Direct Investment in Economic Transition: The Changing Pattern of Investments." *Economics of Transition* 4, no. 2:331–37.

Leblang, David, and Bumba Mukherjee. 2004. "Presidential Elections and the Stock Market: Comparing Markov-Switching and Fractionally Integrated GARCH Models of Volatility." *Political Analysis* 12:296–322.

Lehmann, Alexander. 1999. "Country Risks and the Investment Activity of U.S. Multinationals in Developing Countries." IMF Working Paper 99/133, International Monetary Fund.

Levine, Ross. 1998. "The Legal Environment, Banks, and Long-Run Economic Growth." *Journal of Money, Credit, and Banking* 30:596–613.

Levy, Brian, and Pablo T. Spiller. 1994. "The Institutional Foundations of Regulatory Commitment: A Comparative Analysis of Telecommunications Regulation." *Journal of Law, Economics, and Organization* 10, no. 2:201–46.

Lewis, Charles Paul. 2005. *How the East Was Won: The Impact of Multinational Companies on Eastern Europe and the Former Soviet Union.* New York: Palgrave MacMillan.

Li, Quan. 2006a. "Democracy, Autocracy, and Tax Incentives to Foreign Direct Investors: A Cross-National Analysis." *Journal of Politics* 68, no. 1:62–74.

Li, Quan. 2006b. "Political Violence and Foreign Direct Investment." In *Research in Global Strategic Management*, vol. 12, *Regional Economic Integration*, ed. Michele Fratianni and Alan M. Rugman, 225–49. Amsterdam: JAI Press/Elsevier.

Li, Quan. 2008. "Foreign Direct Investment and Interstate Military Conflict." *Journal of International Affairs* 62, no. 1:53–66.

Li, Quan. 2009. "Democracy, Autocracy, and Expropriation of Foreign Direct Investment." *Comparative Political Studies* 42, no. 8:1098–1127.

Li, Quan, and Adam Resnick. 2003. "Reversal of Fortunes: Democratic Institutions and Foreign Direct Investment Inflows to Developing Countries." *International Organization* 57, no. 1:175–212.

Li, Quan, and Rafael Reuveny. 2003. "Economic Globalization and Democracy: An Empirical Analysis." *British Journal of Political Science* 33:29–54.

Li, Quan, and Dale Smith. 2002. "The Dilemma of Financial Liberalization: State Autonomy and Societal Demands." *Journal of Politics* 64, no. 3:764–90.

Linh, Lam Anh. 2005. "Investment Law Mulls International Input." *VietNamNet Bridge*, November 22. http://english.vietnamnet.vn/interviews/2005/11/514400/.

Linz, Juan. 2000. *Totalitarian and Authoritarian Regimes.* Boulder, CO: Lynne Rienner.

Lipsey, Robert E. 2001. "Foreign Direct Investment and the Operations of Multinational Firms: Concepts, History, and Data." NBER Working Paper 8665, National Bureau of Economic Research.

Lipsey, Robert. 2002. "Home and Host Country Effects of FDI." NBER Working Paper 9293, National Bureau of Economic Research.

Lipsey, Robert E. 2004. "The Labour Market Effect of US FDI in Developing Countries." ILO Employment Strategy Paper 2004/6, International Labour Organization, Geneva.

Lipson, Charles. 1985. *Standing Guard: Protecting Foreign Capital in the Nineteenth and Twentieth Centuries.* Berkeley: University of California Press.

Long, J. S. 1997. *Regression Models for Categorical and Limited Dependent Variables.* Thousand Oaks, CA: Sage.

Loree, David W., and Stephen Guisinger. 1995. "Policy and Non-policy Determinants of U.S. Equity Foreign Direct Investment." *Journal of Business Studies* 26:281–99.

Luo, Yadong. 2001. "Toward a Cooperative View of MNC–Host Government Relations: Building Blocks and Performance Implications." *Journal of International Business Studies* 32, no. 3:401–19.

Luo, Yadong, O. Shenkar, and M.-K. Nyaw. 2002. "Mitigating Liabilities of Foreignness: Defensive versus Offensive Approaches." *Journal of International Management* 8, no. 3:283–300.

Magee, Stephen, William Brock, and Leslie Young. 1989. *Black Hole Tariffs and Endogenous Policy Theory: Political Economy in General Equilibrium.* New York: Cambridge University Press.

Malesky, Edmund J. 2006. "Re-thinking the Obsolescing Bargain: Do Foreign Investors Really Surrender Their Influence over Economic Reform in Transition States." Multinational Enterprises Working Paper 2-2006, Washington University in St. Louis.

Malesky, Edmund. 2008. "Straight Ahead on Red: How Foreign Direct Investment Empowers Subnational Leaders." *Journal of Politics* 70, no. 1:97–119.

Malesky, Edmund. 2009. "Agents of Economic Transition: An Instrumental Variables Analysis of Foreign Investment and Economic Reform." *Quarterly Journal of Political Science* 4, no. 4:1–27.

Mankiw, N. Gregory, David Romer, and David N. Weil. 1992. "A Contribution to the Empirics of Economic Growth." *Quarterly Journal of Economics* 107, no. 2:407–37.

Mardon, Russell. 1990. "The State and the Effective Control of Foreign Capital: The Case of South Korea." *World Politics* 43, no. 1:111–38.

Markusen, James R. 1995. "The Boundaries of Multinational Enterprises and the Theory of International Trade." *Journal of Economic Perspectives* 9, no. 2:169–89.

Markusen, James R. 1998a. "Contracts, Intellectual Property Rights and Multinational Investment in Developing Countries." NBER Working Paper 6448, National Bureau of Economic Research.

Markusen, James R. 1998b. "Multinational Firms, Location, and Trade." *World Economy* 21:733–56.

Markusen, James R., and Keith E. Maskus.1999a. "Discriminating among Alternative Theories of the Multinational Enterprise." NBER Working Paper 7164, National Bureau of Economic Research.

Markusen, James R., and Keith E. Maskus. 1999b. "Multinational Firms: Reconciling Theory and Evidence." NBER Working Paper 7163, National Bureau of Economic Research.

Markusen, James R., and Anthony J. Venables. 1999. "Foreign Direct Investment as a Catalyst for Industrial Development." *European Economic Review* 43, no. 2:335–56.

Marshall, Monty G. 2009. Major Episodes of Political Violence, 1946–2009. Center for International Development and Conflict Management, University of Maryland. http://www.systemicpeace.org/warlist.htm.

Marshall, Monty G., and Keith Jaggers. 2008. Polity IV Project: Political Regime Characteristics and Transitions, 1800–1999. University of Maryland, College Park. http://www.systemicpeace.org/polity/polity4.htm.

Martin, Julie A. 2004. "Commentary on Political Risk Insurance Providers in the

Aftermath of September 11 and the Argentinean Crisis." In *International Political Risk Management: The Brave New World*, ed. Theodore H. Moran, 53–65. Washington, DC: World Bank.

Martínez, Jon I., José Paulo Esperança, and José R. de la Torre. 2005. "Organizational Change among Emerging Latin American Firms: From 'Multilatinas' to Multinationals." *Management Research* 3, no. 3:173–88.

Mataloni, Raymond J., Jr. 1995. "A Guide to BEA Statistics on U.S. Multinational Companies." *Survey of Current Business* 75:38–55.

Mattli, Walter, and Thomas Plumper. 2002. "The Demand-Side Politics of EU Enlargement: Democracy and Application for EU Membership." *Journal of European Economic Policy* 9:550–74.

Mayer, Wolfgang. 1984. "Endogenous Tariff Formation." *American Economic Review* 74, no. 5:970–85.

McCubbins, Mathew, Roger Noll, and Barry Weingast. 1987. "Administrative Procedures as Instruments of Political Control." *Journal of Law, Economics, and Organization* 3, no. 2:243–77.

McKeown, Timothy J. 1999. "The Global Economy, Post-Fordism, and Trade Policy in Advanced Capitalist States." In *Continuity and Change in Contemporary Capitalism*, ed. H. Kitschelt, P. Lange, G. Marks, and J. D. Stephens, 11–35. Cambridge: Cambridge University Press.

Merkle, Daniel, and Murray Edelman. 2002. "Non-Response in Exit Polls: Comprehensive Analysis." In *Survey Non-Response*, ed. R. M. Groves, D. A. Dillman, J. L. Eltinge, and R. J. A. Little, 243–58. New York: Wiley.

MIGA (Multilateral Investment Guarantee Agency). 2002. *Foreign Direct Investment Survey*. Washington, DC: MIGA, World Bank Group.

MIGA. 2004. *Investment Guarantee Guide*. Washington, DC: World Bank Group.

Mikesell, Raymond F. 1971. *Foreign Investment in the Petroleum and Mineral Industries: Case Studies of Investor–Host Country Relations*. Baltimore: Johns Hopkins University Press.

Milhaupt, Curtis. 2008. "Is the U.S. Ready for FDI from China? Lessons from the Japanese Experience in the 1980s." In *Investing in the United States: Is the U.S. Ready for FDI from China?* ed. Karl Sauvant, 1:185–207. Deloitte U.S. Chinese Services Group and Vale Columbia Center for Sustainable International Investment.

Milner, Helen V., and Benjamin Judkins. 2004. "Partisanship, Trade Policy, and Globalization: Is There a Left-Right Divide on Trade Policy?" *International Studies Quarterly* 48, no. 1:95–120.

Minor, Michael S. 1994. "The Demise of Expropriation as an Instrument of LDC Policy, 1980–1992." *Journal of International Business Studies* 25, no. 1:177–88.

Molinas, José, Anabel Pérez Liñan, and Sebastián Saiegh. 2004. "Political Institutions, Policymaking Processes, and Policy Outcomes in Paraguay, 1954–2003." *Revista de Ciencia Política* (Santiago) 24:67–93.

Montero, Alfred P. 2008. "Macroeconomic Deeds, Not Reform Words: The Determinants of Foreign Direct Investment in Latin America." *Latin American Research Review* 43, no. 1:55–83.

Moon, Chul, and Augustine Lado. 2000. "MNC–Host Government Bargaining Power Relationship: A Critique and Extension within the Resource-Based View." *Journal of Management* 26, no. 1:85–117.

Moran, Theodore H. 1974. *Multinational Corporations and the Politics of Dependence: Copper in Chile.* Princeton: Princeton University Press.

Moran, Theodore H. 1978a. "Multinational Corporations and Dependency: A Dialogue for Dependentistas and Non-Dependentistas." *International Organization* 32, no. 1:79–100.

Moran, Theodore H. 1978b. *Multinational Corporations and Dependency: A Dialogue for Dependentistas and Non-Dependentistas.* Princeton: Princeton University Press.

Moran, Theodore H. 1999. *Foreign Direct Investment and Development.* Washington, DC: Institute for International Economics.

Moran, Theodore H. 2003. *International Political Risk Management: The Brave New World.* Washington, DC: World Bank.

Moran, Theodore H., Edward M. Graham, and Magnus Blomstrom. 2005. *Does Foreign Direct Investment Promote Development?* New York: Peterson Institute for International Economics.

Mosley, Layna, and Saika Uno. 2007. "Racing to the Bottom or Climbing to the Top." *Comparative Political Studies* 40, no. 8:923–48.

Mowery, David C., and Nathan Rosenberg. 1989. *Technology and the Pursuit of Economic Growth.* Cambridge: Cambridge University Press.

Navaretti, Giorgio Barba, and Anthony Venables. 2004. *Multinational Firms in the World Economy.* Princeton: Princeton University Press.

Navarro, Marysa, and Susan C. Borque. 1998. "Fault Lines of Democratic Governance: A Gender Perspective." In *Fault Lines of Democracy in Post-Transition Latin America,* ed. Felipe Agüero and Jeffrey Stark, 175–202. Coral Gables, FL: North-South Center Press, University of Miami.

Nelson, Roy. 1999. "Intel's Site Selection Decision in Latin America." Thunderbird, The American Graduate School of International Management, Glendale, AZ.

Neumayer, Eric, and Laura Spess. 2005. "Do Bilateral Investment Treaties Increase Foreign Direct Investment to Developing Countries?" *World Development* 33, no. 10:1567–85.

Norgaard, Ole. 2000. *Economic Institutions and Democratic Reform: A Comparative Analysis of Post-communist Countries.* Cheltenham, UK: Edward Elger.

North, Douglass C. 1990. *Institutions, Institutional Change, and Economic Performance.* Cambridge: Cambridge University Press.

North, Douglass C., and Robert Paul Thomas. 1973. *The Rise of the Western World: A New Economic History.* New York: Cambridge University Press.

North, Douglass C., and Barry Weingast. 1989. "Constitutions and Commitment: The Evolution of Institutional Governing Public Choice in Seventeenth-Century England." *Journal of Economic History* 49, no. 4:803–32.

O'Donnell, Guillermo A. 1978. "Reflections on the Patterns of Change in the Bureaucratic Authoritarian State." *Latin American Research Review* 13, no. 1:3–38.

OECD (Organization for Economic Cooperation and Development). 2004. "Indirect Expropriation and the Right to Regulate in International Investment Law." OECD Working Paper on International Investment 2004/4.

OECD. 2005a. International Direct Investment Statistics. International Direct Investment by Industrial Sector, vol. 2001, release 02. http://www.oecd.org/stats portal.

OECD. 2005b. STAN (STructural ANalysis) Database. http://www.oecd.org/stats portal.

Olarreaga, Marcelo. 1999. "Endogenous Tariffs in the Presence of Foreign Capital." *Journal of Economic Integration* 14:606–24.

Olibe, Kingsley O., and C. Larry Crumbley. 1997. "Determinants of U.S. Private Foreign Direct Investments in OPEC Nations: From Public and Non-Public Policy Perspectives." *Journal of Public Budgeting, Accounting, and Financial Management*, 331–55.

Olson, Mancur. 1993. "Dictatorship, Democracy, and Development." *American Political Science Review* 87, no. 3:567–76.

Olson, Mancur. 1996. "Big Bills Left on the Sidewalk: Why Some Nations Are Rich and Others Poor." *Journal of Economic Perspectives* 10, no. 2:3–24.

Olson, Mancur. 2000. *Power and Prosperity: Outgrowing Communist and Capitalist Dictatorship.* New York: Basic Books.

Oneal, John R. 1988. "Foreign Investment in Less Developed Regions." *Political Science Quarterly* 103:131–48.

Oneal, John R. 1994. "The Affinity of Foreign Investors for Authoritarian Regimes." *Political Research Quarterly* 47, no. 3:565–88.

OPIC (Overseas Private Investment Corporation). 2007. *OPIC Annual Report.* New York: OPIC.

O'Sullivan, Robert C. 2005. "Learning from OPIC's Experience with Claims and Arbitration." In *International Political Risk Management: Looking to the Future*, ed. Theodore Moran, 30–74. Washington, DC: World Bank.

Oxley, Joanne E. 1997. "Appropriability Hazards and Governance in Strategic Alliances: A Transaction Cost Approach." *Journal of Law, Economics, and Organization* 13, no. 2:387–409.

Pearce, John A., II, and Shaker A. Zahra. 1991. "The Relative Power of CEOs and Boards of Directors: Associations with Corporate Performance." *Strategic Management Journal* 12:135–53.

Penrose, Edith. 1987. "The State and Multinational Enterprises in Less-Developed Countries." In *International Political Economy: Perspectives on Global Power and Wealth*, ed. Jeffrey Frieden and David Lake, 218–30. New York: St. Martin's.

Perry, Amanda. 2000. "Effective Legal Systems and Foreign Direct Investment: In Search of the Evidence." *International and Comparative Law Quarterly* 49 (October): 779–99.

Persson, Torsten, and L. E. O. Svensson. 1989. "Why a Stubborn Conservative Would Run a Deficit: Policy with Time-Inconsistent Preferences." *Quarterly Journal of Economics* 104, no. 2:325–45.

Persson, Torsten, and Guido Tabellini. 1994a. "Is Inequality Harmful for Growth?" *American Economic Review* 84, no. 3:600–621.

Persson, Torsten, and Guido Tabellini. 1994b. "Representative Democracy and Capital Taxation." *Journal of Public Economics* 55, no. 1:53–70.

Pinto, Pablo M. 2004. "Domestic Coalitions and the Political Economy of Foreign Direct Investment." PhD diss., University of California, San Diego.

Pinto, Pablo M. 2005. "Does Partisanship Affect the Regulation of Foreign Investment?" Paper prepared for the conference "The Political Economy of Regulating Multinational Corporations and Foreign Direct Investment," Pennsylvania State University, State College, October 14–15.

Pinto, Pablo M. 2013. *Partisan Investment in the Global Economy: Why FDI Loves the Left and the Left Loves FDI*. Forthcoming; Cambridge: Cambridge University Press.

Pinto, Pablo M., and C. M. LeFoulon. 2007. "The Individual Sources of Economic Nationalism: Evidence from Survey Data." Working Paper 3, Saltzman Institute of War and Peace Studies.

Pinto, Pablo M., and Santiago M. Pinto. 2007. "The Politics of Investment: Partisan Governments, Wages, and Employment." Paper prepared for the second meeting of the International Political Economy Society, Palo Alto, CA, November 9–10.

Pinto, Pablo M., and Santiago M. Pinto. 2008. "The Politics of Investment: Partisanship and Sectoral Allocation of Foreign Direct Investment." *Economics and Politics* 20, no. 2:216–54.

Pinto, Pablo M., and Santiago M. Pinto. 2011. "Partisanship and the Allocation of Foreign Investment under Imperfect Capital Mobility." Paper prepared for presentation at the annual meeting of the American Political Science Association, Seattle, WA, Sept. 1–4.

Pinto, Pablo M., and Boliang Zhu. 2008. "Fortune or Evil: The Effects of Inward Foreign Direct Investment on Corruption." Paper presented at the annual meeting of the American Political Science Association, Boston.

Prakash, Aseem, and Matthew Potoski. 2007. "Investing Up: FDI and the Cross-Country Diffusion of ISO 14001 Management Systems." *International Studies Quarterly* 51, no. 3:723–44.

Prillaman, William C. 2000. *The Judiciary and Democratic Decay in Latin America: Declining Confidence in the Rule of Law*. Westport: Praeger.

Przeworski, Adam, Michael E. Alvarez, José Antonio Cheibub, and Fernando Limongi. 1996. "What Makes Democracies Endure?" *Journal of Democracy* 7, no. 1:39–55.

Przeworski, Adam, Michael E. Alvarez, José Antonio Cheibub, and Fernando Limongi. 2000. *Democracy and Development: Political Institutions and Material Well-Being in the World, 1950–1990*. Cambridge: Cambridge University Press.

Przeworski, Adam, and Fernando Limongi. 1997. "Modernization: Theories and Facts." *World Politics* 49, no. 2:155–83.

Pyle, William. 2006. "Collective Action and Post-communist Enterprise: The Economic Logic of Russia's Business Associations." *Europe-Asia Studies*, June, 491–521.

Quinn, Dennis P. 1997. "The Correlates of Change in International Financial Regulation." *American Political Science Review* 91, no. 3:531–51.

Quinn, Dennis P., and Carla Inclan. 1997. "The Origins of Financial Openness: A Study of Current and Capital Account Liberalization." *American Journal of Political Science* 41, no. 3:771–813.

Rajan, Ramkishen S., and Sanjay Marwah. 1998. "The Effects of Policy Uncertainty on the Choice and Timing of Foreign Direct Investment: An Exploratory Firm-Level Assessment." *Journal of Economic Development* 23, no. 1:37–58.

Ramamurti, Ravi. 2001. "The Obsolescing 'Bargaining Model'? MNC–Host Developing Country Relations Revisited." *Journal of International Business Studies* 32, no. 1:23–39.

Resmini, Laura. 2000. "The Determinants of Foreign Direct Investment into the CEECs: New Evidence from Sectoral Patterns." *Economics of Transition* 8, no. 3:665–89.

Resnick, Adam L. 2001. "Investors, Turbulence, and Transition: Democratic Transition and Foreign Direct Investment in Nineteen Developing Countries." *International Interactions* 27, no. 4:381–98.

Riego, Cristian. 2008. "Oral Procedures and Case Management: The Innovations of Chile's Reform." *Southwestern Journal of Law and Trade in the Americas* 14:339–56.

Robock, Stefan H. 1971. "Political Risk: Identification and Assessment." *Columbia Journal of World Business* 6, no. 4:6–20.

Rodrik, Dani. 1991. "Policy Uncertainty and Private Investment in Developing Countries." *Journal of Development Economics* 36:229–42.

Rodrik, Dani. 1999. "Democracies Pay Higher Wages." *Quarterly Journal of Economics* 114, no. 3:707–38.

Root, F., and A. A. Ahmed. 1978. "The Influence of Policy Instruments on Manufacturing Direct Foreign Investment in Developing Countries." *Journal of International Business Studies* 9, no. 3:81–94.

Rosenberg, Gerald N. 1993. *The Hollow Hope: Can Courts Bring About Social Change?* 1st ed. Chicago: University of Chicago Press.

Rosenberg, Gerald N. 2008. *The Hollow Hope: Can Courts Bring About Social Change?* 2nd ed. Chicago: University of Chicago Press.

Rosecrance, Richard, and Peter Thompson. 2003. "Trade, Foreign Investment, and Security." *Annual Review of Political Science* 6:377–98.

Rosendorff, B. Peter, and James Raymond Vreeland. 2006. "Democracy and Transparency: Theory and the Missing Data." Working paper.

Ross, Michael L. 2001. "Does Oil Hinder Democracy?" *World Politics* 53, no. 3:325–61.

Ross, Michael L. 2006. "A Closer Look at Oil, Diamonds, and Civil War." *Annual Review of Political Science* 9:265–300.

Rudra, Nita. 2005. "Globalization and the Strengthening of Democracy in the Developing World." *American Journal of Political Science* 49, no. 4:704–30.

Rummel, R. J., and David A. Heenan. 1978. "How Multinationals Analyze Political Risk." *Harvard Business Review* 1:67–76.

Sabatier, Paul A., and Hank C. Jenkins-Smith. 1993. "The Advocacy Coalition Framework: Assessment, Revisions, and Implications for Scholars and Practitioners." In *Policy Change and Learning: An Advocacy Coalition Approach*, ed. Paul Sabatier and Hank C. Jenkins-Smith, 211–35. Boulder, CO: Westview.

Sachwald, Frédérique. 2003. "FDI and the Economic Status of Korea: The Hub Strategy in Perspective." In *Confrontation and Innovation on the Korean Peninsula*, 5:85–95. Washington, DC: Korea Economic Institute of America.

Saiegh, Sebastian M. 2005. "Do Countries Have a 'Democratic Advantage'? Political Institutions, Multilateral Agencies, and Sovereign Borrowing." *Comparative Political Studies* 38, no. 4:366–87.

Salacuse, Jeswald W., and Nicholas P. Sullivan. 2005. "Do BITs Really Work? An Evaluation of Bilateral Investment Treaties and Their Grand Bargain." *Harvard International Law Journal* 46, no. 1:67–130.

Scheve, Kenneth, and Matthew J. Slaughter. 2001. *Globalization and the Perceptions of American Workers*. Washington, DC: Institute for International Economics.

Scheve, Kenneth, and Matthew J. Slaughter. 2004. "Economic Insecurity and the Globalization of Production." *American Journal of Political Science* 48, no. 4:662–74.

Schmidt, Klaus M. 2000. "The Political Economy of Mass Privatization and the Risk of Expropriation." *European Economic Review* 44, no. 2:393–421.

Schneider, Friedrich, and Bruno S. Frey. 1985. "Economic and Political Determinants of Foreign Direct Investment." *World Development* 13, no. 2:161–75.

Schneiderman, David. 2001. "Investment Rules and the Rule of Law." *Constellations* 8:521–37.

Schultz, Kenneth, and Barry Weingast. 2003. "The Democratic Advantage: Institutional Foundations of Financial Power in International Competition." *International Organization* 57, no. 1:3–42.

Sethi, Deepack, S. E. Guisinger, S. E. Phelan, and D. M. Berg. 2003. "Trends in Foreign Direct Investment Flows: A Theoretical and Empirical Analysis." *Journal of International Business Studies* 34, no. 4:315–26.

Sherwood, Robert M., Geoffrey Shepherd, and Celso Marcos De Souza. 1994. "Judicial Systems and Economic Performance." *Quarterly Review of Economics and Finance* 34, no. 4:101–16.

Shiells, Clinton R. 2003. "FDI and the Investment Climate in the CIS Countries." IMF Policy Discussion Paper 03/05, European II Department, International Monetary Fund.

Shihata, Ibrahim F. I. 1995. "Legal Framework for Development: The World Bank's Role in Legal and Judicial Reform." In *Judicial Reform in Latin America and the Caribbean: Proceedings of a World Bank Conference*, ed. Malcolm Rowat, Waleed H. Malik, and Maria Dakolias, 13–15. Washington, DC: World Bank.

Simmons, Beth, Frank Dobbins, and Geoffrey Garret. 2006. *The Global Diffusion of Markets and Democracy*. Cambridge: Cambridge University Press.

Simmons, Beth, and Zachary Elkins. 2004. "The Globalization of Liberalization:

Policy Diffusion in the International Political Economy." *American Political Science Review* 98, no. 1:171–89.

Spiller, Pablo T. 1995. "Regulatory Commitment and Utilities' Privatization: Implications for Future Comparative Research." In *Modern Political Economy*, ed. J. Banks and E. Hanushek, 63–79. Cambridge: Cambridge University Press.

Spiller, Pablo T., and Mariano Tommasi. 2003. "The Institutional Foundations of Public Policy: A Transactions Approach with Application to Argentina." *Journal of Law, Economics, and Organization* 19, no. 2:281–306.

Staats, Joseph L., Shaun Bowler, and Jonathan T. Hiskey. 2005. "Measuring Judicial Performance in Latin America." *Latin American Politics and Society* 47, no. 4:77–106.

Stasavage, David. 2003. *Public Debt and the Birth of the Democratic State: France and Great Britain, 1688–1789.* New York: Cambridge University Press.

Stolper, Wolfgang F., and Paul A. Samuelson. 1941. "Protection and Real Wages." *Review of Economic Studies* 9, no. 1:58–73.

Stopford, John, and Susan Strange. 1991. *Rival States, Rival Firms: Markets, Competition for World Market Shares.* Cambridge: Cambridge University Press.

Svenson, Deborah L. 1994. "The Impact of U.S. Tax Reform on Foreign Direct Investment in the United States." *Journal of Public Economics* 54, no. 2:243–66.

Swank, Dwane. 2001. Comparative Parties Data Set. http://www.marquette.edu/polisci/faculty_swank.shtml.

Thomas, Jonathan, and Tim Worrall. 1994. "Foreign Direct Investment and the Risk of Expropriation." *Review of Economic Studies* 61, no. 1:81–108.

Tobin, Jennifer, and Susan Rose-Ackerman. 2005. "Foreign Direct Investment and the Business Environment in Developing Countries: The Impact of Bilateral Investment Treaties." Yale Law and Economics Research Paper 293, New Haven, CT.

Tomz, Michael, Jason Wittenberg, and Gary King. 2003. CLARIFY: Software for Interpreting and Presenting Statistical Results. Version 2.1. Stanford University, University of Wisconsin, and Harvard University.

Treier, Shawn, and Simon Jackman. 2006. "Democracy as a Latent Variable." Working paper.

Truitt, J. Frederick. 1970. "Expropriation of Foreign Investment: Summary of the Post World War II Experience of American and British Investors in Less Developed Countries." *Journal of International Business Studies* 1:21–34.

Tsebelis, George. 1995. "Decision Making in Political Systems: Veto Players in Presidentialism, Parliamentarism, Multicameralism, and Multipartyism." *British Journal of Political Science* 25:289–325.

Tsebelis, George. 2002. *Veto Players: How Political Institutions Work.* Princeton: Princeton University Press.

Tufte, Edward R. 1978. *Political Control of the Economy.* Princeton: Princeton University Press.

Tuman, John P., and Craig F. Emmert. 2004. "The Political Economy of U.S. Foreign Direct Investment in Latin America: A Reappraisal." *Latin American Research Review* 39, no. 3:9–28.

Tures, John A. 2003. "The Impact of Instability and Institutions on U.S. Foreign Direct Investment in Developing Areas." *Journal of Conflict, Security, and Development* 3:163–83.

Tybout, James R. 2000. "Manufacturing Firms in Developing Countries: How Well Do They Do, and Why?" *Journal of Economic Literature* 38:11–44.

UNCTAD (United Nations Conference on Trade and Development). 1998. *Bilateral Investment Treaties in the Mid-1990s*. Geneva: United Nations.

UNCTAD. 2000. *World Investment Report, 2000*. New York: United Nations.

UNCTAD. 2002. Data Set. http://www.unctad.org/Templates/Startpage.asp?int ItemID=2921.

UNCTAD. 2003. *World Investment Report, 2003*. New York: United Nations.

UNCTAD. 2005. *World Investment Report, 2005*. New York: United Nations.

UNCTAD. 2007. *World Investment Report, 2007*. New York: United Nations.

UNCTAD. 2008. *World Investment Report, 2008*. New York: United Nations.

UNCTAD. 2010. *World Investment Report: Investing in a Low Carbon Economy*. New York: United Nations.

Uniworld Business Publications. 2005. *Directory of American Firms Operating in Foreign Countries*. 18th ed. New York: Simon and Schuster.

Vaaler, Paul. 2008. "How Do MNCs Vote In Developing Country Elections?" *Academy of Management Journal* 51, no. 1:21–43.

Vaaler, Paul M., Burkhard N. Schrage, and Steven A. Block. 2005. "Counting the Investor Vote: Political Business Cycle Effects on Sovereign Bond Spreads in Developing Countries." *Journal of International Business Studies* 36:62–88.

Vaaler, Paul M., Burkhard N. Schrage, and Steven A. Block. 2006. "Elections, Opportunism, Partisanship, and Sovereign Ratings in Developing Countries." *Review of Development Economics* 10, no. 1:154–70.

Vachudova, Milada. 2005. *Europe Undivided: Democracy, Leverage, and Integration after Communism*. Oxford: Oxford University Press.

Varas, Augusto. 1998. "Democratization in Latin America: A Citizen Responsibility." In *Fault Lines of Democracy in Post-Transition Latin America*, ed. Felipe Agüero and Jeffrey Stark, 145–74. Coral Gables, FL: North-South Center Press, University of Miami.

Vaughn, Scott. 2007. Interview with the general manager and owner of Rocedes Apparel, Managua, Nicaragua, July 11.

Vernon, Raymond. 1971. *Sovereignty at Bay: The Multinational Spread of U.S. Enterprises*. New York: Basic Books.

Vernon, Raymond. 1980. "The Obsolescing Bargain: A Key Factor in Political Risk." In *The International Essays for Business Decision Makers*, ed. Mark B. Winchester, 281–87. Houston: Center for International Business.

Vernon, Raymond. 1998. *In the Hurricane's Eye: The Troubled Prospects of Multinational Enterprises*. Cambridge, MA: Harvard University Press.

Vernon, Raymond. 1999. "The Harvard Multinational Enterprise Project in Historical Perspective." *Transnational Corporations* 8, no. 2:35–51.

Vial, Manuel José. 2003. Interview with the business attorney, Santiago, Chile, June 26.

Viet Lam, and Khanh Linh. 2005. "Investment Law, Not Quite There, Says Chambers." *VietNamNet Bridge*, November 22. http://www.english.vietnamnet.vn/interviews/2005/11/514272/.

Wallerstein, Immanuel. 1979. *The Capitalist World-Economy*. Cambridge: Cambridge University Press.

Weber, Max. 1922. *Economy and Society*. New York: Bedminster.

Wei, Shang-Jin. 2000. "How Taxing Is Corruption on International Investors?" *Review of Economics and Statistics* 82, no. 1:1–11.

Weingast, Barry R. 1993a. "Constitutions as Commitment Devices." *Journal of Institutional and Theoretical Economics* 149, no. 1.

Weingast, Barry R. 1993b. "Constitutions as Governance Structures: The Political Foundations of Secure Markets." *Journal of Institutional and Theoretical Economics* 149:286–311.

West, Gerald T., and Ethel I. Tarazona. 2001. *Investment Insurance and Development Impact: Evaluating MIGA's Experience*. Washington, DC: World Bank Group.

Whitelaw, James A. 2003. Interview with the legal director for the National Chamber of Commerce of Uruguay, Montevideo, Uruguay, January 16.

Wildasin, David E. 2003. "Fiscal Competition in Space and Time." *Journal of Public Economics* 87, no. 11:2571–88.

Williamson, Oliver E. 1979. "Transaction-Cost Economics: The Governance of Contractual Relations." *Journal of Economic Issues* 22, no. 2:233.

Williamson, Oliver E. 1983a. "Credible Commitments: Using Hostages to Support Exchange." *American Economic Review* 73, no. 4:519.

Williamson, Oliver E. 1983b. *Markets and Hierarchies: Analysis and Antitrust Implications; A Study in the Economics of Internal Organization*. New York: Free Press.

Williamson, Oliver E. 1985. *The Economic Institutions of Capitalism: Firms, Markets, Relational Contracting*. New York: Free Press.

Williamson, Oliver E. 1996. *The Mechanisms of Governance*. Oxford: Oxford University Press.

Wint, Alvin G. 2005. "Has the Obsolescing Bargain Obsolesced? Negotiating with Foreign Investors." In *International Business and Government Relations*, ed. Robert Grosse, 251–73. Cambridge: Cambridge University Press.

Wintrobe, Ronald. 1998. *The Political Economy of Dictatorship*. New York: Cambridge University Press.

Woodward, Douglas, and Robert Rolfe. 1993. "The Location of Export-Oriented Foreign Direct Investment in the Caribbean Basin." *Journal of International Business Studies* 24:121–44.

World Bank. 1997. *Improving the Environment for Business Investment in the CIS and Baltic Countries: Views from Entrepreneurs and World Bank Country Economists*. Washington, DC: World Bank.

World Bank. 2005. *World Development Indicators, 2005*. Washington, DC: World Bank.

World Bank. 2008. *World Development Indicators, 2008*. Washington, DC: World Bank.

Yackee, Jason W. 2007. "Do BITs Really Work?" University of Wisconsin Legal Studies Research Paper 1054, Madison, WI.

Yackee, Jason W. 2008. "Conceptual Difficulties in the Empirical Study of Bilateral Investment Treaties." *Brooklyn Journal of International Law* 33, no. 2:405–62.

Zaller, John R. 1992. *The Nature and Origins of Mass Opinion.* New York: Cambridge University Press.

Zamora, Cesar. 2007. Interview with the president of the American Nicaraguan Chamber of Commerce, Managua, Nicaragua, July 10.

Index

Page numbers in italics indicate figures and tables.

Printed and bound by CPI Group (UK) Ltd, Croydon, CR0 4YY

16/04/2025

14658542-0001